Dietrich
Bonhoeffer
and the Theology of a Preaching Life

Michael Pasquarello III

BAYLOR UNIVERSITY PRESS

Contents

III
Consequences

Preface and Acknowledgments

My introduction to Dietrich Bonhoeffer began during the late 1970s in an undergraduate religion course for which I was required to read *The Cost of Discipleship* and *Life Together*. With no prior knowledge of Bonhoeffer, I assumed his popularity among evangelicals was due to his importance as a "devotional" writer. It was only later, during almost two decades of pastoral ministry, that I was "awakened" to appreciate Bonhoeffer as what I will call a "homiletic theologian." This discovery occurred as I sought on a weekly basis to make theological sense of preaching, while also attempting to make homiletic sense of theology. Over the course of many years, I eventually began to realize that homiletic theology involves the integration of theological and practical wisdom, a kind of "knowing how" that unites faith, doctrine, character, and a concrete way of life shared by a community that is attentive and receptive to God, who speaks in the person of Christ.[1]

Through my continuing interest in Bonhoeffer, I began to see that preaching was inseparable from his work as a theologian and as a pastor and from his deep commitment to the church. From his time as a university student to the last years of his life as a prisoner, Bonhoeffer was increasingly committed to preaching, reflecting on preaching, and educating and forming preachers for a church that would confess and proclaim Christ concretely in the whole of life. However, I was puzzled by the way so much otherwise excellent

Bonhoeffer scholarship paid little attention to the significance of his work as a preacher and teacher of preaching for his theology and vice versa.[2] After completing my doctoral work in the history of preaching, and after almost fifteen years as a teacher of preaching, I began to think there could be benefit for the church from recovering Bonhoeffer as a preaching theologian, or "homiletical theologian." This book remembers Dietrich Bonhoeffer both as an exemplar and as a teacher of preaching, who by his single-minded focus on God's address in Christ, and the church's concrete testimony to the reality of Christ, was deeply committed to the life of the world.[3]

My hope is to show how the proclamation of the Word of God in Christ through the word of Scripture provides a necessary, although not exclusive, focus for remembering and learning from Bonhoeffer's wisdom. While his works continue to attract both theologians and preachers, I have found discerning where his theology ends and his preaching begins to be a challenging task, just as his life, preaching, and theology are integrated in a remarkable way. For Bonhoeffer, preaching is at once a theological and practical activity in which God loves, judges, and reconciles the world through the presence of the incarnate, crucified, and risen Lord, who by the work of the Spirit is transposed into the human words of preaching to create a new humanity in Christ.[4] Bonhoeffer's life and work has humbled, challenged, and convicted me at every turn throughout this project. After thirty-five years of preaching, my love and reverence for the God who still speaks an astonishing, life-giving word in Christ has been renewed and deepened by remembering Bonhoeffer's life and work. For this I am truly grateful.

Finally, the title of this book provides a way of seeing Bonhoeffer in a new light: as a theologian who preached with his words and actions; as a preacher who did theology in homiletical form. This book is not a biography, nor is it limited to the study of sermons. Rather, Bonhoeffer's "preaching life" is presented in narrative form in order to allow readers to draw and learn from his abundant wisdom for the challenges of our time.

I owe a debt of thanks to a number of people without whom this book would not be a reality. I am deeply grateful to Carey Newman, editor and director of Baylor University Press, who imagined possibilities for this project and always found creative and insightful ways to keep me focused on what he perceived as the heart of the matter: Bonhoeffer and preaching. Carey has challenged, encouraged, and praised me from the very beginning of the project, offering the kind of support any author would highly value. I am also grateful for his sincere interest in my discoveries and my desire to recover the significance of Bonhoeffer for preachers and for teachers of preachers today. In addition, I also want to thank the editorial staff of Baylor University Press for their good assistance in bringing this project to published form. It is indeed a pleasure to work with such a professional and gracious organization.

I have benefited from a large body of secondary scholarship on Dietrich Bonhoeffer, from the work of those whose careers have been devoted to the study of Bonhoeffer's life, theology, times, and legacy. I could not have even considered working on this project without the fruit of their commitment and expertise. I have also had the joy of working with the critical edition of *Dietrich Bonhoeffer Works* by Fortress Press. This investment by the publishing house of the Evangelical Lutheran Church, and the work of its remarkable team of translators and editors, provides a written "memory" of Bonhoeffer that will serve future generations in new and fresh ways. I am also thankful for colleagues from the Academy of Homiletics and the North American Academy of Liturgy for their responses, comments, and suggestions in responding to parts of my work on Bonhoeffer and preaching. Most of all, I am thankful for their enthusiasm about this book and for their desire to know more about Bonhoeffer and his contributions to the practice of preaching and of teaching preaching that may continue to instruct and encourage the church in its calling to serve God's mission in the world. I also want to thank the Rev. Ron Luckey, friend and pastor, who gladly read chapters as I wrote. I have also been encouraged by my students, at both Asbury Theological Seminary and Fuller Theological Seminary, for their openness to learn from Bonhoeffer's example and wisdom for the great challenge of preaching in our time. Their interest in this book has encouraged me during the long, slow process of research and writing. Lastly, I am indebted to Young Park for her good assistance in compiling the bibliography and index.

I am grateful to my dean and provost, Dr. Joel B. Green, and my president, Dr. Mark Labberton, as well as the administration and trustees of Fuller Theological Seminary for their generous sabbatical support in my initial year on the Fuller faculty. It is a joy to be part of an institution where the importance of preaching, teaching preaching, and scholarship in preaching is valued and supported in significant ways.

I owe more than I can say to my lovely spouse, Patti, for her patience and support, without which it would not have been possible to finish this project. She has waited while I have engaged in long conversations with Bonhoeffer. I am blessed by the joy of our "life together," for which I thank God. Finally, I wish to thank my mentors in the field of homiletics, Rick Lischer, Will Willimon, and Bill Turner, all of Duke Divinity School. Attempting a project like this would not have been possible without their influence and example as homiletical theologians and models of the "preaching life." This book is dedicated to them with my deep appreciation for their encouragement and friendship.

Introduction

> Preaching was the great event in his life; the hard theologizing and all the critical love of his church were all for its sake, for in it the message of Christ, the bringer of peace, was proclaimed. To Bonhoeffer, nothing in his calling competed in importance with preaching.[1]

Since Dietrich Bonhoeffer's death in April 1945, a diversity of interpretive portraits of his life as a Protestant saint have spoken to the questions and concerns of a range of readers and audiences.[2] The memory of Bonhoeffer has become so robust and appropriated in so many ways that it is difficult to identify him with one particular image. Moreover, his reputation as a courageous historical actor, resister, conspirator, prisoner, martyr, Christian hero, and even saint may actually have contributed to the neglect of other authentic appropriations of his life and work.[3]

Bonhoeffer has become one of the most widely known Christian figures of the twentieth century, both within and beyond the boundaries of the church. The integrity of his life and thought has continued to inspire and challenge Christians of many traditions and others with no religious commitment. Moreover, his range of interests as well as the quality of his accomplishments continue to attract not only pastors and theologians but also dramatists, novelists, various types of artists, and filmmakers. The scope and character of Bonhoeffer's memory, joined with the diversity of those attracted by him, have encouraged multiple approaches to his reception.[4]

While knowledge of the various ways Bonhoeffer has been remembered is helpful, it cannot replace engaging with his writings. Images of Bonhoeffer as a scholar, teacher, ecumenist, pastor, philosopher, and ethicist have become so established that each is capable of determining how his work should be remembered and understood. In addition, each interpretive image is also capable of controlling the unique place and importance of a particular writing or writings by Bonhoeffer for the contemporary religious imagination. Yet each image highlights and represents the significance of only one particular aspect of his work as a whole. A consequence is that recognizing the full scope of Bonhoeffer's contributions is obscured by the influence of important, but also limiting, ways of appreciating his work.

A fuller appreciation of Bonhoeffer requires acknowledging that established ways of understanding his work are both plausible and problematic. On the one hand, established images of Bonhoeffer are plausible: he was highly respected in the academic world; he was a popular and effective teacher; he was a prominent voice in ecumenical circles; he was a pastor to children, youth, students, and congregations; he was a learned philosophical thinker; he was a wise and insightful ethicist. On the other hand, each particular image of Bonhoeffer is problematic since the importance of his legacy continues to exceed any one way of remembering him.

For example, an appreciation of Bonhoeffer's occasional and contextual writings—particularly his sermons, biblical meditations, lectures, essays, and correspondence—has not been prominent. Moreover, the fragmentary and occasional nature of much of Bonhoeffer's work represents an open-ended character, rather than a closed system, that invites further appropriation to discern his continuing importance.[5] An example of this kind of appropriation can be seen in recent attention to Bonhoeffer's work as a practical theologian.[6] Bonhoeffer's engagement in pastoral ministry is recognized as being closely related to his work as a theologian of the church. His theology is understood as serving preaching, worship, prayer, the study of scripture, ministry with children and young people, pastoral care, and the church's witness in the world.[7]

Arguably, the most neglected aspect of Dietrich Bonhoeffer's work is his single-minded commitment to the proclamation of the Word revealed in Scripture as the heart of the church's existence in the world.[8] However, his reputation as a courageous historical actor, resistor, conspirator, prisoner, martyr, Christian hero, and even saint has contributed to neglect of the homiletical significance of his work.[9] From his time as a university student, Bonhoeffer was a deeply committed preacher who eventually became a teacher of preachers.[10] A persistent theological and pastoral concern for him was the necessity of proclaiming the word of God to establish the church as the presence of Christ in the world.[11] Recovering him as a preaching theologian, a "homiletical theologian," is a necessary—although insufficient—way of remembering him, since his was a theology made for the service of preaching.

In *Act and Being*, his most technical academic work, Bonhoeffer argued for the necessity of preaching theologians and of theological preaching in the life of the church:

> For preaching it follows that preachers must be theologians. The way of knowing of preaching differs from theological knowing because of the particular situation in which preachers have to speak the word to the just-now-gathered historical community of faith. The object of the way of knowing of preaching is no longer the already spoken word but the one to be spoken just now to this community of faith. This word is not spoken from the pulpit as existential confession, nor as theologically pure doctrine; everything depends on the office. Preachers who know that—just here, just now, precisely through them—Christ seeks to speak to the community of faith, proclaim the gospel by the full power of the authority of the community of faith.[12]

Bonhoeffer viewed preaching as the activity of Christ—the incarnate, crucified, and risen Lord whose presence is mediated by the Spirit in the word of Scripture to form the church as a visible community in the world.[13] He sought to make theological sense of preaching and homiletical sense of theology in both his academic and his pastoral work. For Bonhoeffer, discerning the relation of preaching and theology required a kind of practical wisdom joining faith and the pastoral vocation, theological knowledge, and homiletical wisdom in service of the church as a community created by the ministry of word and sacrament.[14]

Bonhoeffer shared his developing thoughts about preaching with a friend during his time as assistant to the pastor of a German-speaking congregation in Barcelona, an assignment that was part of his preparation for ordination:

> I have long thought that sermons had a center that, if you hit it, would move anyone or confront them with a decision. I no longer believe that. First of all, a sermon can never grasp the center, but can only itself *be grasped* by it, by Christ. And then Christ becomes flesh so much in the word of the pietists as in that of the clerics, or of the religious socialists, and these empirical connections pose difficulties for preaching that are absolute, not merely relative. At the most profound level, people are simply not all one, but are individuals, totally different people, people "united" only by the word in the church. I have noticed that the most effective sermons have been those in which I have spoken about the gospel in an enticing manner, the way one tells children a fairy tale about a strange land.[15]

Bonhoeffer understood preaching as a form of confessing faith that is generated by the Spirit where the gospel is heard, believed, and reflected upon within the life of the church.[16] Preaching is a conversation in which God gives himself to the church through the proclamation of Christ for the sake of the world.[17] Preaching requires discerning not only what to speak but how to speak by perceiving the reality of God and the world reconciled in Christ:[18]

> One cannot understand and preach the gospel concretely enough. A real evangelical sermon must be like holding a pretty red apple in front of a child or a glass of cool water in front of a thirsty person and then asking: do you want it? We should be able to talk about mattes of our faith in such a way that the hands reach out for it faster than we can fill them. People should run and not be able to rest when the gospel is talked about, as long ago the sick ran to Christ to be healed when he was going around healing (but Christ, too, healed more than he converted). That is really no stock phrase. Shouldn't it really be that way whenever the good news of God is spoken of?[19]

The divine address and human answer identified as "sermon" is learned best from the exemplary work of preachers who speak the gospel from and to the church. Bonhoeffer viewed such wisdom as the fruit of attentiveness to the reality of God in Scripture and the reality of the world.[20] Discerning the reality of God and the world occurs by the guidance of the Spirit in the practices of praying, reading, speaking, hearing, meditating, discerning, and obeying as God's people.[21] Preaching, then, is ultimately bound to the church as a creature of the word. As Bonhoeffer writes,

> The church is constituted through the word of God in Christ's redemptive act. The word, and nothing else, is constitutive! The church is always already there. What comes from Christ comes out of the church and is directed toward the church. Because there is the word, there is the church; because there is the church, there is the word. The word exists only in the church! "Outside the church there is no salvation"; that is Protestant! The church is always already included when we talk about the word. The holy community speaks to the church-community in the word. The Protestant concept of the congregation is built upon the church because the church is built upon the word.[22]

Hearing God's word in Christ gives preaching a peculiar shape, sense, and sound, which Bonhoeffer described as a "strange glory." The strangeness of the external word, *externum verbum*, is the bodily presence of the incarnate, crucified, and risen Lord, who in preaching speaks to generate the knowledge and affection of faith:[23]

> Christ, who could make anyone do anything, comes to us as one who asks, as a poor beggar, as if he needed something from us. That he comes to us in this way is the sign of his love. He does not want to make us contrary but rather wants to open our hearts so that he can enter. It is a strange glory, the glory of this God who comes to us as one who is poor, in order to win our hearts.[24]

The external word is appropriated inwardly and manifested outwardly in a way of life that is both receptive and reflective. Bonhoeffer viewed this way of knowing as appropriate to preaching, which makes a path for God into the life of the congregation by proclaiming the concrete presence of Christ.[25] An example of this knowledge can be seen in a lecture to seminarians that begins with an astonishing theological claim: "The sermon derives from the incarnation of Jesus Christ and is determined by the incarnation of Jesus Christ. . . . Hence the sermon is actually Christ. God as human being. Christ as the Word. As the Word, Christ walks through the church-community."[26]

For Bonhoeffer, preaching is inseparable from the interpretation of Scripture. Biblical exegesis, theological reflection, and faithful action in the world are woven into a way of life that is established, judged, and enabled by the reality of Christ. Bonhoeffer did not begin with a methodology that fit the Bible into a preconceived world of understanding, but rather he approached Scripture with the conviction that all of reality is created and redeemed through and toward Christ. Preaching thus invites the church to hear the miracle of God speaking through Scripture in and for the world:[27]

> This is what makes a sermon something unique in all the world, so completely different from any other kind of speech. When a preacher opens the Bible and interprets the word of God, a mystery takes place, a miracle: the grace of God, who comes down from heaven into our midst and speaks to us, knocks on the door, asks questions, warns us, puts pressure on us, alarms us, threatens us, and makes us joyful again, and free, and certain. When the Holy Scriptures are brought to life in a church, the Holy Spirit comes down from the eternal throne, into our hearts, and the busy world outside sees nothing and does not realize at all that God could actually be found here.[28]

The publication of *Dietrich Bonhoeffer Works* in English makes it possible to read the sermons and homiletical writings within the context of Bonhoeffer's work as a whole.[29] Sermons, homiletical lectures, biblical meditations, and other occasional writings may now be understood as integrally related to more-familiar publications such as *Sanctorum Communio, Act and Being, Lectures on Christology, Discipleship, Life Together, Ethics,* and *Letters and Papers from Prison.*

Reading Bonhoeffer in a more integrative manner will serve to illumine how his theological development was shaped by preaching and how his preaching was informed by his theological work.[30] Bonhoeffer's sermons provide concrete descriptions of reality for the church as a people called to be conformed to Christ by the Holy

Spirit through the word of Scripture. Theological convictions rather than pragmatic concerns were the basis of Bonhoeffer's opposition to abstract preaching that lacked the form of the whole humanity of Christ taking form in the church for the world. He expressed this conviction in response to German Christians who supported Hitler's National Socialist agenda as good for both the nation and the church. But he was also critical of "orthodox" Christians who chose to limit the church's ministry to a "neutral" sphere of doctrinal purity removed from public confession and resistance to all that threatened proclaiming and living the gospel within the brutal conditions of Nazi Germany:

> We are tired of Christian agendas. We are tired of the thoughtless, superficial slogan of a so-called practical Christianity to replace a so-called dogmatic Christianity. We have seen that the forces which form the world come from entirely other sources than Christianity, and that so-called practical Christianity has failed in the world just as much as so-called dogmatic Christianity. Hence we must understand by "formation" something quite different from what we are accustomed to mean, and in fact the Holy Scripture speaks of formation in a sense that at first sounds quite strange. It is not primarily concerned with formation of the world by planning and programs, but in all formation it is concerned only with the one form that has overcome the world, the form of Jesus Christ. Formation proceeds only from here. . . . Christian people do not form the world with their ideas. Rather, Christ forms human beings to a form the same as Christ's own.[31]

There is historical precedence for remembering Bonhoeffer as a preaching theologian.[32] For the majority of Christian tradition, the church's greatest theologians were its most influential preachers, who gave concrete shape and specificity to the Word of God for particular times and places. The person and work of Christ cannot be separated, since discerning what is to be spoken as true and good, for faith and life in the present, requires attentiveness to God's revelation that is given in the reality of Christ.[33] Bonhoeffer addressed this matter in *Act and Being*:

> The preachers, as preachers of the community of faith, must "know" what they preach: Jesus Christ the crucified (I Cor. 2:2). They have been given authority to proclaim the gospel to the

hearers, to forgive sins in preaching and the sacrament. There may be no uncertainty here, no not knowing; everything must be made plain from the given word of God, from the bound revelation. For in the sermon, which creates faith, Christ lets himself be proclaimed as the "subject" of the words spoken. I preach, but I preach in the power of Christ, in the power of the faith of the community of faith, not in the power of my faith.[34]

Remembering Bonhoeffer as a preacher includes acknowledging his place within the preaching tradition of the whole church. The history of participation in a tradition entails a particular ethos or character at the heart of the practice, an ethos demonstrated not only by competence and skill but by exemplary virtues, qualities, and habits embedded in the practice as displayed by its members.

The wisdom of the past is handed down within a shared world of language in which thinking is illumined by the path set forth by God speaking in Scripture. Preachers are called to honor the gifts received from the past, even as they seek to discern anew God's path in the present. Bonhoeffer sought to escape neither his historical place nor his indebtedness to the past, even in conditions of devastating moral, social, and cultural loss under the tyrannical reign of Hitler. He therefore struggled to be true to the church's calling as a community shaped by the Word in and for the world.[35]

Illuminating the importance of Bonhoeffer's homiletical work also warrants reading him in conversation with a select company of preaching theologians: Augustine of Hippo, Martin Luther, Karl Barth, and Martin Luther King Jr. Attending to Bonhoeffer in this manner will lead to a greater appreciation of him as a figure who not only instructs and inspires but also provokes and challenges. Such understanding emerges by allowing the other to speak while listening with both humility and love. Such differences are not merely signs of historical distance that render others irrelevant but must be seen as gifts that assist in understanding better how a person such as Bonhoeffer has something to say only as he is recognized in his difference.[36]

Bonhoeffer once noted that an important theme in preaching should be "God's path through history in the church of Christ." He identified Hebrews 12:1 as a fitting text for this task since it follows the climax of chapter 11: "Therefore, since we are surrounded by such a cloud of witnesses."[37] Remembering Bonhoeffer within a "great cloud of witnesses" will contribute to a more robust understanding of preaching as a historical practice that is remembered in the present and thus extended into the future. Readers, particularly preachers and teachers of preaching, are encouraged to see themselves within a community that receives and reflects upon its life in light of God's self-communicative Word in the present and not merely as a relic from the past.

Bonhoeffer could not have anticipated what this would look like in the future, since, as a form of "theology on the way," preaching will always be incomplete. Writing from a Nazi prison cell near the end of his life, Bonhoeffer expressed hope that, in the future, preaching would once again be characterized by a reconciliation of the church's language and life within the concrete reality of Christ taking form in the world. His words point to a persistent concern for recovering the visibility of the church as a necessary condition for proclaiming the gospel in the whole of life:[38]

> What reconciliation and redemption mean, rebirth and Holy Spirit, love for one's enemies, cross and resurrection, what it means to live in Christ and follow Christ; all that is so difficult and remote that we hardly dare to speak of it anymore. In these words and actions handed down to us, we sense something totally new and revolutionary, but we cannot yet grasp it and express it. This is our own fault. Our church has been fighting during these years only for its self-preservation, as if that were an end in itself. It has become incapable of bringing the word of reconciliation and redemption to humankind and to the world.[39]

I

Preparation

1

Learning a Theology of Preaching from Luther and Barth
Berlin 1925–1927

In 1924, after a year of study in Tubingen, Dietrich Bonhoeffer matriculated to the University of Berlin, center of the German liberal Protestant tradition. He had decided to pursue a career in theology, entering the university during a time of political upheaval and social change in post–World War I Germany. He adjusted quickly, however, establishing himself as a bright student, open to intellectual challenges and capable of learning from both old and new ways of thinking theologically.[1] It was an exceptionally influential time in Bonhoeffer's formation as a theologian and preacher: a homiletical theologian. Moreover, Bonhoeffer's education at Berlin led him to engage with the theology of Martin Luther in what could be described as a turn "back to the future." Bonhoeffer's extensive conversation with Luther, coinciding with an introduction to Karl Barth's early work, marked the beginnings of a persistent commitment to recovering the social reality of the church as a necessary condition for proclaiming the gospel.[2]

To understand better Bonhoeffer's formation, it will be helpful to consider some key theological and cultural aspects of the University of Berlin.[3] It was Friedrich Schleiermacher, a theologian, who served as the principle architect of the first modern German university at Berlin. The modernization of Germany blurred the lines between church and state and greatly diminished the church's importance as an institution and concrete historical reality. A consequence was that religion was increasingly spiritualized as an immanent power within the general experience of humanity and, thus, removed from ecclesial commitments and practices—a division that had the effect of diminishing the social reality and visibility of the church.

The challenge of the Enlightenment imagined reason's sovereignty to rule not only its domain but also everything else, thus transforming, respectively, the foundation of Christian teaching and preaching—Scripture and tradition—into history and experience. Bonhoeffer would eventually conclude liberal religion and a correlative homiletic offered little to either theology or preaching. Because the historical and scientific study of Scripture left it as unreliable, scholars thus looked elsewhere to validate historical events behind the text that could be made available to anyone with appropriately informed interest. Scripture, as the church's canon, was no longer the subject of theological and pastoral wisdom through both its liturgical enactment and its ecclesial embodiment. Here Schleiermacher's influence was far-reaching, contributing to a transformation of Protestant theology that gave shape to what would become a form of cultural Protestantism.[4]

An additional factor is that some of the most distinguished members of the Berlin theological faculty were ideologically driven in their support of military expansion to return Germany to a position of leading world political power. But they were also instrumental in supporting this goal with persuasive theological justification. Adhering to the philosophies of Kant and Hegel, this theological orientation was determined by an interpretation of world history that convinced them God was on Germany's side, that God was active in history for the German people. World War I was thus seen in apocalyptic terms—an interpretation of history that was supported by the Protestant educated classes and Protestant churches. Those who were opposed, such as the Social Democratic Party and the Roman Catholic Centre Party, including the working classes, were perceived as being like vagabonds without a homeland.[5]

At the time of Bonhoeffer's arrival in Berlin, the faculty was consumed by an intense theological debate on the nature of theology between Karl Barth (then a professor at Bonn) and Adolf von Harnack (Barth's former teacher in Berlin). Harnack thought the ideals underlying theology should be identified with those that gave birth to the modern university—the ideal of humane culture as the aim and context of study that must be objective, in effect the study of history rather than religion, and religion as a historical object of study.[6] Barth, however, contended that the historical-critical method served best when acknowledging its limitations. The task of theology was not to mirror the norms of culture but when necessary to confront and even contradict them since it was free to pursue its own dogmatic and ecclesial tasks. What was most necessary was the word of God and faith awakened by God. As Barth wrote, "The task of theology is one with the task of preaching. It consists in the reception and transmission of the Word of Christ."[7]

The significance of this debate was not lost on Bonhoeffer.[8] The conflict between Barth and Harnack is an important element for understanding better his path to becoming a homiletical theologian whose attention was turned to the action of God's Spirit through the scriptural word that constitutes the social reality of the church. Moreover, God's initiative in preaching would remain a constant mark of all his subsequent work. Although Bonhoeffer was indebted to Barth for recovering an emphasis on divine revelation as the starting point for theology and preaching, he retained an independence in seeking to establish the historical reality of revelation. From Luther he would also learn how the practices of the church and its means of grace, particularly word and sacrament, not only bear witness to the action of the Spirit but are a social embodiment of the Spirit's work in the new humanity established by the word of Christ, the body of Christ on earth.[9]

Homiletical Beginnings

Bonhoeffer preached his first sermon in October 1925.[10] He was called upon to substitute for the ill pastor of a congregation on the south side of Berlin. His text was Luke 17:1-10. The sermon begins with a theological claim: "Christianity entails decision, repentance, renunciation, yes, even enmity toward the old humanity that is past." Quite possibly echoing Barth, Bonhoeffer asserts that this decision entails acknowledging that "God remains God, and humans remain human. It is God who can demand things from humans, not humans from God. It is not that humans take, but God gives." The heart of the sermon is a sober call to repentance that Bonhoeffer identifies as a gift of the Holy Spirit, who enables the "holy self-recognition" leading to prayer in the presence of a merciful God. The assumption is that the comfortable lives of self-assured, self-satisfied people, like the Pharisees in the Gospels, must be shaken by the coming of Christ: Bonhoeffer turned the light of the text toward his listeners, issuing an invitation to see themselves as participants in the story. "Truly we can give to charity over and over again, go to church every Sunday, and read the Bible at home every day; but as terrific and wonderful as this may be, the moment that we believe we have a claim on God, we are trying to grab God's omnipotence and holiness with unholy hands, and with this we slander God."[11]

The problem is that human beings do not desire what God commands and wills, as Bonhoeffer notes: "With our moral lifestyle we want to have a claim on God, to speak first and not wait until God speaks. We want to strike a bargain with God for our salvation, we want to forestall God's sentence. We want to intrude into God's judgments, although we know 'a servant should not know his master's secrets.'" Bonhoeffer turns to Luther to announce a way out of this dilemma: "We find it impossible to accept, yet we must acknowledge that if it is God's will that we be among the unjustified and condemned, we must accept our condemnation as completely legitimate. We should joyfully acknowledge it, just as Luther always advocated. We want peace and self-satisfaction, and not the saving divine unrest that is effected by the Lord."[12]

Following Luther, Bonhoeffer asserts that Christian preaching ends with a recognition of humanity's worthlessness and sinfulness before God, since without this insight there can be no conversation with God. But there is great promise in the words of Jesus—"unworthy servants"—that gladly acknowledges the mercy of God, who steps in to help: "We confess that we are worthless and that, in our relationship with God, God alone is the one who demands, speaks, and gives, while we are ones who perform, listen, and receive." If this were not so, human beings would have a claim on God, especially in attempting to assume a self-deprecating stance of repentance and contrition, which in actuality is a kind of false humility. The good news is that God extends divine assistance that is received and realized in prayer: "This is not the prayer of the Pharisee but the prayer of the tax-collector who prayed in the Temple, 'God be merciful to me, a sinner.'" The sermon concludes by proclaiming God's promise of mercy: "God defends humanity. God comes to humanity so that humanity can come to God in prayer."[13]

On the one hand, the sermon reads like the work of a student preacher. The language is quite dense and conceptual, the style rather rough and unpolished, the tone urgent and assertive. On the other hand, the sermon is marked by an intense commitment to God, to God's honor and mercy, which reflects Bonhoeffer's newly kindled passion for theology. This God is pleased to hear the prayers of sinners and servants. This God must be acknowledged and believed in rather than understood and proved. Human beings are dependent on this God for all they are and have—life, labor and work, and even their renunciation. Human existence is limited, bounded by a God who reigns at an infinite distance and directs the lives of his servants.[14]

That the sermon coincided with Bonhoeffer's discovery of Barth's early writings was undoubtedly an important factor. However, Luther's influence may also be seen in the conviction that the truth that is believed and actualized by the Spirit is demonstrated in the prayer and worship of the church: "God defends humanity. God comes to humanity so humanity can come to God in prayer."[15] In addition, Luther's apocalyptic interpretation of the gospel and history would have provided a theological perspective from which to challenge the optimistic liberal theology of Berlin.[16] The church's proclamation must do more than inspire religious experience or awaken consciousness of God. The proclamation of the gospel provokes a genuine existential crisis for the church: "Christianity entails decision, repentance, renunciation, yes, even enmity toward the old humanity that is past."[17]

Bonhoeffer's homiletical beginning is truly significant given the state of preaching in early twentieth-century Germany.[18] There was an established Protestant homiletic tradition that provided a dominant understanding of the purpose of preaching. Schleiermacher's work continued to be influential, so that the study of homiletics was related to the other theological disciplines in the university—philosophical theology and historical theology—with preaching placed under practical theology. Since the study of theology was for the purpose of producing leaders for a church that served a modern society, the practical disciplines were constituted by principles of art, or theories of practice.[19]

As defined within this modern intellectual framework, the task of preaching was to communicate the "essence" of Christianity. Schleiermacher's influence continued to affect the three main traditions in Germany: Enlightenment rationalism, Lutheran orthodoxy, and pietism. According to Schleiermacher's homiletical theory, the sermon was the preacher's outward expression of his own inward consciousness of God. The aim was to arouse in listeners a similar awakening by communicating the religious experience of the preacher or the characters of the Bible. However, preaching as a testimony of the preacher's religious consciousness was central.[20] In *The Christian Faith*, an immensely popular work, Schleiermacher writes,

> The whole work of the Redeemer Himself was conditioned by the communicability of his self-consciousness by means of speech, and similarly Christianity has always and everywhere spread itself solely by preaching. Every proposition which can be an element of the Christian preaching is also a doctrine because it bears witness to the determination of the religious self-consciousness as inward certainty. And every Christian doctrine is also a part of the Christian preaching, because every such doctrine expresses as a certainty the approximation to the state of blessedness which is to be effected through the means ordained by Christ.[21]

The influence of this approach was felt in the homiletic reformation that emerged in the early decades of the twentieth century—a time of considerable political, economic, and social change in German culture. A consequence of this change was the emancipation of the culture from the established church. This divide precipitated increasing concern among church leaders that Christian preaching had lost contact with the circumstances of hearers, leading to the emergence of a new way of preaching known as "modern." The modern approach sought to identify with listeners more closely, to place more emphasis on the preacher's personal testimony and religious experience, and to make the content of religious sermons useful in the practical sense of liberal Christianity.

Because the German state church was formally open to all people, it was assured that those who heard sermons were not necessarily a believing audience. Scripture was thus read in lesser amounts, presumably a consequence of historical-critical methods and a history-of-religions approach to the study of Christianity. Most important was that sermons should be life oriented and practically applicable, touching the happenings, feelings, and experiences of people. Topical preaching was popular, although not necessarily very religious or focused on Christian topics. The hope was that preaching should help the church to recover its numerical and political influence in German culture, a hope shared alike by liberal Protestants, orthodox Lutherans, and pietist pastors.[22]

An additional development was that many "political theologians" and nationalist Protestants desired to see preaching promote the new republic and its system of social democracy as a threat to the old unity of a Protestant church and the German people. They were of the opinion that the church should use preaching to establish its relevance in the new Reich, preaching a gospel tied to "common blood, nationality and culture."[23] The problem with these arrangements was that they separated theology from the faith and practice of the church. This would become increasingly evident to Bonhoeffer through his introduction to Barth's early works and study of Luther's theology and life.[24]

The Re-turn to Luther

The German Protestant church that Bonhoeffer knew was essentially a Lutheran church, a church of the Reformation. Indeed, Luther is present more than anyone else at every stage of his path and in every dimension of his thought, so that even his alignment to and arguments with Barth have their origins in the influence of Luther. In addition, it is more than a coincidence that during Bonhoeffer's student years, Luther was an exemplary figure who demonstrated how the work of a theologian can be united with the ministry of preaching. Barth, too, was influenced by particular aspects of Luther's theology in his theological development. Without discounting the importance of Barth for Bonhoeffer, it is necessary to remember the significance of Luther's influence for both.

Barth engaged with Luther's thought throughout his career in what would be an ambivalent relationship with the Reformer. In spite of his vehement criticism of Luther, he was deeply indebted to his courageous defense and bold proclamation of the gospel. Barth thus followed Luther in perceiving that the source and substance of salvation is Christ himself and Christ alone. A similar connection can be seen in Barth's strong commitment to a theology of the Word of God, which in its primacy holds undivided precedence over human reason and experience, authenticating itself from faith to faith. Christ is proclaimed by faith and cannot be grasped through any means other than by faith.[25] As Luther wrote in the *Small Catechism*, "I believe that by my own reason or strength I cannot believe in Jesus Christ, my Lord, or come to him. But the Holy Spirit has called me through the Gospel, enlightened me with his gifts, and sanctified and preserved me in true faith."[26]

Bonhoeffer became a student of Luther during a time of increasingly renewed interest in the Reformer's life and work. In addition to a "Luther renaissance" in Berlin, Barth's attention to Luther and the Reformation, especially the primacy of God's word, provided a perspective from which Bonhoeffer could critically assess the tendencies of modern Lutheran interpretation. This timely discovery of Barth inspired Bonhoeffer to read Luther against liberal Protestantism to gain a fresh hearing of the Reformer that would allow the norm for assessing the truth of particular claims to be the gospel itself.[27]

Bonhoeffer's seminar papers on Luther reveal the beginnings of a theological and homiletical reorientation that would be given fuller expression in his doctoral dissertation, *Sanctorum Communio*.[28] One of the earliest of these essays was written for Karl Holl, the church historian whose work on Luther was extremely popular in Germany. The paper was titled, "Luther's Feelings about His Work as Expressed in the Final Years of His Life Based on His Correspondence of 1542–1546."[29] Bonhoeffer responds critically to Holl's interpretation of Luther's faith as a "religion of conscience." In Holl's view, Luther's doctrine of justification, the dynamics of judgment and forgiveness, occur in the human conscience, which is the location of revelation; God's will meets the human sense of moral obligation. This approach led Holl to analyze Luther's autobiographical accounts of *anfechtungen* (temptations, inner conflicts, and spiritual trials) as a source for both theology and psychologically observable phenomenon. However, Bonhoeffer had begun to have concerns about the limitations of Holl's approach to Luther. As he commented in handwritten notes on a copy of Luther's lectures on Paul's letter to the Romans, "Theological logic intends to set itself free from psychologism. It does not speak of sin and revelation as contents of consciousness. Instead, it speaks of them as realities of revelation: acknowledgment of what is spoken in revelation and by the authorities."[30]

Bonhoeffer interpreted Luther's sense of being propelled by a higher power and an accompanying feeling of astonishment in contemplating his calling and life's work. This self-understanding was created by the call of God to the service of the gospel, a vocation carried out through "difficulty, earnest prayers and much suffering." Luther's most precious gifts were prayer and the "dear word of God" that focused his attention on God's command rather than his own conscience. As Bonhoeffer notes,

> Because he [Luther] serves God's command, God works through him. These are certainly only two different expressions of the same significance, whether Luther says, God, whom we serve as servants, or who works in us. God works in and through us, i.e., the work that "we" do is God's work. Our work is not our work, our preaching is not ours. Amidst the many intense death and life conflicts, we leave our human words behind, because God desires to speak through us. Therefore, it is not Luther who speaks. Instead, anyone who hears him hears God, "because I do not want to speak my own, but God's word."[31]

The paper condenses Luther's work into three areas: "spiritual assaults, prayer, and sermons." These are also essential aspects for any who desire to share Luther's work since "the entire history of the world is to be seen under the aspect of this battle between the gospel and devil. This was especially true in this final crisis that had emerged as the gospel was proclaimed anew, i.e., in Luther's work."[32]

Bonhoeffer affirmed Luther's conviction that proclaiming the gospel is a divine task that is fulfilled by the grace of the Holy Spirit. While the Holy Spirit has no need for human assistance, the Spirit desires that human servants share in the service of prayer and preaching. But proclamation cannot be limited to or controlled by a preacher's experience and existential condition.[33] As Luther notes, "The office of preacher, the office of pastor, and the gospel are not ours, nor any person's, not even an angel's. Instead, they belong solely to God our Lord." Bonhoeffer saw this as the "paradox of the Reformation." The peace Luther longed for in his life and ministry was a particular peace, "[for which] you must pass through the world with the sword of the divine word."[34]

In the summer of 1925, Bonhoeffer submitted a seminar paper to Rudolph Seeberg on the word of God and historical-critical research. Seeberg's interpretation of Luther was different from that set forth by Karl Holl in that the former argued that the Reformer accepted religious experience as a "canon of truth" in addition to Scripture. The paper shows the influence of Barth's theology of God's transcendence in its description of Scripture as more than a word about God but as God's word itself. However, Bonhoeffer was also indebted to Luther's insistence that the location of truth is found within the historical reality of the church through the word of God, through Scripture alone. In a real sense, Bonhoeffer found himself moving toward a mediating position between Barth and the Berlin theologians, particularly Adolf Harnack, the distinguished historian who had expressed great admiration for his seminar work.[35]

The paper argues that a pneumatological interpretation of Scripture must be taken seriously as historical reality. It therefore begins with a theological claim: "Christian religion stands or falls with the belief in a historical and perceptibly real divine revelation."[36] The following questions are addressed: history and the Spirit (which refers to the letter and the Spirit) and Scripture and revelation (that is, human words and God's word). Bonhoeffer asserts the Bible is not one book among others but quite simply the "ultimate book which narrates the most significant of events." The problem with historical criticism is twofold, in that its principles are based on a scientific-mechanistic worldview and thereby dependent upon epistemological methodologies taken from the natural sciences.[37]

Although Bonhoeffer was trained in historical-critical methodology, he concluded for theological reasons that it was a modest servant but a bad master.[38] A strictly historical approach causes the concept of the biblical canon to disintegrate, leveling the content of Scripture and rendering it meaningless, thus forcing its alignment with knowledge derived from scientific study. On the other hand, when revelation is discovered, "the extraordinary enters and its power is self-evident."[39] As did Luther, Bonhoeffer claimed revelation is found only in Scripture, where God is pleased to speak and the word is heard, experienced, and proclaimed. While Scripture is not itself revelation, it is a document that bears witness to revelation that is silenced if objectified by rational science. Scriptural understanding of Christ, the Word of God, is not a priori and interior to human understanding but a gift conferred by the Spirit. Christ appears in verbal form, the Spirit appears in personal form, and the past of Scripture becomes present in human form. Such understanding depends upon the Spirit, who inspired and disclosed to its writers that revelation is found in the person of Jesus within the framework of ordinary events.[40]

Bonhoeffer followed Luther's lead in defining the words of Scripture as written-down proclamation or "good tidings and report." In the *Preface to the New Testament*, Luther offered a concise summary of "good news":

> For "gospel" [*euangelium*] is a Greek word and means in Greek a good message, good tidings, good news, a good report, which one sings and tells with gladness.... Thus the gospel of God ... is a good story and report, sounded forth into all the world by the apostles, telling of a true David who strove with sin, death, and the devil. Without any merit of their own he made them righteous, gave them life, and saved them, so that they were given peace and brought back to God. For this they sing, and thank and praise God, are glad forever, if only they believe firmly and remain steadfast in faith.[41]

For Luther, proclamation is the center of all the church does and the central point of its theology and mission. The oral address of the gospel, in both divine and human form, communicates God's gracious promises in Christ for the salvation of the world. In this particular form of Christian speech, which is derived from Scripture and enlivened by the Spirit, Christ gives himself and his gifts— the "joyful exchange" of his righteousness for human sin that opens the "gates of heaven" for all the continued gracious workings of the Triune God.[42]

Bonhoeffer, too, sees Scripture as a witness to the gospel. The written words of the Bible are of the Spirit and mediate understanding of the facts as incarnate images of Christ as God's revelation, judgment, and will: "Christ is the speaker and the doer of the word." The standard of biblical exegesis is received with the word that is Scripture's revelation and foundation or "what drives toward Christ." He comments, "Because God speaks . . . by means of the authentic witness of historical revelation, God must personally also have spoken in historical events." While these historical events are embedded in the faith of the prophets, the apostles, and the historical person of Christ, "in order, however, to be comprehended as Spirit, he must appear in verbal form."[43] Theologians and preachers, too, are dependent upon the Spirit, since every attempt to speak God's word in human words remains a prayer to the Spirit, who confers understanding, speaking, and hearing: *Veni creator spiritus*, "Come, Creator Spirit!"[44]

Listening to the Spirit with Luther

In the fall of 1926, Bonhoeffer submitted a seminar paper on the topic of the Holy Spirit and Luther.[45] He drew primarily from two disputations by Luther during the period of 1535 to 1545: "Theses concerning Faith and the Law" and "The Disputation concerning Justification." The background of the disputations is Luther's desire to provide clarity concerning the gospel in light of attacks from theological opponents whom he viewed as antinomian. According to Bonhoeffer, the important elements for Luther are justification, law and gospel, and faith and love. The Reformer's approach to the Spirit followed Paul and the early church, thus departing from the metaphysical way of thinking favored by medieval scholastic theology. Rather than adhering to a systematic or speculative approach that works its way down to human faith and religious experience, Luther begins with the Spirit and means of grace that lead to the knowledge of God that is grasped by faith.[46]

Bonhoeffer introduces his topic by affirming God's desire for sinners; the gift of the Holy Spirit and the reason for grace are of God. The Spirit is the unity of law and gospel that puts sinners to death and brings forth new creatures in Christ. Grasping the truth of Christ—as for us and in us—requires the work of the Spirit and faith. As Bonhoeffer notes, "So, faith from the Spirit, Christ in faith, the Spirit from Christ, and therefore in faith, Christ gives the Spirit." Through faith, the Spirit creates a new person and a new self, bringing forth a new will and new heart that desire what the Spirit desires.[47] This change occurs through the medium of human words and the capacity of human understanding, in which "the Holy Spirit speaks the Word of God as a gift, as the effective reign of God." For theological reasons, those who interpret, preach, and listen need the Spirit as the subject of faith that grasps God's saving knowledge:

> This spiritual understanding, however, can only originate from the word. Therefore, faith arises only from the spiritually understood word. This, however, assumes faith. Spirit out of faith, faith out of Spirit. . . . Like can be understood only by like. God only through the Spirit; hearing the word or "receiving faith" cannot be one's own deed, instead it can only be the effect of the Spirit.[48]

Biblical interpretation and preaching are the activity of the Spirit, who addresses the church through the word of Scripture that has Christ as its meaning. Bonhoeffer summarizes this truth: "The Spirit is in truth in the word and, according to the content, the word is the word of the Holy Spirit as God, or the word of the Spirit that gives itself as a gift." This is the "holy circle" in which the church is established and built up.[49]

The hermeneutical and homiletical gifts of the Spirit create a way for Christ to enter into the congregation, which is also a way for the congregation to hear the word of Christ. This is dependent upon the promise of Isaiah 55, which the Spirit fulfills. As Bonhoeffer acknowledges, "I will never be able to convince through the words of my sermon unless the Spirit comes and makes my word into the Spirit's word." It is the Spirit who establishes the church through the instrument of preaching. However, to see the church truly, as a creation of the word, is possible only through faith granted by the Spirit and confessed in the creed: "I believe in the Church."[50]

Bonhoeffer learned from Luther that the Spirit's work through Scripture and preaching is generated by the gospel itself. This is why Luther could write with confidence, "We should not live in fear of poor preachers and should not rely too heavily on good ones." Thus, wherever the word is the Spirit is effective, and there is the church. The word of Scripture is the means by which the Spirit brings forth theologically informed thinking and speaking that springs from the present presence of Christ. Bonhoeffer concludes by affirming Luther's Trinitarian vision of the economy of salvation: "God the Father, in God's integrity, sends the Son and the Holy Spirit as gifts."[51]

Pneumatology, Christology, and ecclesiology mutually co-inhere within a "holy circle" of Trinitarian self-giving. Worship is the act of the church through the efficacy of the Spirit, who bonds with the "external Word" in the bodily and sensory practices of word and sacrament. As means of grace, these acts make known the presence of God in Christ, who freely communicates himself and converses in "revelatory signs."[52]

Sanctorum Communio: An Ecclesial Turn

In 1925, Bonhoeffer began plans for his dissertation, *Sanctorum Communio* ("The Communion of Saints"), under the supervision of Rudolph Seeberg.[53] Completed in 1927, it seeks to provide a study of the church as a theological community that embodies God's will and purpose for humanity in history by exploring the social intention of basic Christian concepts:[54] "In order to establish the clarity about the inner logic of theological construction, it would be good for once if a presentation of doctrinal theology were to start not with the doctrine of God but with the doctrine of the church."[55] An additional aim was to develop a specifically Christian sociology as an alternative to the liberal assumptions of his Berlin teachers. This led Bonhoeffer to challenge and reject the categories established by the historian Ernst Troeltsch—church, sect, and mysticism—in order to reclaim the concrete visibility of the church.[56] The church is neither a voluntary association nor a compulsory organization, categories that fail to take into account revelation, the reality of the essential relation between Christology and ecclesiology made visible in the world:[57]

> Revelation enters into time not just apparently but actually, and precisely by so doing it bursts the form of time. If, however, for this reason one regarded revelation only as beginning (potentiality), and not at the same time also as completion (reality), this

would take away what is decisive about the revelation of God, namely that God's word became history.[58]

Bonhoeffer's emerging homiletic theology is best understood from within the relation of Christology and ecclesiology, the hermeneutical space in which human words and actions are interpreted through the Spirit, who confers the reality of God's word in Christ. The visibility of the church, or "Christ existing in community," is the necessary condition for preaching that is both generative and demonstrative of revelation.[59] Although Bonhoeffer's christological starting point reflects Barth's insistence that revelation occupy a space in the world, his work also reflects a concern that the social reality of the church must be taken seriously in light of the humanity of Christ. A premise of his work is that the justification and renewal of humanity has as its life principle the gratuitous, self-giving love of Christ. Through the power of the Spirit, Christ himself calls forth and constitutes an ecclesial way of being with and on behalf of others that participate in his vicarious action in and for the world.[60]

Bonhoeffer's description of community is both theological and social; God sees the natural state of communication between human beings, human history is the history of human community, and the individual and community coexist and rest in one another. Community is therefore "from God to God," since the call to all humanity is communicated in the story of Christ. As completed in Christ, the church is God's revelation in Christ *and* in the church-community under the form of historical life. However, to truly "see" the church requires the gift of revelation that makes God's will visible in history as the work of the Holy Spirit. Bonhoeffer writes,

> In and through Christ the church is established in reality. It is not as if Christ could be abstracted from the church; rather, it is none other than Christ who "is" the church. Christ does not represent it; only what is not present can be represented. In God's eyes, however, the church is present in Christ. Christ did not merely make the church possible, but rather realized it for eternity. . . . This is accomplished by the Spirit-impelled word of the crucified and risen Lord of the church. The Spirit can work only through this word. . . . The word is social in character, not only in its origin but in its aim. Tying the Spirit to the word means that

the Spirit aims at a plurality of hearers and establishes a visible sign by which the actualization is to take place.[61]

The Spirit's actualization through the word "turns" or transforms Christians into one another through self-giving love. By seeking the good of others, the marks of division, which are consequences of sin, are exchanged and transformed. The true sociological structure of the church, then, is a participation in Christ's vicarious representation on behalf of one another.[62]

An early sermon by Luther ("The Sacrament of the Body and Blood of Christ") supports this thesis. As Luther writes, "In this sacrament, therefore, one is given through the priest a sure sign from God himself that he or she is united with Christ and his saints and has all things in common with them, that Christ's sufferings and life are one's own, together with the lives and sufferings of all the saints." The sacramental nature of the church is constituted by and embodies the vicarious action of Christ in the world, the "gracious exchange" of Christ's righteousness for the believer's sin:

> See to it that you give yourself to everyone and by no means exclude anyone in hatred or anger. For this sacrament of fellowship, love, and unity cannot tolerated discord and enmity. You must take to heart the infirmities and needs of others, as if they were your own. Then offer to others your strength, as if it were their own, just as Christ does for you in the sacrament. This is what it means to be changed into one another through love, out of many particles to become one bread and drink, to lose one's own form and to take on which is common to all.[63]

Bonhoeffer's "theology of sociality" cannot be separated from the sacramental reality of the church, the communion of saints, which was central for Luther.[64] As Luther comments in the *Large Catechism*, "Likewise the word *communio*, which is appended, should not be translated 'communion,' but 'community.' It is nothing but a comment or interpretation by which someone wished to explain what the Christian church is." He continues,

> This is the sum and substance of this phrase: I believe that there is on earth a little holy flock or community of pure saints under one head, Christ. . . . Until the last day the Holy Spirit remains

with the holy community or Christian people. Through it he gathers us, using it to teach and preach the Word. By it he creates and increases sanctification, causing it daily to grow and become strong in the faith and in the fruits of the Spirit.[65]

Bonhoeffer describes the work of the Spirit through preaching in a similar manner: "Preaching is an act of the whole community in whom scripture becomes a living word through which the Spirit confers the truth of the gospel as a social reality. . . . Preaching is a divinely ordained activity *of the church for the church.*" Entrusted by the Spirit to the *sanctorum communio*, the word is the creator and instrument of its life: "For it is the word preached according to the will of God and the church-community that is the means through which this will is actualized."[66]

The final part of *Sanctorum Communio* includes a discussion of the empirical church: "The whole theological reflection thus far not only leads to the discussion of the *sanctorum communio*, but is possible and meaningful only from the perspective of the *sanctorum communio*." Bonhoeffer's approach is neither exclusively historical nor sociological; rather, it seeks to embrace both. However, acknowledging the church's grounding in the reality of God and revelation requires the Spirit's assistance: "The church of Jesus Christ that is actualized by the Holy Spirit is really the church here and now . . . Christ existing as church-community."[67]

This vision of the church is a reality and not an ideal. While acknowledging the contingent, imperfect, and sinful nature of human speech, Bonhoeffer maintained the word of proclamation actually bears the Spirit's social activity. The basis of this claim is the work of the Spirit as the source of the church and the charismatic significance of preaching. As a social practice, then, the church proclaims its faith *and* embodies the Spirit's work as both a means to an end *and* an end in itself: "God makes the divine self the means to God's own end."[68]

The last section of *Sanctorum Communio* offers a series of judgments in relation to the church's mission of proclaiming the gospel as God's will and purpose for humanity. Bonhoeffer viewed the church's loss of access to ordinary people as a failure to bring the gospel into contact with their lives. The church was inattentive to the great number of people who were suffering from isolation and longing for a life with others, a condition that was recognized by competing social and political movements in Germany.

Bonhoeffer saw this as a homiletic problem, as a matter of *how* the church proclaims the gospel. The gospel should be proclaimed concretely for both those within the church and those who reject the church. In his judgment, too many sermons aimed to reach only the bourgeois class (i.e., civil servants, skilled workers, and merchants). As an expression of the "modern" style, this preaching was directed to people who lived "relatively securely and comfortably, in orderly families and circumstances, who are relatively educated and relatively stable morally." Their expectation was to hear a beautifully crafted, learned, and moral speech by an educated pastor with the status of a civil servant. Such preaching sought to display the preacher's literary expertise in order to connect with the inward experiences and (self-)interests of an audience.[69]

Learning the Practice of Preaching

In his work as a student preacher, Bonhoeffer went against the homiletical norms and expectations of the German church and culture. In November 1927, he submitted a sermon with an accompanying meditation and outline for his first theological examination and ordination.[70] The sermon text was Luke 9:51-56. Bonhoeffer begins with an invitation to the gospel narrative by directing attention to the passion of Jesus: "He set his face to go to Jerusalem." This establishes the focus of the sermon: "Yet they [the disciples] have not yet understood that Jesus' path is the path of divine love, not the path of divine judgment." His vivid retelling of the story highlights the difficulties of the disciples in order to proclaim the identity and action of Jesus.[71]

Although Bonhoeffer was relatively inexperienced as a preacher, the sermon displays a quality of theological and pastoral discourse that would increasingly characterize his preaching. He pays close attention to the plot of Luke's narrative; Jesus sent messengers to Samaritan territory to find lodging, but they were not welcomed; upon hearing this news, James and John called down fire from heaven to consume the Samaritans. He announces the significance of Jesus' response ("For the Son of Man has not come to destroy the lives of human beings but to save them") in order to pose a question ("How does this affect us?") that points to the reality of the gospel ("until the walls of the centuries that divide us from it disappear and we comprehend the timeless kernel of the story").[72]

Bonhoeffer had argued earlier for a way of reading that treats the Bible as "the ultimate book that narrates the most significant of events." He adhered to this approach in preaching from Luke. He describes the response of the Samaritans and their hostility toward the Jews. He then describes the reaction of the disciples and their anger toward the Samaritans. His close attention to the narrative leads to the most astonishing turn of the story—that Jesus expressed more anger toward the disciples than the Samaritans. Bonhoeffer takes this a step further—"They had completely misunderstood and failed to obey"—a failure that calls for a response: "No overdone enthusiasm! No excess emotion! . . . Instead, pay attention to the word. Be obedient. . . . Truly honoring Jesus is not a matter of attending to and cherishing his physical life but obeying his commandment." He calls the church to hear the word of Jesus: "Now all the facets of the picture are clear and transparent. We face Jesus eye to eye."[73]

The sermon concludes by exhorting the church to welcome Jesus, who is present and waiting, "a controlling, willful guest . . . [who] will not tolerate competition to his rule." Bonhoeffer's sermon narrated the German church into Luke's story of the Samaritans and disciples. On the one hand, they were filled with anger and pain; on the other, they were filled with zeal for calling down judgment on all who resist Christ and his mission: "In our midst, the story comes alive for the millionth time in the history of the world." The church must open itself to the gospel: "What does that mean? What is going on?"[74]

The gospel is a summons to believe the promises of God, whose word affects what is spoken: "When we begin to doubt our own power, it is then that we place our whole trust in the eternal power and love of God and our Lord Jesus Christ." Thought and action are one in faith, which is given and guided by the word of Jesus: "The Son of Man has not come to destroy the lives of human beings but to save them."[75]

This claim is established by proclaiming the true identity of Jesus: "[He is not] a religious genius, an ethical thinker, or a philosopher, but . . . [is] the Lord of death and life . . . the Word of God made flesh, for whom command and promise are the same." The command of love is accompanied by a promise of its fulfillment; receptivity to the word of Christ transforms the church to perceive the world with eyes illumined by his alluring love. By living from the love of Christ and the Father, Christians become "Christ to our brothers and sisters." Bonhoeffer closes with a prayer requesting that the eyes, ears, and hearts of all be opened and receptive to the rule of Christ: "Amen. Come, Lord Jesus."[76]

The theological authority of the sermon is worth noting in that Christology, ecclesiology, and preaching are drawn together into a "holy circle" through the medium of the scriptural word. The experience of human figures is not primary but rather presented in light of the presence and action of Jesus as God's Word of judgment and mercy. This focus on the identity of Christ undoubtedly reflects the theological influence of Barth. However, Bonhoeffer also follows Luther in affirming that God's word is realized in faithful and responsible action extended into the full range of human existence, including suffering, failure, limit, and need: "With the alluring love of Jesus Christ let us look at our time, the suffering out there in the world and the suffering here in the church, the suffering of blindness and deafness, both here and there."[77]

Berlin superintendent Dr. Bronish was examiner for the sermon. He commended Bonhoeffer for "gratifying evidence of intensive thought and thoroughgoing effort to comprehend the text from every perspective. It gives serious evidence of a struggle to utilize these points of view and groups of thoughts in a fruitful homiletical manner." Bronish's evaluation lists external and internal weaknesses related to punctuation, grammar, style, coherence, and unity. He even suggests that Bonhoeffer study model sermons by experienced preachers to cultivate a straightforward simplicity for delivering his message. But with regard to the actual delivery of the sermon, Bronish comments, "The sermon was preached with great assurance and vitality."[78]

As a university student, Bonhoeffer displayed an increasing independence in thought and practice. He began to move toward a vision of preaching in which the Spirit speaks God's Word through Scripture to create the social reality of the church. The discovery of Barth's early works and extensive study of Luther's theology and life were significant for his decision to challenge contemporary assessments of the gospel, which had submitted to the terms of German nationalism, culture, and intellectual respectability. Reading Luther against his modern interpreters, Bonhoeffer was led to a fresh discovery of the Reformer's confidence in God's Spirit to generate preaching and hearing of the word as Christ's act in the church that is actualized through the obedience of faith. A consequence of this "Lutheran" conversation was increasing awareness of the need for reclaiming the visibility of the church as a necessary condition for preaching the gospel: "Christian religion stands or falls with the belief in a historical and perceptibly real divine revelation."[79] This would be a persistent concern for the remainder of his life and work as a theologian and preacher—a homiletical theologian.

2

Reconciling Pastoral Ministry with Preaching
Barcelona 1928–1929

In December 1927, still only twenty-one years old, Bonhoeffer received a doctoral degree summa cum laude from the University of Berlin. Karl Barth would describe the dissertation, *Sanctorum Communio*, as nothing less than a "theological miracle."[1] Bonhoeffer had reached a vocational crossroads: Should he pursue the work of practical ministry and preaching or the academic career of a professor?[2] Max Diestel, the Berlin church superintendent, suggested Bonhoeffer spend a year as a vicar, a pastoral assistant in a congregation, to gain more practical training. Bonhoeffer agreed and received a year-long assignment with the German-speaking congregation in Barcelona. He viewed this dramatic change in environment as an opportunity to "stand on my own two feet for a longer period completely outside my previous circle of acquaintances."[3] Surprisingly, leaving his church work as a student assistant in Berlin was the most difficult factor in the move. The farewell on his last Sunday—when the pastor, children, and congregation prayed for him—sent shivers down his spine: "Where a people prays, there is the church; and where the church is, there is never loneliness."[4]

There was much to learn about the German-speaking church of about three hundred members in Barcelona, to which Bonhoeffer would refer as "the colony." He was immediately introduced to the children and youth and found they were open to receiving him. Attendance jumped dramatically, from one to fifteen girls and boys, after he led the children's service for the first time. The children were "wonderfully fresh and lively. . . . I showed them the splendid things that the children's service could offer, and that caught fire." Bonhoeffer was obviously affected by the response: "This service has virtually transformed me; the light anxiety that I couldn't get going with the practical work has vanished." He began making plans to offer religious instruction to the church's school and to continue building the children's service.[5]

Bonhoeffer lamented to friends about the lack of theological conversation partners like those he had enjoyed in Berlin. His initial impressions of the young people in Barcelona were not very favorable; they were spoiled, poorly brought up, cliquish, disrespectful, too comfortable, and lacking ambition in life. In addition, they did not appear to be very serious, having experienced little in comparison to their counterparts in Germany, especially in relation to the war, political revolution, and suffering that followed.[6]

Bonhoeffer was confident he had begun to make his mark with the congregation even before preaching his first sermon. Newcomers among the children were already quite responsive to his teaching, although he was warned they were "lazy bones, good for nothings, precocious, etc." He began working with the children on Sunday mornings, looking for opportunities to engage with their families during the week. By the time of his first sermon, a number of children, young people, and adults had already gotten to know him. He commented on the effect establishing such relationships was having on him: "My theology is beginning to become humanistic; what does that mean?"[7]

He had spent the previous four years in an academic environment where theology was studied as a "science." But he was now being drawn to experience more deeply the humanity of the church, a central topic of *Sanctorum Communio*. He was surprised to discover becoming more acquainted with the people of the congregation provided opportunities to reflect on the relation of theology, preaching, and the church.[8] He found the people defied his attempts to classify them, since many had worked their way up from simple beginnings to become competent in the German language and culture. He had the most difficulty understanding those who were willing to support the church without participating in its life. There was much gossip, moreover, a rather unpleasant experience for him.

He wrote to his parents about this problem, telling of the need to be cautious, since new people provided "inexhaustible conversation fodder" for the gossip mill: "There seems to be many factions within the colony, and the best tactic seem to be to know nothing about it and take as little interest in it as possible."[9]

As pastoral supervisor, Pastor Olbricht would be a constant factor in Bonhoeffer's Barcelona experience. He was not only distant from Bonhoeffer in age and experience but also different in temperament, training, and culture. He was a German patriot who made an annual pilgrimage to the homeland. Bonhoeffer came to view the older pastor with sympathy. He sensed Olbricht was a man without pathos, with neither a blasé manner nor arrogance, but a person who enjoyed material pleasures like "a good cigar or glass of wine rather than a bad sermon." Bonhoeffer was appalled by the pastor's intellectual habits: "He read little and studied less." In his estimation, Olbricht was "not exactly a dynamic pulpit presence."[10]

Olbricht possessed a temperament that was volatile and lively, prone to outbursts of anger and rants, especially at children and women. Bonhoeffer writes, "He typically first yells at those in need, assuring them they will secure nothing from us, and yet in the end never sends away any without something." Bonhoeffer also witnessed Olbricht's anger at the confirmands when they raised questions, incidents the pastor tended to forget rather quickly. He thought Olbricht was better suited for the army or work as a forest ranger. His assessment of the pastor's preaching was equally critical: "His sermons are uninspired and scandalously boring."[11]

Yet Bonhoeffer also observed in Olbricht a certain kind of humility, an honest assessment of himself and others, a capacity to relate openly and freely with the members of the congregation. He was impressed with how Olbricht seemed as at home outside the walls of the church as within. He notes the year with Olbricht raised no theological questions between them, and, on an intellectual level, they remained strangers. They liked each other in spite of their differences. Pastor Olbricht may have been the right supervisor for Bonhoeffer, since the pastor's manner of working provided ample time for his young assistant to reflect on his work, his calling, and his future plans: "He granted me all the freedom I wanted, and for that I was grateful to him."[12]

Bonhoeffer wrote to a friend in Berlin after his first sermon, stating that the change in church culture was beginning to challenge his theological convictions. He repeated his concern that many of the German-speaking people in Spain had not experienced the trauma and loss the German homeland knew from the war. He began to wonder if he should rethink his theology "from the ground up." The children continued to touch him with their openness and desire to learn, which was for him both frightening and beautiful. His involvement in the congregation had also begun to challenge some of his deeply held convictions about piety and devotion, even though the religious expression of the people had initially overwhelmed him.[13]

Bonhoeffer took great pride in his academic training at Berlin. He complained to a friend when the Evangelical High Church Council in Berlin suggested he attend one of the church's preacher's seminaries to equip him more practically for ministry:

> How dare these presumptuous consistory bigwigs suggest they can train a person better in a preacher's seminary than when such a person is already prepared for an academic career? That takes gall at that! . . . Those spiritual gray beards. Just don't be taken in by them, hide behind the university; surely the dean would have to intervene in this matter.[14]

He was discovering that the easygoing Spanish way of life that seemed so charming was also counterproductive to serious scholarly work. However, after several months in Barcelona and regular opportunities to taste its cultural life, a dearth of intellectual conversations and questions was becoming more acceptable. Bonhoeffer perceived the Spanish way of life as one in which "everything is so logical and regulated and lacks any real spirit." On the other hand, a pleasant aspect of this lack of ambition was that he saw very few signs of arrogance: "People don't try to be something they are not!"[15]

Bonhoeffer wrote to Max Diestel after his first few months in Barcelona. He reported there was little work for him apart from the services on Sunday: no Bible study, religious instruction, lectures, or young adult fellowship. In addition, there was too much business, gossip, and moralizing, and just a dab of religiosity. On the other hand, Bonhoeffer reported observing an "enormous amount of honesty and decency, without posturing and arrogance": "I must say I really like being with most of the people. You can see I am glad to be here. . . . Let me thank you for helping me along into this period, which will certainly be important for my entire life."[16]

He remained ambivalent about his future plans in spite of increasing confidence in doing pastoral work and a growing fondness for the Barcelona congregation. He wrote to his most respected professor, Adolf von Harnack, approximately halfway through his assignment:

> Here amid all my purely practical work, where as a scholar I am completely dependent on myself and my books, where I must live without any exchange of ideas in this regard, I think back to those hours in your house and to those afternoons in [Berlin] with a certain sense of longing and melancholy, and often wish I could sit again for but a single hour in your seminar circle or have a conversation with you of the unforgettable kind that I remember from seminar celebrations, outings, and various other occasions. Only here have I come to realize completely what I had and what I have lost, both in a scholarly and human sense.[17]

He was looking forward to the possibility of returning to Harnack's scholarly circle. He acknowledged his longing was accompanied by a growing awareness that the obsessive nature of academic pursuits had its limitations. His immersion in pastoral work was bringing a certain amount of necessary freedom for appreciating the goodness of life in other ways.[18]

Bonhoeffer shared similar thoughts with Reinhold Seeberg, his doctoral mentor, regarding his vocation and future. He expressed his gratitude for Seeberg's influence, expressing hope that they would someday be reunited in their academic endeavors. He was appreciative of the opportunity to be in Barcelona; it was good for him to work with such a mixture of people far removed from his own circle of interests and view of life. The settled Spanish way of life was marked by an apparent absence of tension, anxiety, and restlessness, conditions he perceived as pervasive in Germany. He saw the congregation as free from intellectual affectation, the "mannerism of the sort we enjoy in such abundance in Germany and which is considered so essential to good form." He repeated his admiration for the decency, honesty, and simplicity he observed in people, as was their lack of arrogance and pride: "Not to be anything one is not . . . puffed up [or] posing . . . I fear we have forfeited a great deal abroad."[19]

Learning to Preach with "Real People"

Bonhoeffer shared his musings on theology, preaching, and pastoral ministry in a letter to Walter Dress, a friend and former classmate. Preaching from 2 Corinthians 12:9 left him wondering about particular matters he had always found theologically ambiguous. He was beginning to view these questions from a different angle in light of his work with the congregation: "Can one refer to sin as God's will with regard to human beings, and in this way reassure people about themselves and have them look to Christ alone?" His confusion concerned the sufficiency of Christ, not only to human misfortune, but also to sin. Bonhoeffer had had a strong sense of the reassuring nature of the text while preparing the sermon, but he began to doubt his judgment as to whether he wanted the text to be too reassuring. He found help in Luther's dictum *pecca fortitor* ("sin boldly, but believe and rejoice in Christ even more boldly").[20]

Bonhoeffer had begun reading the text in light of his pastoral responsibilities. He sensed that without acknowledgment of sin, people would be left to despair of themselves, completely ruined and "with a God who does nothing." He was confronted by a theological and practical dilemma: "Is the gospel then only for those 'outwardly weak' and not rather for those who are weak in will? Is strength and will a path to sinlessness? Whoever abides in Christ sins no more." He was questioning whether this claim should be taken seriously. Should people be encouraged to look away from their sin and conscience to Christ in both the present and the future?[21] He suggests to Dress that such thoughts must sound rather "un-Barthian." He found them quite liberating, however, describing this way of thinking as "eudaemonistic." He was wondering if God does not think this way as well. He concludes by asking Dress for his thoughts, noting it was a matter of great importance "compared to academic theology."[22]

Bonhoeffer's first preaching opportunity came on March 11, 1928, the third Sunday in Lent. His sermon text was Romans 11:6: "But if it is by grace, it is no longer on the basis of works; otherwise grace would no longer be grace" (ESV). He begins with a direct reference to Paul and his significance for the congregation: "He is talking about God's will to grant us salvation, that is, about justification." He suggests the text possesses a rather "unpretentious" character that can be easily overlooked, that any number of matters could have occupied their attention. To do so, however, would demonstrate how much their thoughts had moved beyond Paul and the early Christians, falling "far below the sublime thoughts that stirred early Christianity."[23]

Bonhoeffer's introduction to the reality of justification, a matter that is "neither trivial nor comical," acknowledges "God's honor and goodness, God's seriousness and goodness." His plan was to divide the text into two clear "strong lines." The first line, "works," leads from human beings to God; the second line, "grace," leads from God to human beings. Paradoxically, although "grace" and "works" belong together, they are also opposed to each other, a mystery that makes possible conceiving of "God and the human being together." The stage was set for Bonhoeffer's exposition of "the miracle of the Christian faith we must fathom."[24]

The heart of the sermon is a lengthy discourse that builds upon a quote from Augustine's *Confessions*: "You have made us for yourself, and our heart is restless until it rests in you."[25] Bonhoeffer offers his understanding of restlessness:

> "Restless," this is the word that concerns us. Restlessness is the characteristic feature distinguishing human beings from animals. Restlessness is the power that creates history and culture. Restlessness is the root of every spirit that elevates itself to morality; restlessness is—let us go ahead and say it—the most profound meaning and the bloodlike power in all religion. Restlessness—not in any transitory human sense, where all we find is nervousness and impatience—no, restlessness in the direction of the eternal. Instead of restlessness we could also say dread, anxiety, yearning, love.[26]

The great problem that haunts human beings is a desire to transcend the self, to experience the power of the eternal, to control the infinite so to be rid of anxiety and restlessness. The sermon has the feel of a lecture, the sound of a recently graduated theology student demonstrating his knowledge. Bonhoeffer concludes his rather lengthy description of human restlessness with a theological assertion that, presumably, echoes Barth's critique of religion: "God is God, and grace is grace." This is the "great disturbance" of all human illusions, illustrated by the ancient myth of the Tower of Babel: "But if it is by grace, it is no longer on the basis of works, otherwise grace would no longer be grace."[27]

Bonhoeffer returns to the text of Romans, marking a shift in the direction of the sermon: "For another path emerges, the path of God to human beings, the path of revelation and grace alone. It is not religion that can make us good before God, but God alone who makes us good." The movement of the sermon continues to labor under the weight of its wordiness. A sermon on the topic of restlessness, on how human beings long for the eternal, must have seemed like an eternity to the congregation. Bonhoeffer finally concludes, "Only one thing remains, namely, that God comes to human beings and bestows grace." The gospel is the path of grace from eternity into time, the path of Jesus Christ that is the paradoxical message that moved with such power through the ancient world.[28]

Bonhoeffer's initial sermon offered much in analysis and explanation; it is dense and wordy, intellectually rigorous, grand, and expressive. The sermon reads like what might be expected of a newly graduated doctor of philosophy in theology, learned in his field, a product of the University of Berlin, the pride of the German academic tradition. Yet Bonhoeffer was still relatively inexperienced as a preacher and was a newcomer to his audience. The sermon offers a Lutheran exposition of grace and works that points to God's judgment and mercy revealed in the events of Good Friday and Easter. It concludes with a brief word from Luther: "We are beggars in spirit."[29] A Lenten sermon reflecting on the condition of human restlessness may have also reflected something of a young preacher's own restlessness during a time of uncertainty and change in his vocation and life.

Bonhoeffer preached on the first Sunday of Easter, choosing as his text Matthew 28:20: "Remember, I am with you always, to the end of the world."[30] He begins by rehearsing the story of humanity's rebellion against God and the consequences of sin. He reminds the congregation of the events of holy week, when the hope of redemption was "radically demolished" by Good Friday—the crucifixion of

Christ. The sermon follows the movement from death to life, when "God took up dwelling among human beings anew and for all eternity, the day when the outstretched but unholy hand of humanity was filled, against all hope, with divine grace, the day when Christ was raised!" The Easter message is good news of a God who is not distant but nearby.[31]

The sermon seeks to unfold the remarkable message of Easter. The goodness of God's creation and the destiny of humanity as communion with God provide the context for Bonhoeffer's interpretation. "I am with you always" is the reality of Jesus Christ, the One Word of God speaking: "Remember, I am there. . . . Whether we see Jesus or not, feel him or not, want him or not—none of this makes any difference over against the fact that Jesus is here with us, that he is simply wherever we are, and we can do absolutely nothing. I am with you always." Because of the great recapitulation of the creation stories and the rebellion of human beings, the reality of God is now found among the abandoned, homeless, and lonely of the world. The great wonder of Easter is that the world is transfigured by its light. He assures the congregation that God walks among them. They can speak with God; they can walk down the street with God; they encounter God in the stranger on the road, in the beggar at their door: "The world is God's world; wherever we go, we encounter God, and Jesus, the Resurrected, is with us."[32]

The sermon brings the congregation into the drama of the Easter story. Children, boys and girls, adults, men and women, parents and the most mature, even the elderly, are addressed by God's Word. The various stages of life and all its circumstances are seen in light of the One Word of Jesus Christ: "Our entire life stands under that word and is sanctified by that word. . . . Remember, I am with you." Bonhoeffer adds, "This applies *whether we want it to or not.*" The promise of God is followed by the judgment of God, emphasizing both the gift and the burden of the promise "I am with you always." There is assurance in knowing that the judgment of the nearby God is accompanied by grace.[33]

Bonhoeffer identifies the climax of the sermon as a "fairy tale," as a story that sounds too good to be true but has become reality: "Remember, I am with you. Jesus Christ, God himself, speaks to us from every human being; the other person, this enigmatic, inpenetrable You, is God's claim on us; indeed, it is the holy God in person whom we encounter." The miracle of Easter illuminates Matthew 25: "Just as you did it to the least of these, you did it to me." Life in the human community acquires divine meaning in Christ and becomes a form of God's revelation in the world: "The most profound meaning of our ties to social life is that through it we are tied all the more securely to God."[34]

A simplicity characterizes the sermon in light of the proclamation of Easter. Bonhoeffer's interpretation is informed by a vision of Easter that addresses the life of Christian people in the present, where God is encountered. The sermon is a confession of faith in God, whose mercy and judgment are revealed in Christ through the ordinary circumstances of life. There is a homiletical clarity that illumines rather than obscures, reflecting Bonhoeffer's attentiveness to Scripture in shaping the sermon for the life of the church. If the God who raised Jesus from the dead does not exist, the sermon makes no sense; neither does the church; nor does the world as God's creation. Theology, exegesis, and preaching function as interrelated parts of the whole. The congregation is encouraged to discern what being Christian people entails for them in the day-to-day circumstances of their lives: "Jesus Christ is with us to the end of the world. This we owe to Easter."[35]

Summer was a time when many parishioners visited the German homeland. Bonhoeffer wrote to Superintendent Diestel regarding his plans: "Things around me are starting to quiet down now. For the first time, services this year will continue through the vacation as well, albeit only every two weeks and with no guarantee anyone will attend. . . . I will be one of the few who sees things through." He concludes, "I must say that I really like being with most of the people and have an extremely nice social life. I especially enjoy the children's service here, which I had to reestablish and which has started off well."[36]

An early summer sermon was from Psalm 62:2 (Ps 62:1 NRSV): "My soul is silent before God, who helps me." Bonhoeffer begins with a lengthy description of the Psalter's power to speak deeply within the human soul: "Like a song from ancient times, like a medieval picture, painted on a gilt background, like a childhood memory, this strange, alien statement about the soul drifts down to us in the twentieth century." He invites the congregation to consider if the psalm still has any relevance for them: "Is there still something like the soul in an age such as ours, an age of machines, of economic competition, of the dominance of fashion and sports? Is this nothing more than a cherished childhood memory, like so much else?"[37]

The heart of the sermon addresses what it means to have a soul and to be silent before God: "Well, of course, some might say, you are telling us all of these wonderful things, but why is it that so few actually get this far? It must be something that requires special power or grace." There is a fear of silence that is marked by boredom and busyness—a lethargic and lazy spirit that plagues the religious life. Moreover, human beings often fear God might actually disturb them by acting in their lives. They may lack discipline in relation to God. They may be reluctant to practice their faith, to learn the language of faith, to learn to speak with God in prayer, since faith requires work: "Confusing religion with emotional daydreaming is a grievous, fateful error. Religion takes work, perhaps the hardest and certainly the most sacred work a person can undertake."[38]

The congregation is exhorted to be faithful, to take up a life of prayer, to practice silence, to expose themselves daily to God's word. Bonhoeffer offers encouragement from his own modest experience, noting it is possible to spend a few minutes each day reading Scripture and being in God's presence. Although there is difficulty in getting started, even feeling funny or empty at first, those who apply themselves will eventually be rewarded with an abundance of fruit.[39]

Bonhoeffer returns to Augustine's *Confessions*, to a key passage from his initial sermon: "You have made us for yourself, and our heart is restless until it rests in you." Human restlessness must be understood within a basic law of the universe that determines there can be no rest or satisfaction in itself. Rest can be only where the whole has been attained, which means rest can be found only in God: "May God grant something of this rest to all of us, may God draw us into his stillness and solitude, and we will be grateful to him."[40]

Bonhoeffer wrote to Walter Dress approximately halfway through his assignment. The letter provides a window into what he was seeing, thinking, and learning in pastoral work: "I am getting to know new people each day, at least their life stories." He valued this kind of experience, since it afforded him the privilege of seeing more deeply into the reality of others' lives: "One encounters people here the way they are, far from the masquerade of the Christian world." Those whom he met comprised a rather diverse cast of characters, especially in the city of Barcelona, including criminals, vagabonds, vagrants, and assorted misfits. He was discovering they possessed a variety of passions, while many were small-minded, with limited desires, ambitions, and goals—he adds, "all in all, people who feel homeless in both senses, people who thaw a lot when you speak to them in a friendly manner—*real people*." He was drawn to them, to understand their condition, sharing generously of his time and attention. He perceived them as standing under grace rather than wrath. In his judgment, it was the "Christian world," presumably a reference to the church, which stood under wrath rather than grace. A passage in Isaiah had been helpful in making sense of such things: "I am sought out by those who did not ask . . . to those who did not call on my name I said, 'Here I am'" (Isa 65:1).[41]

Bonhoeffer's daily encounters with "real people" had a profound effect on his thinking as he prepared to assume the summer preaching responsibilities: "I don't know where to begin with the precious half hour one has." He sensed his preaching was beginning to change: "I am preaching much differently from what I have thought possible for myself." He was considering a number of texts for future sermons and was grateful for initial signs of success in his preaching that brought "a mixture of personal joy, let's say self-awareness, and objective gratitude."[42]

The experience of preaching was joining the personal and vocational elements of his life. Standing in the pulpit prompted awareness of his pride, of his desire to excel, and that such feelings were inseparable from his calling. It was a struggle that

> one can perhaps ennoble but cannot fundamentally eliminate, a mixture under which one suffers doubly as a theologian—but on the other hand, who wouldn't be pleased about a full church, or that people are coming who haven't come for years? And on the other hand, who analyzes this joy to determine whether it is completely untainted?[43]

A consequence was that his mind was being changed with regard to the nature of preaching and function of sermons. He was questioning his tendency to classify people, to assess others on the basis of their religious or social status and background, but without sufficient consideration of their identity as members of the body of Christ:

> I have long thought that sermons had a center that, if you hit it, would move anyone or confront them with a decision. I no longer believe that. First of all, a sermon can never grasp the center, but can only be grasped by it, by Christ. And then Christ becomes flesh as much in the word of the pietists as in that of the clerics, or of the religious socialists, and these empirical connections actually pose difficulties for preaching that are absolute, not merely relative. At the most profound level, people are simply not all one, but are individuals, totally different people "united" only by the word in the church.[44]

Bonhoeffer was thinking about the effectiveness of preaching. He found his best sermons were spoken in an enticing manner, similar to telling children fairy tales about a strange land. His fear was that the task of presenting milk was easily turned into offering sugar water instead. He had reflected on this challenge in light of 1 Corinthians 3:2: "I fed you with milk, not solid food, for you were not ready for solid food. Even now you are still not ready." He had been contemplating preaching from the Beatitudes in Matthew 5, of which he notes, "I have never approached a sermon with such trepidation."[45]

Later in the summer, Bonhoeffer preached from 1 Corinthians 12:26-27: "Now you are the body of Christ and individually members of it." The sermon begins with a brief description of the importance of the church for Catholics: "It stirs profound religious feelings, ranging from awe and dread to the bliss of God's presence." "Church" is a word that evokes feelings of home, feelings that only a child might feel in gratitude, reverence, and selfless love toward a mother. Bonhoeffer contrasts a Catholic love for the church with that of Protestants, which he describes as "banal, indifferent, and superfluous." He continues, "Church is a word that does not make a [Protestant's] heart beat faster . . . a word that in any event does not lend wings to our religious feelings."[46]

The sermon focuses on the necessity of recovering the God-given significance of the church for the continued existence of

Protestantism: "Yes, the word whose glory and greatness we want to examine today is 'church.'" The congregation is prompted to consider the possibility of ". . . [beholding] in our service today something of the radiance and luster, the shining splendor that is the church. Ah, so much dust has settled on this word over the centuries that I hardly dare to hope."[47]

The sermon is a stirring exposition of the church as the body of Christ. Bonhoeffer echoes the astonishing claim made by Paul to the Christians in Corinth, a congregation plagued by questions, filled with problems, a people who doubted the resurrection, lived in incest and sin, and were dominated by weak faith: "Paul now writes the words, 'you *are* the body of Christ'; not 'you should be,' no, precisely that 'you *are.*'" The sermon draws from *Sanctorum Communio* to affirm the miraculous nature of the church as a creature of the Word. Bonhoeffer asserts, "Apparently the text is saying this to us, as well, 'you are the body of Christ,' you need only behold it; you need do nothing for it. God has already done everything; through God's grace we are the body of Christ." To this he adds, "But this also means that God has fused us together into a single life whose strength, breath, blood, and spirit is Jesus Christ."[48]

Bonhoeffer's aim was to depict the beauty or form of the church as the body of Christ. The church is the pilgrim people of God—neither a building nor a bell tower, neither an organization nor an activity. "Church" is only understood in terms of belonging to "God's chosen people through the world under the banner of Christ, and that means from within God from eternity. . . . Church means community with the people of God in God himself."[49] Bonhoeffer called the congregation to embrace an identity exceeding national and ethnic origins—to see themselves as a people in the true sense of the word, with its own laws and justice. Three strengths characterize the miraculous existence of the church. The first is the greatest power on earth: "We are able to sacrifice for others with a joyous heart." The second is, "We are able to pray for one another." The third, however, is the most "sublime, miraculous, mysterious and sacred . . . namely, that we forgive one another's sins."[50]

Bonhoeffer concludes the sermon with the urgent need for a Protestant recovery of "church." "Church" means recovering sacrifice, intercession, and the confession of sins as miraculous powers that are summed up in the word "love," the kind of love God showed the world, which is "becoming Christ for the other person."[51] The congregation's calling in Christ is a sign of the world's destiny in God: "Our world should become part of the people of God; it should become church." The necessary remedy for the current age in its feeble, weak, and homeless state is "back to the church, back to where a member bears the other in love, where one lives the life of the other, where there is community in God, where there is home because there is love."[52]

In August, Bonhoeffer followed through with his plan to preach from the Sermon on the Mount. His text was "Blessed are the pure in heart, for they will see God" (Matt 5:8). He began by calling attention to the sacred nature of the text: "Those who come too close to today's text lose their lives to it." The best response is "to behold and be silent, to allow ourselves to be seized and conquered by this text." Bonhoeffer returns to an earlier theme, that of yearning and restlessness, the cry of the world to see God in the midst of its godlessness and godforsakenness. Israel's entire existence was a cry for God, which was joined by the voices of Plato, Socrates, Kant, and German philosophy. The great problem, however, is that while humankind longs to gaze upon the face of God, it finds itself fixated with the world and things, "dreary, gloomy, gray, ugly, as if we were no longer able to lift our eyes or look in a different direction."[53]

Bonhoeffer suggests the congregation consider if there is anyone from whom they could receive such sight without being blinded by its light. The stage was set for the words of Jesus: "Blessed are the pure in heart, for they will see God." The vision of God requires a conversion of the heart, to become like the One it loves and beholds, since a pure heart reflects and takes in God. Purity is a beautiful word that is full and mature, "a word causing the heart momentarily to skip a beat, a word prompting a bit of melancholy to come over us." Clarity is "the mark of purity, clarity of vision that beholds the beauty of creation, the innocence of a child, the love of a spouse, a couple at the altar, the thoroughly transfigured conscience that radiates from the eyes of the mature. . . . Purity, it overwhelms us when we look with Jesus's eyes and heart."[54]

The sermon moves forward with a question: "What is here that moves us so?" And it is followed by the promise of Christ: "Blessed

are the pure in heart." Only Jesus removes the darkness brought by
sin, the loss of clarity and purity, the spiritual and moral blindness
that exists, opening the eyes of the heart to God: "Become simple,
clear, genuine, natural, straightforward, pure, and your hearts will
reflect God's own parental heart." The distressing realization of
every Christian is their loss of purity and need for grace: "Lord, I
cannot do it alone. . . . If you made me pure, then I am impure."
Bonhoeffer shifts the focus from the self to God, since to see God
means to recognize God: "It means beholding in astonishment and
child-like awe God's mysteries being revealed." Although the vision
of God in the present is partial and yet to be fully revealed, beholding God is "to become a piece of eternity ourselves in love, gratitude,
and purity." When the world cries out to God, the voice of Jesus is
louder: "Blessed are the pure in heart, for they will see God."[55]

Sermons were occupying an increasing amount of Bonhoeffer's
time. He commented on the serious nature of homiletical work in
a letter to his parents, apologizing for the delay in writing because
of his preaching responsibilities: "Preparing sermons still demands
much of my time. Actually I work on them the entire week, every
day."[56] He shared his plans to deliver a lecture on the essence of
Christianity in December. He was pleased how recent conversations
with the young people had revolved around the theme of the lecture
and pleased that their work together included reading assignments,
reports, and group discussions. He mentions again his impressions
of the young people: "There is not much intellectual arrogance or
self-importance. In any event, intelligence is not overrated. One has
the impression of greater honesty and clarity."[57]

Bonhoeffer preached his last two sermons to the congregation
in December 1928 and February 1929. The December sermon was
from Revelation 3, a call to wait upon God in the season of Advent,
"an art our impatient age has forgotten." The greatest and most profound things in life require patience; nothing good happens in a
rush—it happens only according to divine law. Waiting, moreover,
is impossible for those who are full and satisfied. Bonhoeffer returns
to the theme of restlessness and yearning, emptiness and poverty:

> Only people who carry a certain restlessness around with them
> can wait, and people who look up reverently to the One who is
> great in the world. Hence, only those whose souls give them no

peace are able to celebrate Advent, who feel poor and incomplete and who sense something of the greatness of what is coming . . . the Holy One, God in the child in the manger. God is coming, the Lord Jesus is coming . . . !⁵⁸

Advent is a time to acknowledge the condition of homesickness, a time of yearning for the eternal house of the Father. Homesickness weighs upon the world as "the curse of eternally having to sojourn without goal and without end." Bonhoeffer inquires if anyone can offer such help and redemption. His answer is a prayer: "Come, God, Lord Jesus Christ, come into our world, into our homelessness, into our sin, into our death, come, you yourself, and share with us, be a human being as we are and conquer for us."⁵⁹

The sermon concludes with a passionate announcement of God's nearness in Christ: "You are searching for him, would perhaps give anything to have him with you sometimes, genuinely, actually with you, not just inwardly, but physically, in reality." Bonhoeffer points to Matthew 25, the parable of the sheep and goats, which depicts Jesus standing at the door, knocking, in the figure of the beggar, the degenerate, and every other person: "Christ walks the earth as long as there are people, as your neighbor, as the person through whom God summons you, addresses you, makes claims on you." Life is a perpetual time of Advent, a time of restlessness and waiting for the final Advent when a new heaven and new earth will emerge. Human beings will then be brothers and sisters, joined with the angels to proclaim "peace on earth and goodwill among people."⁶⁰

Bonhoeffer preached his final sermon in February 1929. The text was Philippians 4:7: "And the peace of God, which surpasses all understanding, will guard your hearts and your minds in Christ Jesus." The sermon begins with the familiar theme of restlessness, the thirst for a peace that the world was created to desire: "We sense the rift between us and the infinite and know that this rift, that is, our own godlessness and godforsakenness, is the basis of our weakness, our restlessness; and all our activities are basically trying to do nothing other than to overcome this rift."⁶¹

Bonhoeffer affirms Paul's exhortation to peace as a summons to be reconciled with God, a reality transcending all beautiful and well-intentioned hopes for world peace. The peace of God is discerned by looking to the transitory as a sign pointing to the in-transitory. There are forms of peace for which all human beings long: feeling supported, loved, and protected, being able to count on others' loyalty, and having a home amid the restlessness of the world. The congregation's greatest need, however, is to hear God speaking: "Leave the rush and anxiety and restlessness of the world, come to me and to my peace. Give me your tormented, outcast heart, and I will heal your wounds and give your heart the peace of God. Come to me, all you that are weary and are carrying heavy burdens, and I will give you rest, and you will find rest for your souls."[62]

Words of blessing to the congregation follow. Bonhoeffer offers thanks for the opportunity to learn the beauty and serious nature of his calling. He singles out the experience of preaching for special mention. His comments offer a glimpse into the growth of his self-understanding as a preacher:

> Having to speak about God is indeed a great thing when one yet knows that with human words one can at best merely touch the hem of God's holy garment, and that it is God's grace when God initiates something to his own glory. Many a time I have come to the pulpit with an anxious heart. Would I find the right words? In such cases, the message of God's peace has always helped, the peace that surpasses all understanding and works and creates in its own free way.[63]

The Formation of a Homiletical Theologian

Bonhoeffer delivered a lecture to the Barcelona community in early December: "Jesus Christ and the Essence of Christianity." The lecture pulls together a number of key convictions that informed the aim, rigor, and intensity of his sermons. There is the problem of religion as a separate compartment of life, a view he saw as having severe consequences: "We all know that, for all practical purposes, Christ has been eliminated from our lives." However, knowing Christ is an either-or commitment. Christ is not a "spiritual" Lord but rather claims the whole of life for God's will. Bonhoeffer acknowledges there are many popular religious views of Christ that put him into a worthy position according to aesthetic categories—a religious genius, a great ethicist, a sacrificial hero, one who is committed to a great idea: "The only thing these attempts do not do is take him seriously. That is, they do not draw the center of their own lives into contact with Christ's claim to speak and to indeed be [the] revelation of God."[64]

The serious matter of God speaking has been lost by the church. Since God's word once became present reality in Christ, it is Christ who possesses urgent significance: "To understand Christ means to understand this claim: taking Christ seriously means taking seriously his absolute claim on human decision." The problem is shared by all Christians, lay and professional, since for many pulpits and lecterns the primary source of what is spoken could actually be "Plato, Buddha, or Goethe." But a "history of religions" approach quickly loses sight of Christian uniqueness. Christianity is reduced to a historical manifestation of a general category called "religion" and defined essentially by Hellenistic culture.[65]

The "history of religions" approach had led to a century and a half of attempts to write the life of Jesus. Bonhoeffer asserts, "The main reason for this situation is that our New Testament originated in a church-community that worshiped Jesus not as a historical personality but as Kyrios, the Lord . . . and thus as God, himself." The way forward will be found only by allowing the New Testament to speak rather than reconstructing historical portraits of Jesus and the early church. Moreover, hearing the claim the New Testament makes in its entirety means coming to terms with history on the unsettling basis of Christ as God's revelation in the world. This means God's claim is heard in the whole of the gospel narrative—in the incarnation, ministry, suffering, death, and resurrection of Christ. Bonhoeffer concludes, "In all these episodes, we thus see Jesus up on the icy heights of that unrelenting demand on human beings. Who will dare to follow him? Who will enter his discipleship?"[66]

The movement of the Gospel narratives yields a rather astonishing picture. Jesus looks to the unnoticed, those who are hidden beneath the surface—the children, the morally and socially least of these, all who are viewed as less worthy. The whole of the gospel story points to a God who does not want those who already know, the strong and moral heroes, or the saints, but rather the unrighteous, foolish, and sinners. All human claims on God, therefore, are at an end. Bonhoeffer alludes to both Luther and Barth to make this point: "There is absolutely no path leading from human beings to

God." All attempts to bring about such a path amount to building another Tower of Babel.[67]

The lecture reflects the influence of Luther's theology of justification and Barth's critique of religion, particularly as it was defined by liberal Protestantism.[68] Christianity is not a historical manifestation of religion contained in a separate sphere of life. A Barthian critique of human religious pride is thus joined with a Lutheran vision of God, who graciously comes close to those who make no claims. God chooses what is foolish and weak in the eyes of the world. God chooses people who listen and receive; people who see themselves far removed from God; people who do not live with the illusion that they are entitled to make claims on God through religion or morality: "The Christian religion is basically amoral and irreligious." The gospel is the most dangerous criticism of a church that presents itself as a human way to God. The lecture, as do the sermons, stops short of offering concrete ethical direction for obeying God's command to serve Christ in the neighbor, particularly those who suffer at the margins of life:[69] "Christ's gift is not the Christian religion but God's grace and love, which culminate in the cross."[70]

The strength of Bonhoeffer's preaching in Barcelona is a passionate focus on the need of all people for the gospel, for humble faith in God's grace revealed in the nearness of Christ crucified. The sermons are marked by serious engagement with Scripture and the influence of Barth and Luther. Only God's grace and love in Christ are able to satisfy human restlessness, yearning, homesickness, and godlessness—especially for those engaged in the practice of religion. Human hunger and desire for rest in God was an orientating focus in Bonhoeffer's interpretation of Scripture, understanding of people, and framing of sermons. But he had not yet begun to wrestle seriously with the political and social implications of this claim in light of his pride and status as a German citizen and academic theologian.

He found that his thinking about preaching began to change as he made himself available to know and be known by strangers within and outside the church. He was surprised to discover that work in practical ministry, in being with others whom he described as "real people," could be a means of deepening theological understanding. On the other hand, he was disappointed in not finding the kind of theological conversation partners he enjoyed in Berlin. Most surprising to Bonhoeffer was how Barcelona offered opportunities for a different kind of learning, the primary text of which was a willingness of others to share their lives with him. His reflection on this experience in light of his academic training prompted him to reconsider two primary elements of his dissertation—theology and sociology, Christ and humanity in community—in much closer relationship. His reflection on preaching accompanied and contributed to a gradual shift toward language that was more personal and social, less abstract and individualistic. He was learning the integral relationship of theological content and homiletical form, the shape preaching takes to be heard as the word of God in a particular time and place.[71]

Bonhoeffer was learning that the pastoral vocation has a sense of personal truth and participatory knowledge, a form of practical wisdom that orients the life of the church in and through its present circumstances toward its final end in communion with God.[72] Augustine, whose *Confessions* Bonhoeffer cited on several occasions, exemplified a way of knowing that springs from faith that rests upon the humble love of God. Augustine wrote in the *Confessions* of an intensive seeking for wisdom and understanding prior to his conversion to Christianity. A passionate love of philosophy and learning in pursuit of eternal truth entailed his commitment to a way of life—an intellectual, moral, and emotional awakening and inner healing facilitated by the spoken or written words of ancient sages.

Augustine was able to describe the intellectual vanity fostered by his love of philosophy only after his baptism and incorporation into the body of Christ. He confessed his prideful illusion that human reason is capable of ascending unaided to divine wisdom and happiness.[73] The doctrine of the incarnation revealed in the church's "folly of preaching" and the correlative way of life shaped by Christ's humble self-giving were significant factors in this conversion. Later, as a pastor and bishop, he would proclaim God's Wisdom incarnate in Christ as the principle of creation and as both the means and the end of its redemption:

> And so it was in the Wisdom of God that the world was unable to come to know God through wisdom. So why did she come, when

she was already here, if not because it was God's pleasure through the folly of preaching to save those who believe? . . . That is how the Wisdom of God treats the ills of humanity, presenting herself for our healing, herself the physician, herself the psychic. So because man had fallen through pride, she applied humility to his cure.[74]

Augustine was no stranger to the healing power of God's Wisdom in the fellowship of the church. Through an extended time of repentance, confession, and forgiveness, his mind was changed to see how human loves and desires point to a deeper restlessness that seeks certitude and control through attachment to created things instead of the Creator. Restless human beings find satisfaction when reoriented by grace toward a life of love—for God and others—in the communion of the church.[75] Augustine confessed this truth in a prayer that was particularly helpful to Bonhoeffer in Barcelona: "You have made us for yourself, and our heart is restless until it rests in you."

Following Bonhoeffer's return to Berlin, Pastor Olbricht praised his work as a preacher in a report to the German Evangelical Church Committee:

During my own leave, which I spent in Germany from July to September, a time when services used to be canceled because of the heat, he preached every two weeks and was able to excite his listeners to such an extent that they came regularly. His sermons were well thought through and contained profound and rich ideas; in his presentation he developed a self-confidence remarkable for his young age and gave the impression of a pastor with many years of experience.[76]

Olbricht's glowing assessment notwithstanding, Bonhoeffer's experience as a preacher was still limited, comprising a few sermons as a student and less than twenty opportunities as a pastoral assistant. However, his letters and sermons reveal the important role Barcelona played in his formation as a theologian and preacher—as a homiletical theologian.[77] The challenge he had yet to address was that of reconciling faith in God's revelation in Christ for all people as "neighbors" with love for Germany—a patriotic "piety" he shared with the expatriate church in Barcelona.[78] This question, which was both professional and personal in nature, would increasingly command his attention.

3

The Discovery of a Black Jesus
New York 1929–1931

Bonhoeffer bid farewell to Barcelona in February 1929. His desire for a sense of clarity concerning the future remained unfulfilled.[1] The return to academic life in Berlin was less than satisfying: "Everything seems so banal and dull. I never before noticed what nonsense people speak in the trams, on the street—shocking. Only one thing is important now: never to forget that this kind of life is unworthy, regardless of whether one is able to overcome it or not."[2] He served as assistant for systematic theology to Wilhelm Lutger, successor to his mentor, Reinhold Seeberg. Bonhoeffer writes, "It's murderously hot and humid here now, and yet I am supposed to be intellectually creative and grade excruciatingly dumb seminar papers!" The real task was finding a "place to stand":

> All of us are searching for this. But wherever we seek it, whether in the tasks of our daily lives, in educational ideals of this or that sort, or wherever—one thing remains clear, or at least sensed: doubt and temptation [*Anfechtung*] about the meaningfulness of being cast to and fro, of being at the mercy of things, will not cease as long as we remain focused on ourselves, as long as in one form or another "the other" does not step into our lives. Only then . . . do we find the stability that receives its potential and its strength from elsewhere.[3]

Because Bonhoeffer was not yet qualified to offer his own seminars, he began work on his postdoctoral dissertation, or habilitation, to qualify for an appointment in the German university system. *Act and Being: Transcendental Philosophy and Ontology in Systematic Theology* is a rigorously argued philosophical and theological work addressing modern understandings of revelation, salvation, humanity, and the church, including a critical response to the work of Karl Barth.[4]

Barth had sought a way to approach preaching that would be more attentive to Scripture and, thus, more attentive to God, who speaks. He had been deeply shaken by the failure of his esteemed theological teachers in Berlin to stand against the ideology of German nationalism that led to World War I. He saw these failures as primarily theological in nature and recognized an urgent need in his own preaching for a homiletical starting point beyond politics, morality, ethics, religious experience, or human consciousness.[5] Bonhoeffer would write of Barth's path toward recovering preaching as a theological activity, "Barth's initial move in theology was not to be explained in terms of the collapse of the war . . . but in terms of a new reading of Scripture, of the Word which God has spoken in God's self-revelation. . . . This is not war psychosis but listening to God's word. Barth does not come from the trenches but from a Swiss village pulpit."[6]

Barth's subsequent turn to Scripture, beginning with Paul's Epistle to the Romans, produced a provocative reading of the apostolic witness to the gospel.[7] Barth's *Romans* focused on the word of God as the paradoxical message of the church, as the power of the unknown God. This gospel is not one truth among many truths but a question mark against all truths: "The Gospel proclaims a God utterly distinct from men. Salvation comes to them from Him, because they are, as men, incapable of knowing Him."[8] The place of the congregation in relation to the preaching of the gospel is "no more than a crater formed by the explosion of a shell and seeks to be no more than a void in which the Gospel reveals itself."[9] The gospel brings the end of religion as a human message, form of seeking, spiritual experience, or moral consciousness. Faith in the living God is a miracle, not the pinnacle of human knowledge or experience.[10] *Romans* was nothing less than a hermeneutical manifesto launched by Barth into the world of German theology.[11]

From the time of the war (1914–1918) to Hitler's rise to power (1933), Barth vigorously opposed all attempts to deify human reason and culture.[12] Spurred by Barth's influence, Bonhoeffer's formative years as a theologian and preacher were marked by a growing awareness of needing to maintain the integrity of a church that confessed the gospel in the preaching of the word and the integrity of a church that took seriously a responsible witness in the world. *Act and Being* is in basic agreement with, even indebted to, Barth's assessment of the need and promise of Christian preaching, a primary topic of the latter's 1925 Göttingen Lectures on Christian dogmatics.[13]

Barth left his Swiss pastorate in 1921 to become honorary professor of Reformed theology in Göttingen. Without a doctoral degree, he immersed himself in Christian tradition, especially the Reformed dogmatic tradition, to reconceive a revelational theology of the Word-disclosing role of the preacher as Christian witness.[14] He determined that the Word is disclosed in three forms: as revelation, as Scripture, and as preaching: "Revelation is from God alone, scripture is from revelation alone, and preaching is from revelation and scripture."[15] In all three instances, however, the Word is always God speaking. The study and interpretation of Scripture serves the church's proclamation. Although dogmatics is not preaching, it is necessary that preachers know doctrine and the language of Christian faith. Theology, however, must have its starting point and goal in preaching:[16]

> The divine address to which dogmatics reflection must relate directly is preaching, that is, the proclamation of the Christian church which has its basis in revelation and scripture. This reflection is twofold. It involves first the hearing of the Word of God which is actually spoken in this proclamation, and it then involves the task of truly speaking the Word of God in this proclamation. Both take place as we work back from preaching itself to the underlying scripture and revelation. Dogmatics is the methodical execution of this movement.[17]

There is a Trinitarian logic to Barth's thinking, since the Word becomes present to human hearers in the same manner the Spirit makes God present in Christ:[18] "What is given is the wonderful song of praise of the Christian church as we may hear it each Sunday or even each weekday."[19]

Act and Being interprets Barth as locating the *externum verbum*, the externality of the Word of God, in the deity of Christ. The eternal Son of God, true God, cannot be contained in any creaturely form. Christ is the freely acting subject who, according to God's will and pleasure, assumes human flesh and speaks in the man Jesus so the world may know God is God and the world is not. For Barth, the reconciliation effected by God in Christ with humanity is not of being but of act, as event that occurs as a miracle of divine grace. Bonhoeffer, however, construed Barth's approach as too formal. He chose instead to follow a Lutheran way of thinking, locating God's redemptive and commanding Word in the undivided person of Christ's incarnate humanity and the community of the church.[20] His primary interest was the question of "who" rather than "what" or "how."

Easily overlooked in the abstract language and academic structure of *Act and Being* is Bonhoeffer's solution to the relation of revelation, theology, and preaching within the continuity of the church, prompted largely by his response to Barth. For Bonhoeffer the key to revelation is that of a person rather than subject. The necessary condition for uniting act and being is the person and work of Christ, who himself constitutes the enduring witness of the church through space and time. The Spirit—rather than human reason, knowledge, or experience—resolves the apparent ambiguity of the identity of Christ, past, present, and future, in the church's confession of faith in him. As a confessing community, the church is led to conform its life to Christ's death and resurrection wherever and when he is present to faith in word and sacrament.[21]

Bonhoeffer chose to define the problem by discussing the gift and demand of faith, which, only in light of revelation, is capable of acknowledging the reality of human pride and sinfulness— the relentless, self-centered "I." The gracious act of God's Word is required to place the wholeness of human existence into the truth of being "in Christ" rather than the untruth of being "in Adam":[22]

> This is knowledge from revelation, which can never be had apart from it, that is, precisely, in Adam. For "in Adam" means to be in untruth, in culpable perversion of the will, that is, of human essence. It means to be turned inward into one's self, *cor curvum in se* [the heart curved in on itself]. Human beings have torn themselves loose from community with God and, therefore, also from that with other human beings, and now they stand alone,

that is, in untruth. Because human beings are alone, the world is "their" world, and other human beings have sunk into the world of things. . . . God has become a religious object, and human beings have become their own creator and lord, belonging to themselves. It is only to be expected that they should now begin and end with themselves in their knowing, for they are only and utterly "with themselves" in the falsehood of naked self-glory.[23]

Luther also has a place in the discussion, and this is particularly true with regard to the heart curved in on itself. Bonhoeffer's concern was the freedom of God, who is bound to nothing, but in relation to everything, given and contingent, but without absolute possession. As Luther states, "It is in the honor of our God, however, that, in giving the divine self for our sake in deepest condescension, entering into flesh and bread, into our mouth, heart and bowel and suffering for our sake, God be dishonorably handled, both on the altar and the cross."[24]

For Bonhoeffer a key presupposition is that all human beings are part of a community, existing either "in Adam" or "in Christ." He thus argues from revelation—the reality of the church community, those "in Christ," whose existence is to make revelation concrete and intelligible, particularly in preaching: "Revelation should be thought of only in reference to the concept of the church, where the church is understood to be constituted by the present proclaiming of Christ's death and resurrection—within, on the part of, and for the community of faith." Christ is the content of proclamation and is interpreted corporately, as the present Christ in whom the church exists, and who is in the church as the community that lives and speaks by faith in him. God freely gives himself in Christ to the church in terms of both act and being: "Here Christ has come in the closest proximity to humanity. Here Christ has given Christ's own self to the new humanity in Christ, so that the person of Christ draws together in itself all whom Christ has won, binding and committing Christ to them and them to one another."[25]

Act and Being defines the church as a visible, concrete person and community created by the Word: "It is the Christian church that hears the preaching and believes it." The concreteness of the church is word and sacrament; its action is believing and loving, its being and continuity rooted in Christ's self-giving through space and time:[26] "Through believing, praying, and proclaiming, they bear the new humanity; at the same time, they know themselves borne in all their actions by the community of faith, by Christ."[27] Preaching springs from God's revelation in Christ—a believing way of knowing, speaking, and hearing in the church. Doctrine is not the aim but the presupposition of preaching.[28]

The object of faith is neither an institution nor the self, neither a book nor system of belief, but Christ present and proclaimed in the community of faith: "I preach, but I preach in the power of Christ, in the power of the faith of the community of faith, not in the power of my faith."[29] Theology functions as the church's memory, with the task of fostering understanding of the doctrinal presuppositions of preaching: "All the happenings held in remembrance in the Christian community of faith; in the Bible; in preaching and sacrament, prayer, confession; in the word of the person of Christ." However, God's revelation in Christ is primary; the doctrine on which preaching builds is subject to the judgment of the gospel whenever Christ himself speaks in proclamation.[30]

Embedded in the academic argument of *Act and Being* are important existential issues relating faith, doctrine, and preaching to divine revelation given by the external Word and inward work of the Spirit. Bonhoeffer was insistent that the *extra nos* and *pro nobis* of salvation must be proclaimed from and in a form of living faith that is integral with life. The reality of the church requires preaching theologians called to a believing way of thinking and speaking that sustains a community of faith through space and time. Preachers are "those who know that just here, just now, precisely through them, Christ seeks to speak to the community of faith, proclaim the gospel by the full power of the authority of the community of faith that is borne by Christ himself."[31]

Bonhoeffer submitted the dissertation in March 1930 and gave his trial lecture before the university faculty of theology in July. He had arrived at a critical juncture in his vocational path. Only twenty-four years old, he was too young for either a university position or a pastoral call. He had yet to resolve his competing interests in academic and pastoral work; the pull of both the university and the church; his desire to honor the reality of the Word and the world to which the Word is given. The inaugural lecture offers a glimpse into Bonhoeffer's ongoing reflection on the self in relation to God's act and being in the church—the mystery in which the self is seized by Christ: "The church is the hidden Christ among us. Hence the human being is never alone; instead he exists only through the church-community that brings Christ, a community incorporating the human being, drawing that person into its life. . . . Only here is the continuity of that person's existence in Christ guaranteed."[32]

Bonhoeffer also remained committed to ordination, which required he demonstrate progress in homiletical competence. Soon after completing *Act and Being*, he submitted a paper called "The Meaning and Choice of a Biblical Text for the Sermon in the Worship of the Congregation" for his second examination. The essay is a theological reflection on the pastoral responsibility for preaching as an activity that creates and sustains the church. Bonhoeffer asserts the necessity of preaching from biblical texts rather than the use of literature that may impress the "cultural world." Examples of cultural preaching can be seen in sermons that look to Goethe or Nietzsche as sources of authority; here the wisdom of the world is placed above the foolishness of the cross. However, the "heart of the matter" is the sufficiency of Scripture, which becomes God's revelation in Christ in living fashion within the *sanctorum communio*.[33]

Bonhoeffer's discussion of scriptural sufficiency has derivative significance for preaching since the sermon carries God's revelation in Christ. As God's word to the present, preaching draws the divine word out of the biblical past: "The God of Christ is our God, the God whom the Bible reveals, which in its own turn is given to the church as the *communio sanctorum*." Bonhoeffer adds, "That precisely the Bible is God's word, however, and a religious poem by Nietzsche is not, is the irresolvable mystery of God's revelation in hiddenness."[34] The proclamation of God's revelation in Christ from Scripture binds the church, past and present, with ecumenical significance: "God is speaking to us from within his historical revelation and thus overcomes the ages." A related hermeneutical issue is how God's revelation speaks to the present situation of the congregation: "How today can I become a Jew to the Jews, [a Gentile] to the Gentiles, a German to the Germans, a liberal to the liberals, a merchant to the merchants, and a worker [to the] workers, and yet at the same time remain . . . [under Christ's law] (1 Cor 9:18-21)?"[35]

Bonhoeffer suggests a lectionary is the first good means of assistance available to young preachers, since it offers relief from having to choose texts but ties sermons to the whole canon of Scripture. Although the lectionary possesses variety and coherence, it also has limitations, especially after several cycles. The free selection of texts may also serve as a way of ordering the ministry of the word. Bonhoeffer envisions a plan of preaching through the entire church year: "God's path through the old covenant in Christ." Here the Old Testament, especially the prophets and psalms, is the primary source of preaching texts and it is interpreted as pointing to the reality of Christ.

A second plan, "Our Path to Christ," addresses the present life of a congregation. Topics could include religion, work, marriage, Christian obedience, and morality. Here, the Sermon on the Mount is primary. The liturgical framework of the church's festival days (Easter, Christmas, Pentecost, etc.) provides theological direction for preaching. A third plan, "God's Path through History in the Church of Christ," begins with Hebrews 12:1, the "cloud of witnesses," and moves progressively through church history. Christian feast days again inform a theological interpretation of Scripture in sermons. There is also a need for occasional sermons to address general circumstances and events. In all cases, however, the starting point is Scripture and revelation in the church. Bonhoeffer concludes, "And now, when the congregation sees the contemporary questions are also questions of the Church of Christ, the pastor and the congregation will come together on the foundation of an ancient and yet ever new and inexhaustibly rich word."[36]

Homiletical matters held his attention. He lamented to a friend about the poor state of preaching in Berlin, even criticizing his doctoral mentor, Reinhold Seeberg, for a sermon that was "shameful . . . shallow religious babble [that lasted] forty-five minutes; it was painful." Bonhoeffer viewed Seeberg's sermon as representative of the preaching he had heard since returning to Berlin.[37] Finding the concrete existence of the church as a necessary condition for proclaiming the word remained a challenge and concern.

Max Diestel, Berlin church superintendent, who had taken a personal interest in Bonhoeffer, was instrumental in securing a stipend for a year of study as a Sloane Fellow at Union Theological Seminary in New York. Diestel wrote of Bonhoeffer, "His academic training to this point has been very good, although his practical skills (sermon, catechesis, etc.) should not be underestimated either."[38] Bonhoeffer revealed his varied interests in applying for the position: "I would like to take advantage of an opportunity to study my own particular scholarly discipline, systematic theology, as it has developed under completely different circumstances. . . . The subject of my dissertation was the systematic foundation of a sociology of the church. Hence I would especially view a solid familiarity with the circumstances of the church in the United States of America as being of enormous value for my entire scholarly and ecclesiastical work."[39] Prior to leaving for New York, Bonhoeffer confided to a friend, "I feel in general that academic work will not hold me for long. But I do acknowledge that it is quite important to acquire beforehand the best academic training possible."[40]

"There Is No Theology Here"

Bonhoeffer traveled to America in hope of finding a reality that he primarily knew in academic and theoretical form. He longed to join what was taught in the classroom with what was lived in the community of faith. Union Theological Seminary was the center of progressive social thought in America, the flagship theological school of liberal Protestantism, a diverse composition of students and teachers.[41] The form of social theology taught at Union, particularly the ethics of Reinhold Niebuhr, would challenge his Lutheran belief in justification as a "formal doctrine" detached from responsible, public action. The year in New York would be a time of awakening to the need for uniting faith in God's grace and ethical obedience in the world. Bonhoeffer's arrival in New York was just one year after the Wall Street crash that sparked a worldwide depression. Life in the city would expose him to widespread unemployment and poverty, while surrounding him with signs of American optimism and progress: the Statue of Liberty, towering corporate centers of commerce, and the recently constructed Riverside Church, pastored by Dr. Harry Emerson Fosdick.[42]

Bonhoeffer wrote to Diestel following the fall semester. After a few personal comments, he shared his initial impressions of

America. His experience thus far had been informative and stimulating; the students and professors were cordial and sociable. He was of the opinion, however, that the numerous conversations around the Union campus yielded little in the way of actual theological substance: "They talk a blue streak without the slightest substantive foundation and with no evidence of any criteria." Attempts to be profound were, in reality, just frivolous. Bonhoeffer observed that most students, many of whom were between the ages of twenty-five and thirty, were "clueless" with respect to dogmatics and the most basic of questions. Christ was dealt with rather lightly and then done with, while Luther was neither appreciated nor respected. He perceived American religion as an optimistic and sentimentalized version of German liberal theology, which was in his view more honest and rigorous than what he had found in New York.[43]

Conditions in the church were not much different. Sermons were reduced to parenthetical remarks about news and current events: "As long as I have been here [three months], I have heard only one sermon in which you could hear something like a genuine proclamation, and that was delivered by a Negro (indeed, in general I am increasingly discovering greater religious power and originality in Negroes)."[44] The state of preaching raised fundamental questions, including whether it was possible to still speak of Christianity and where the criteria for this might be found: "There is no sense to expect the fruit where the Word really is no longer preached. But then what becomes of Christianity per se?" The dearth of preaching in America prompted a reference to himself: "Once again, I enjoy preaching so much. . . . Because the people here have and hear so little, it's a special task."[45]

Bonhoeffer received numerous invitations to speak as a German Christian, particularly about the war. He shared freely of the widespread suffering, loss, grief, and hardship he had observed in his homeland, including effects on his immediate family:

> I will tell you from my own personal experience, two brothers of mine stood on the front. The older one, 18 years old, was wounded, the younger one, 17 years old, was killed. 3 first cousins of mine were also killed, boys of 18 to 20 years old. Although I was a small boy, I never can forget those most gloomy days of the war. Death stood for the door of almost every house and called for entrance. . . . Germany was made a house of mourning.[46]

He was invited to preach on Armistice Day, November 9, 1930, at Memorial Methodist Church in Yonkers. His sermon text was 1 John 4:16: "God is love; and he that dwelleth in love dwelleth in God, and God in him." He began by announcing the gospel as good news about God for all nations: "In and Germany, in India and in Africa, there is not any difference before God, as Paul sais [*sic*]: there is neither Jew nor Greek, there is neither bond nor free, there is neither male nor female, for ye are all one in Christ Jesus." The cross is the sign planted by God, "a strange, miraculous and wonderful sign where we all could find him." As the sign of God's suffering love, the cross binds all Christians together in one need and hope, ending all human differences: "A human being with all his suffering and all his joys, with sorrows and with desires, with disappointments and fulfillments—and most important a human being with his sin and guilt, with his faith and hope."[47]

Bonhoeffer's sermon was Lutheran in its interpretation of the gospel and ecumenical in scope. The gospel creates "the marvelous mystery of the people of God. . . . There is One God, One Lord, One Spirit, One hope." Proclaiming the gospel prepared the way for addressing the reality of the church as an international community: "Now I stand before you not only as a Christian but also as a German, who loves his home the best of all, who rejoices with his people, and who suffers when he sees his people suffering, who confesses gratefully, that he received from his people all that he has and is."[48] A personal confession of Germany's moral and spiritual failings follows:

> I as a Christian see the main guilt of Germany in a different light. I see it in Germany's complacence, in her belief in her allmightiness, in the lack of humility and faith in God and fear of God. It seems to me, that this is the meaning of the war for Germany: we had to recognize the limits of man and that means: we discovered anew God in his glory and allmightiness, in his wrath and his grace.

He concluded with an appeal for Christians from all nations to strengthen the witness of peace—the fruit of faith that is demonstrated in love for one another as brothers and sisters in Christ: "It must never more happen, that a Christian people fights against a

Christian people, brother against brother, since both have one Father."[49]

The sermon reveals Bonhoeffer's emerging ecumenical perspective, a change undoubtedly influenced by fellow Union student Jean Lasserre, a French Reformed pastor and pacifist. Lasserre's serious attention to the Sermon on the Mount, the command of Jesus to make visible the reality of God's peace, challenged Bonhoeffer to reconsider his thinking about the church as an international body. Lasserre and Bonhoeffer shared a commitment to the nearness of God's grace in the person of Christ. After a difficult beginning, given the relations between France and Germany following the war, their friendship became a catalyst for Bonhoeffer to begin conceiving anew the relation of the Word spoken in Christ and the practice of faith in all of life. Conversations with Lasserre turned Bonhoeffer's attention to the reality of discipleship, which would increasingly reorient his life and work.[50]

Life in America was nothing like what Bonhoeffer had experienced in Barcelona. Christmas time in the Barcelona congregation had been meaningful, but New York was different. He wrote of his difficulty in getting into the Christmas spirit. It was like a person who, standing and observing the whole world, sees "something infinitely depressing." His impressions of church life in America were not encouraging either. It was a church "smiling in desperation," a frivolous attitude that bitterly disappointed his hope of finding Hebrews 12:1 fulfilled: "Therefore, since we are surrounded by so great a cloud of witnesses, let us also lay aside everything that burdens us."[51]

Bonhoeffer visited Havana over the Christmas break, where he was invited to preach for a German-speaking congregation. The sermon text for the Fourth Sunday in Advent was Deuteronomy 32:48-52. Moses was standing on Mount Nebo, peering at the promised land from afar. Bonhoeffer interpreted the present in light of the story: "Advent is a serious matter. . . . You know, we are a strange people." There are similarities between Advent remembrance, Christmas celebrations, and Moses: "Moses died on the mountain from which he was permitted to greet the promised land from a distance. Wherever the Bible talks about God's promises, it is always a matter of life and death."[52]

The narrative of Moses on Mount Nebo is a type of God's people sojourning through history with hope in God's promise. They, too, long to inhabit the promised land, but, like Moses, they know they must also die. Bonhoeffer comments, "If we had composed this story, we would have made him [Moses] the first to enter the promised land with rejoicing. But God says: Ascend the mountain and die. . . . Jesus says, 'Blessed are those who hunger and thirst for righteousness.'" The congregation is part of the story. "The language this ancient story is speaking is quite clear." Great things are promised that human beings can neither attain nor grasp on their own, since the message of Advent ends with a question: Are you prepared for God? "The kingdom of heaven has come near, God the Lord is coming, the Creator and Judge is approaching humankind in love and will take us home to the eternal festival meal. God is coming. Are you prepared?"[53] Bonhoeffer was not particularly pleased with the sermon—with neither the presentation of himself nor his message to the congregation. He would describe it as a "time of crisis," declaring himself a victim of the hot sun.[54]

Helmut Rossler, a friend and pastor, wrote in the spring to report on conditions in Germany. He responded to Bonhoeffer's complaints about the "theologically grotesque nature of the American church," commenting, "From that you can probably see what a frightful illusion world Protestantism can be as an ecumenical ideal: But are things much different in our [German] church?" Rossler lamented the troubled state of the church in Germany. After seeing twenty years of improvement in theological work, he was still waiting for its effects to be seen "in practice, particularly the proclamation of the gospel." There had been a strong surge in nationalistic fervor and desire that the gospel be utilized for that end. Rossler describes the alarming changes he had observed:

> A war of liberation, the renewal of the Prussian idea of the state . . . racial purity, war on the Jews and on the Young Plan [German reparations for World War I], death to Marxism, the "third Reich" of German freedom and righteousness (an eschatological-chiliastic remnant)—those are the ideas moving the German rural population today, who are themselves currently highly agitated. And directly in the midst of all of this the preaching of the cross.[55]

Rossler viewed Bonhoeffer as "unpolitical" by nature and removed from the brewing turmoil in Germany: "It's easier for you from your high vantage point to examine Ephesians 3:18-19. This is not to say I fail to recognize your own temptations. They are perhaps more comprehensive but perhaps not as concrete as among us 'frontline soldiers in the filthy trenches.'" Rossler depicted a powerful Volkisch movement, "purified red hot nationalism with a new paganism . . . clothed in Christian garb." Religion was united to race, particularly the Aryan race. There was strong social resentment toward Christianity—that the church justify itself on the basis of national customs, tradition, and race. This religious syncretism was for "all God-believers of good will." Humanitarian idealism mixed with faith in God and love for the fatherland, a historical mysticism uniting the destiny of the spirit and the Volk by an act of the will.[56]

The millennial, chiliastic nature of German Volk religion favored the Third Reich, while directing its hatred toward Jews and capitalists. Rossler's comments are striking:

> The world has become smaller. Nations are moving closer to one another. The same ideas and intellectual movements are drawing all nations under their spell. And the tragedy of our own age is the clash between two fundamentally related fronts: the rigorous secularism of a conscious focus on the here and now, and religiously colored secularism for which only the pragmatic understanding of religion is still accessible. And placed in the middle of it all: the church of Christ, together with all religions . . . consciously assaulted by the former front, and yet wooed by the latter to enter into the battle.[57]

The only hope for the world is the proclamation of Christ; the old humanity has exhausted all hope and expectation. The "old" way of preaching—threatening people with fear, distress, and hell first—will no longer suffice: "The great hope, Jesus Christ, is proclaimed to this hopeless, suffering humanity. . . . Must we not bring the realism of love to those who are lost?" Rossler concedes that some form of penance may be necessary to address the self-glorification of modern people drunk on progress. But repentance cannot be separated from the hope of the gospel, which must be erected above "the essential hopelessness of the current generation."[58]

Bonhoeffer submitted his final report to Diestel in the spring. He had concluded that the theological preparation of American students was poor, hindered by excessive emphasis on community living that failed to encourage a necessary independence: "This characterizes all American thinking, something observed especially with regard to theology and the church; they do not see the radical claim of truth on the way one structure's one's life. Community is based less on truth than on the spirit of fairness."[59]

Preaching in America also fit this characterization; the question of truth was viewed largely in light of the practical community. Sermons are "edifying narrations of examples, willing proclamation of their [preacher's] own religious experiences to which, of course, they assign no substantively binding character." Bonhoeffer perceived a stark difference between preaching in Germany and the United States: the former focused on dogmatic positions, the latter on the religious experience of the preacher. He was appalled by the lack of theological content among American pastors, who preferred to function as organizational leaders but remained ignorant of what was at stake in their work: "The theological spirit at Union Theological Seminary is accelerating the process of the secularization of Christianity in America."[60]

Bonhoeffer was taken aback by the pragmatic spirit of Union's curriculum, especially the influence of William James and John Dewey. The effects of this kind of thinking subordinated truth to what is "useful in the long run," "effective truth," or "truth that works." In his view, the consequence of this approach to reality was a "radically immanent ethical humanism" that was simply inimical to Pauline and Lutheran Christianity. He saw Americans as people "for whom justification by faith is of no importance." Most alarming was the tendency toward "a churchless, individualistic character" accommodating the influence of pragmatism.[61]

His exposure to preaching in America was deeply distressing. The *New York Times*, which published Monday-morning sermon reviews, provided a survey of contemporary preaching. Topics were posted in advance to attract listeners: "Science finds void compared to faith," "Virtues stressed," "New freedom," "Put needs above creeds." The focus of preaching was on the present, shaped along political, social, and apologetic lines. Bonhoeffer viewed this strategy as creating an illusion of unity that was nothing more than agreement. He was astonished by the pervasive spirit of optimism and trust in progress: "In New York, they preach about virtually everything; only one thing is not addressed, or it is addressed so rarely that I have as yet been unable to hear it, namely, the gospel of Jesus Christ, the cross, sin and forgiveness, death and life."[62]

The roots of this problem stemmed from "ethical and social idealism; faith in progress had displaced the church's message." Bonhoeffer questioned whether such preaching was deserving of the name "Christian." He was dismayed by the lack of catechesis and Christian education in favor of "new methods" that aimed to make Sunday school and church more attractive. Prizes were awarded; advertising was up-to-date; revivals were scheduled to fill feelings of burdened emptiness. Pastors played with the emotions of people, using psychological devices to draw them into their "enthusiastic-eschatological-radical sects." There were teas, lectures, concerts, charity events, sports, games, bowling events, and dances. He wondered how such a distorted form of church, as a "social corporation," could have arisen in the first place.[63]

Bonhoeffer was struggling to make theological sense of Christianity in America. He concluded that the Spirit of God was not tied to the word; the significance of sermon, confession, dogma, church, and community had never been grasped. An example of this ignorance was evinced in the way Christian doctrine was attacked by preachers. During a Good Friday sermon, he had heard one of New York's best-known preachers claim, "I deny the reconciliation of the cross. I don't want that kind of Christ." Bonhoeffer comments on this remark, "Note the use of 'I.'" Americans misunderstood the theological nature of the church: "The church is no longer the place where the congregation hears and preaches God's word, but rather the place where one acquires a secondary significance, as a social entity for this or that purpose. . . . People confuse the role of the church with that of a religious association."[64]

An Unexpected Theological Education

Adding to Bonhoeffer's confusion was an unexpected opportunity to learn outside the classroom by participating in American community building and organizing. He had been introduced to a number of faith-based social reformers who were passionate to continue the social-gospel tradition, living out Christian faith in its public and communal expression. These "progressive Protestants" included professors at Union and ministers in the community who refused to separate pastoral from political matters.[65] He was surprised by the nature of American "practical theology." Service was an integral part of learning, a sharp contrast to the German academic method of theological study. He was joined with others in on-site social ministry that led to numerous conversations around such ethical matters as unemployment, urban poverty, labor relations and union organization, juvenile crime, conscientious objection, civil rights, and social justice:[66]

> The most valuable experience I had at the seminary was a practical course on "Church and Community" with Mr. Webber, former pastor at the Church of All Nations, and a radical socialist. We made weekly visitation to the various socio-pedagogical or so-called character building agencies in New York. We saw settlements, night schools, YMCAs, church organizations, the Association for the advancement of coloured people, among many others. . . . This ongoing personal contact with Americans in the context of social work was of enormous value to me.[67]

Bonhoeffer's impressions of the church continued to improve as he became increasingly involved in the black church. There he would experience a transformation that was profoundly affected by the religious and cultural gifts of the "Harlem Renaissance."

Between the late nineteenth century and the mid-1930s, there was increasing black mobility that led to a "Great Migration" to New York, a movement that was both intellectual and ideological, leading toward a new black identity for the twentieth century. A proliferation of art, literature, and music was part of an emerging political and theological black self-understanding and culture in Harlem, a "Harlem Renaissance."[68] Bonhoeffer viewed the black church, a "church of the outcasts of America," as largely untouched by the theological and ecclesial conditions he observed in white congregations.[69] He had traveled earlier with Frank Fisher, an African American student at Union, to Washington, D.C., where he was personally exposed to the ugliness of racism. He writes, "In Washington I lived completely among the Negroes and through the students was able to get acquainted with all the leading figures in the Negro movement, was in their homes, and had extraordinarily interesting conversations with them. . . . The conditions are really unbelievable. Not just separate railway cars, tramways, and buses south of Washington, but also, for example, when I wanted to eat in a small restaurant with a Negro, I was refused service."[70]

Bonhoeffer was surprised by the way the Spanish population in Havana got along much better with Negroes than did Americans. He thought the segregation of blacks and whites in the southern United States was shameful; the way whites spoke of blacks was repugnant to him; even pastors were no better in their speech: "It is a bit unnerving that in a country with so inordinately many slogans about brotherhood, peace, and so on, such things still continue uncorrected."[71] Bonhoeffer wrote to his brother, Karl-Friedrich:

> I want to have a look at church conditions in the South, which allegedly can still be quite peculiar, and get to know the situation of the Negroes in a bit more detail. I don't quite know whether I have not perhaps spent too much time on this question here, especially since we don't really have an analogous situation in Germany, but I've just found it enormously interesting, and I've never for a moment found it boring. And it really does seem to me there is a great movement forming, and I do believe that the Negroes will still give the whites here considerably more than merely their folksongs.[72]

Bonhoeffer was eager to learn about life in the black church, to acquire an intimate understanding of the "Negro problem." This new awareness would help him to see white churches from the vantage of its "hidden perspective."[73] Moreover, Frank Fisher had introduced him to Abyssinian Baptist Church, the largest black Baptist congregation in the city. Abyssinian was led by Adam Clayton Powell Sr., who in his sermons interpreted and proclaimed Jesus as "an outcast among outcasts" hidden in suffering and weakness.[74] Bonhoeffer writes,

> I was in one of the large Baptist churches in Harlem every Sunday at 2:30 in the afternoon, and together with my friend, and often as his substitute, had a group of young Negroes in the Sunday School.

> I conducted Bible study for some Negro women and once a week
> helped out in a weekday church school. I also visited their homes
> several times. This personal acquaintance with Negroes was one
> of the most important, gratifying events of my stay in America.[75]

Bonhoeffer was astonished by Powell's preaching. He was captivated by its power to effect what was spoken, to awaken intense feeling and moving response to the good news of the gospel. He heard
black preachers "speaking in a Christian sense about sin and grace
and the love of God and ultimate hope," essential matters ignored
by established white churches. He concluded that black preaching
was fitting for the reality of Christ present with and for his suffering,
oppressed people: "In contrast to the often lecture-like character of
the white sermon, the 'black Christ' is preached with captivating
passion and vividness."[76] A fellow student at Union described Bonhoeffer's display of emotion after returning from a visit in Harlem:

> Early one Sunday afternoon . . . Bonhoeffer came in from the
> Abyssinian Baptist Church where he was teaching a Sunday
> School class. He was excited and talkative, and instead of going
> to his room he described the preaching with excitement and
> audience participation and especially the singing of black spiri-
> tuals. He was very emotional and did not try to hide his feelings,
> which was extremely rare for him. He said it was the only time
> he had experienced true religion in the United States, and was
> convinced that it was only among blacks who were oppressed
> that there could be any real religion in this country.[77]

Bonhoeffer was deeply moved by Negro spirituals: "I still believe
that the spiritual songs of the southern Negroes represent some of
the greatest artistic achievements in America."[78] He perceived spirituals as mixing melancholy and eruptive joy, characterizing the
worship of a people whom he saw as a truly "proletariat" church
in America.

Bonhoeffer's concern for the black church was similar to his
observations in *Sanctorum Communio* regarding the failure of the
church in Germany to reach young people. He saw the disdain of
black young people for the kind of preaching that made their ances-
tors submit willingly to their fate. He understood what this would
mean: "White Americans will have to take the blame that these

black masses became godless. Here we are standing at a powerful crossroads."[79] Harlem afforded him a unique perspective on life in America, a theological context for learning to see the world and himself in a new way as he was "evangelized" into the life of the black church:[80]

> Here I had the opportunity to get to know America quite inten-sively at one of its delicate points without being in a position where someone might dazzle me. And the results of such an experience are, I must say, deeply distressing. Here one gets to see something of the real face of America, something that is hid-den behind the veil of words in the American constitution saying that "all men are created free and equal."[81]

Albert Frank Fisher was from Birmingham, Alabama, where his father, Charles Fisher, was pastor of 16th Street Baptist Church, the center of Birmingham's black community. Charles Fisher preached and led his congregation in worship, but he was also deeply involved in the black community, advocating for justice in protest against humiliating Jim Crow laws. In 1930, Charles Fisher became dean of the School of Theology of Selma University. His son (Albert, or Frank) moved to New York to attend Union Seminary, where he met Dietrich Bonhoeffer.[82]

More than thirty years later, 16th Street Baptist Church would be singled out and bombed by white racists, resulting in the deaths of four young girls soon after Martin Luther King Jr. delivered his "I Have a Dream" speech. Martin Luther King Jr. was born in Atlanta in 1929, the year before Bonhoeffer visited America and met Frank Fisher. King had a deep connection with Fisher's hometown of Bir-mingham, especially its black churches and community. After com-pleting seminary and pursuing a doctorate in theology, King was called to pastoral ministry in 1954 by Dexter Avenue Baptist Church of Montgomery, Alabama. A few years later, both Fisher and King were arrested in Atlanta for sitting in the whites-only section of the city's buses. The two black pastors would continue as partners in the Civil Rights Movement.[83]

King was arrested in 1963 for leading civil rights demonstra-tions in Birmingham. His open letter—"Letter from Birmingham City Jail"—was written as a prophetic response to white liberal clergy who publically called on him to seek more moderate means of change, patiently allowing local and federal court systems to end the problem of segregation in America. King's response from jail is helpful for understanding how Bonhoeffer, given his theological and political convictions, would have found the concrete form of life and speech he encountered in the black church as both startling and life changing. King had been warned that his public advocacy for civil rights was "unwise and untimely." His letter was an answer to this criticism in "patient and reasonable" terms. He had gone to Birmingham because of injustice, interpreting this turn of events in light of his call to proclaim the Word of God:[84]

> I am in Birmingham because injustice is here. Just as the eighth century prophets left their little villages and carried their "thus saith the Lord" far beyond the boundaries of their hometowns; and just as the Apostle Paul left his little village of Tarsus and carried the gospel of Jesus Christ to practically every hamlet and city of the Graeco-Roman world, I too am compelled to carry the gospel of freedom beyond my particular hometown. Like Paul, I must constantly respond to the Macedonian call for aid.[85]

King expressed deep disappointment with the clergy of Birmingham for their failure to see his nonviolent efforts as a "more excellent way" he learned as a member of the Negro church. He was accused of being extremist but countered this charge by appealing to the narrative of Scripture—to Jesus, Amos, and Paul, who were extremists for love, justice, and the gospel.[86]

He reiterated his disappointment with white churches and their pastors, claiming his authority to do so was as a minister of the gospel who deeply loved the church. But he was deeply distraught by the indifference of white churches to injustice, especially in light of their preoccupation with "pious irrelevancies and sanctimonious trivialities." King was weary of being told the gospel had no real concern with social issues, a form of Christianity that made a distinct separation of "body and soul, the sacred and secular."[87]

He was left to ask himself, "What kind of people worship here? Who is their God?" King's sobering conclusion bears striking similarities to the concern for the black church that Bonhoeffer had expressed more than thirty years earlier:

But the judgment of God is upon the church as never before. If the church of today does not recapture the sacrificial spirit of the early church, it will lose its authentic ring, forfeit the loyalty of millions, and be dismissed as an irrelevant social club with no meaning for the twentieth century. I am meeting with young people every day whose disappointment with the church has risen to outright disgust.[88]

A major factor in Bonhoeffer's change of perception was his exposure to the striking image of the "black Christ" in Harlem. He was confronted with a radically different way of thinking and speaking of Christ: as the One who is hidden in the suffering, excluded people, whose life he freely enters and shares as Savior and Lord.[89]

A course with Niebuhr had addressed the "social and Christian problem": "That was extremely informative. I learned much from my own experiences in Harlem. The impressions I got of contemporary representatives of the social gospel will remain determinative for me for a long time to come."[90] Niebuhr introduced Bonhoeffer to "The Black Christ," a poem by Countee Cullen that tells of a black man tortured and hung by a southern mob. In his suffering, a black man, hung on a tree, becomes the Anointed One. Cullen's poem depicts Jesus as the first in a succession of lynched black men in the South, a counternarrative to white racist Christianity, and a figure of theological and social triumph for the marginalized.[91]

Cullen's poetic depiction of Christ became reality for Bonhoeffer through his empathic participation in the life of the Abyssinian Baptist Church. There he experienced the fellowship of a people whose faith and life embodied the message proclaimed in "The Black Christ." Bonhoeffer had spoken of Christ's hiddenness as a student and with the Barcelona congregation, referring to Christ's presence in others as a sign of God's disruptive grace. His experience in New York challenged him to see hiddenness by standing in a different place. Christ does not merely hide himself among humanity in general but is concealed in the fellowship of suffering women, men, and children forgotten and despised by the world.[92] Bonhoeffer sensed he had found the "cloud of witnesses." In Harlem he saw "true religion" preached and lived.

Life with the black church had illumined the heart of Luther's *theologia crucis*—the reality of the redemptive and commanding

Word that has been poured out fully in history.[93] Bonhoeffer's theological education in America entailed both continuity and change. The abstract theological arguments of *Sanctorum Communio* and *Act and Being* were fleshed out in the words and deeds of black people who, as a worshiping community, displayed the reality of Christ in Harlem: "Through believing, praying, and proclaiming, they bear the new humanity; at the same time, they know themselves borne in all their actions by the community of faith, by Christ."[94] Experiencing the presence of Christ among marginalized black folk was a true awakening for Bonhoeffer. Immersing himself in the black church was not only life changing; it would have enduring significance for him as a theologian and preacher—a homiletical theologian.

II

Preaching

4

Preaching as Theology
Berlin 1931–1932

Bonhoeffer's transition from New York to Germany was not without its challenges.[1] He immediately found himself in the midst of a rising tide of nationalistic fervor that looked to the church to rehabilitate the soul of a once-great but defeated nation. The "German spirit" was to be revived and celebrated, necessitating an Aryan church and Aryan Jesus freed from the distortions of the Old Testament and Paul. This "folk" Christianity was a purified version of faith well suited for an emerging National Socialism and those who would soon identify themselves as "German Christians." In the name of nationalism, evils such as communism, secularism, capitalism, immorality, internationalism, and pacifism were attacked as serious threats to the German spirit and "folk" revival. The church was seen as obligated to support a German production of the gospel—a message adapted to what advocates believed was Germany's unique destiny.[2]

The pressure for the church to make its existence intelligible in light of nationalistic aspirations was intense, fueled largely by a fear of alienating people who united the German spirit and morality. The National Socialists presumed to support the importance of the church but sought to limit its authority in relation to the state and German nationalism as the will of God. As the Nazi Party continued to make strides in succeeding national elections, the question of the church's identity and mission—the nature of the gospel and proclamation—became increasingly urgent in conditions where to speak of God, church, and Scripture without mentioning God's "German-ness" would be seen as positively sinful.[3]

Bonhoeffer quickly discovered that the recent work of dialectical theologians, of which Karl Barth was the most prominent, had had little effect on preaching in Germany. Other than early pieces on theology and the Word of God, Barth would not produce a homiletic, a study of the art of preaching, until 1933. There was, however, a particularly intense renewal of preaching during this time among nationalistic theologians. Sermons providing a theological framework that increasingly merged the language of the pulpit with that of political propaganda were published widely. Bonhoeffer found himself in a world increasingly dominated by a "homiletic" oriented to contemporary German life and by a correlative "hermeneutic" that guided interpretation of the Bible's words, ideas, and images in service of this "positive" end. The goal was to assuage the fears of Christian people, thereby winning their support, while countering and even mitigating those aspects of the church's confession of faith that were perceived as "negative."[4]

This period in Bonhoeffer's life marks a transition from years of study, research, writing, and apprenticeship in practical ministry to new responsibilities of teaching, leading, and mentoring others. His sermons, lectures, letters, ecumenical addresses, and pastoral writings should not be seen as merely preliminary steps toward later and better-known commitments and works. Rather, his activity during the critical years of 1931–1932 evinces a maturing and deepening of faith in divine revelation that generates a way of thinking, perceiving, and speaking shaped by Christ. His life was changed dramatically through a diverse but interrelated mix of commitments that fully tested his capacities, gifts, and energies. The outcome was a stronger commitment to integrating faith, theology, and devotion with preaching in and for the church as the present Christ.[5]

Bonhoeffer's first priority in returning to Germany was to visit Karl Barth in Bonn. He turned down the opportunity for spending a holiday with his family to sit on Barth's lectures and to engage with him around the relation of theology and ethics in the church's proclamation. In a letter to Edwin Sutz, a Swiss friend from Union Seminary who was instrumental in introducing him to Barth, Bonhoeffer wrote of his "bastard origins" in relation to Barth's students at Bonn. His overall impression, however, was good and reveals a continued strong interest in learning from Barth's work: "You can breathe freely. You are no longer afraid you will die for lack of oxygen in the rarified atmosphere. I have, I believe, seldom regretted not having done something in my theological past as much as I now regret that I did not go to hear Barth sooner."[6]

Bonhoeffer found himself at a distance from Barth in relation to ethics, on the church's authority to proclaim the concrete commandment of Christ that calls the church to faithful obedience, since Barth was ambivalent in this matter. But he was grateful for the conversations with the older theologian, as the situation at home was very different: "One sits in poor, desolate Berlin and is discouraged because there is no one there from whom one can learn theology and some other useful things along with it."[7]

By November 1931 Bonhoeffer's slate of commitments were in place. He was appointed as special adjunct assistant for systematic theology in the University of Berlin, as part-time chaplain to students in the Berlin Technical College, and as a young-adult delegate in the German church's ecumenical connections, and he was ordained and sent to be assistant pastor with a Berlin congregation. He wrote to Sutz in October, describing the pressures he felt: "Sometimes I simply cannot see how I will be able to do all these things right. The cheap consolations that one just does what one can, and that there are others who would do it even worse, isn't always enough." This pressure was compounded by worsening conditions in Germany's economic and political life. But Bonhoeffer was also deeply concerned by the demise of the church: "But will our church survive another catastrophe? Will it not reach the end of its existence then, if we do not change immediately, speak and live completely differently? But how?"[8]

He wrote to Rossler about the deteriorating situations all around him, particularly the weakening condition of the church: "The mother church itself is dying. . . . Is our time over? Has the gospel been given over to another people, perhaps proclaimed with completely different words and actions? How do you see the eternal nature of Christianity in light of the world situation and our own way of living?" He questioned the possibility of ministering in such conditions: "How do I preach such things to these people [students]? Who still believes that anymore?" His questions revealed an intense concern for the necessity of the church's concrete witness to the reality of Christ, something he saw as conspicuously absent in Germany: "Invisibility is ruining us."[9]

An additional disappointment was the inferior quality of theological students, many of whom took up theology because of limited opportunities provided by other professions. Bonhoeffer feared for the church, blaming a selection process that was turning loose students of such poor quality that, in his opinion, not even a Barthian theology would be of help. Remembering his strong criticisms of Union Seminary, he acknowledged that even it did well in comparison to the state of theology in Berlin.[10] Nationalism already had a strong historic foothold in the universities and was fueled even more by the humiliation of the war and the Treaty of Versailles. German professors lived with the memory of a strong imperial Germany that had nurtured them professionally and supported their academic achievements. They returned this loyalty by supporting the war efforts and criticizing the peace settlement, expressing publically their concern about the "Jewish threat." Many academics insisted they were above such political matters, interested only in intellectual pursuits, while betraying their aggressive nationalistic, antidemocratic assumptions.[11]

Conditions in the university were not insignificant to Bonhoeffer, since he began his teaching career at a time when many students had been shaped by a romantic idealism that resisted much of modern industrial life and its effects. Young people were turning to the beauty of the natural world, to conservative, monarchist, and nationalistic values. As part of Germany's "youth movement," student clubs and values supporting these strong militaristic and nationalistic aspirations were common. In addition, the upturn in university enrollment and its adverse effects due to economic conditions created a deep sense of dissatisfaction among both students and professors, who were more than willing to blame the struggling Weimar Republic. Students were quick to protest and condemn the presence of faculty members who held views sympathetic to pacifism, socialism, or any other perspectives they perceived as opposed to their nationalistic ideals and desires. Bonhoeffer expressed his frustration with theology students in particular: "This leads many to theology today who should not touch it."[12]

Bonhoeffer's first lecture course, offered in the winter semester 1931–1932, provided an opportunity to establish the landscape of recent theology and to position himself within it.[13] "The History of Twentieth-Century Systematic Theology" begins with the nineteenth-century background, primarily the influence of Schleiermacher, and it moves both forward and backward in time, presenting key figures in modern philosophy and theology, including critiques of his former teachers—Seeberg, Harnack, and Holl. However, Luther's Reformation theology and Barth's radical challenge to liberal Protestantism were most important. Bonhoeffer reiterates his previous assessments of Barth, while showing his appreciation for the "turning point" brought about by Barth's commitment to divine revelation, a renewed desire "to speak rightly of God": "To the extent Barth no longer wants to confuse religion with God, this indicates that the turning point has been reached; it is not psychosis resulting from the war but rather listening to God's word. . . . Barth's theology comes from preaching; this is his only concern."[14]

The seminar concludes with Bonhoeffer's comments on ethics. He takes exception to Barth's habit of referring to this subject as demonstration—that Christian action in love of neighbor points only to a recognition of God's reign but not to the reality of required visible human action. Bonhoeffer was looking to find a place for concrete commandments in preaching, the coordination of gospel and law—the proclamation of Christ that calls the church to obedient faith. The lectures left students to ponder how theology could function as a church discipline and whether this was still possible within the present academic system. Bonhoeffer wondered aloud, "Who will show us Luther?"[15]

Bonhoeffer's first sermon in Berlin is from Psalm 63:3—"Your steadfast love is better than life"—for the occasion of Thanksgiving Sunday. He begins by describing the psalm as "one of those Bible passages that never lets go of anyone who has once understood it." It is "a word from the world of the Bible and not from our world." Clearly echoing Barth, he announces that the steadfast love of God is known only by the risk of faith that dares to live within "the strange world of the Bible," which would be the consistent focus of his preaching in Berlin.[16] This world is expansive, as wide as God's love, and includes tax collectors, the suffering and abandoned, the weary and heavy laden, the sick and oppressed, the unemployed and hungry, and all kinds of sinners.[17]

The character of God's love cannot be known without surrendering to God's claim on the whole of life: "If you want my loving-kindness, give the last thing you have, your life!" Bonhoeffer points to signs of God's steadfast love: the goodness of creation, God's abundant provision, God's faithful preservation of life. But he also points to the judgment of God's steadfast love that, paradoxically, is revealed in the needs of people throughout the world, in the sufferings of the neighbor that are evinced at every turn. Knowing God's loving-kindness is thus attained by risking one's self for the other. The sermon concludes with a call to believe in the greatest miracle known to the world:

> Where we have fallen away from God, where we have become dead and unreceptive to God in our guilt, that is where God's loving-kindness follow us and reveals itself to us as the eternal promise of God in Jesus Christ, beyond all guilt and beyond all life. Only one who in the depths of the darkness of guilt, of disloyalty, of enmity toward God has felt touched by the love that never ends, that forgives all and points the way beyond all suffering into the eternal world of God, knows truly and completely what God's loving-kindness is.[18]

Bonhoeffer returned to the "strange world of the Bible" for the first Sunday of Advent. The sermon was from Luke 12:35-40, a parable about servants waiting for the return of their master. The blessing at the center of the text comprises the heart of the sermon: "Blessed are those slaves whom the master finds alert when he comes." Bonhoeffer acknowledged circumstances in Germany had made the world of the Bible, the world of Christ, seem like so much foolishness apart from the reality of Christ himself. This led to a long exposition of the parable and the human vocation of waiting for God.

Waiting for God to fulfill the divine promises is distinguished from political or ethical activity that seeks to take hold of history to produce its own outcomes. Since the end of the world and history are God's, no one knows the hour he will come. The sermon brings out the strangeness of living by faith, and it addresses objections that it is an ideal that has been imposed on life. Bonhoeffer presumes God is the One who has come, who comes, and who will come again, "the First and the Last." Moreover, God is not a static deity that can be controlled, but a God who speaks and commands the church to believe, to be prepared at all times to welcome God's salvation and judgment, God's love and peace. The surprising outcome of the parable is the patient, gracious God who shares his blessedness with those who wait, not in their own power, but by grace alone.[19]

In February 1932, Bonhoeffer preached on Memorial or "Reminiscere" Day. The text for the sermon was Matthew 24:6-14: "And you will hear of wars and rumors of wars; see that you are not alarmed; for this must take place, but the end is not yet." The sermon asserts the eschatological nature of the gospel and church that exists under God's reign. Bonhoeffer chose Matthew 24 on a day when Germans gathered to remember all who had sacrificed their lives in war for the nation. This topic was particularly poignant in 1932, when the pain of remembering the war, Germany's defeat, and the conditions that followed continued to be deeply humiliating for the nation, stirring passionate desire for a return to greatness. Bonhoeffer's sermon did not measure up to the standards set for nationalistic, "positive" Christianity.[20] He distinguished the church from the German nation, establishing its first loyalty as knowing God and God's will—as a people called to see the world truly and without illusion. This is the true love of one's nation: "It [the church] does so out of love. . . . The one who loves the most is the one who sees deepest, sees the greatest danger. A seer has never been popular. That is why the church will also not be popular, least of all on days like this."[21]

The sermon proclaims Christ crucified as the truth by which the church is enabled to see itself, the nation, and the world more truly. Although Bonhoeffer spoke respectfully of the occasion, he announced that the church is built on the gospel and therefore must have more to say. The church itself is this: "The sign of God's judgment and triumph over the powers of darkness is the sign of Christ's strange nearness." From the perspective of the cross, the war was a sign of the great disintegration of Christianity. The church was torn apart by attacks against Christ and his people that caused untold numbers to doubt and disbelieve. Many saw the war as an occasion to turn away from faith as foolishness, while millions were filled with hatred as their love grew cold.[22]

The way forward is the word of the cross, Christ's way of peace, a way that leads through suffering and death. The church lives from a different memory and hope than the world, from the gospel of God's reign made present in Christ, the gospel that must be proclaimed to all nations until the end comes. As Bonhoeffer concludes, "Mourning the dead is done by passing on the message of peace; that means that God in the cross is near us, that means knowing that Christ alone wins the victory. Amen."[23]

Bonhoeffer was also deeply involved in the ministry of Zion Church in Berlin, preparing young people for confirmation. He told a friend that preparing for Christmas with the boys was as important as preparing for theological lectures at the university. His deepening investment in the lives of the boys was similar to the ministry he had observed and contributed to with Abyssinian Baptist Church in Harlem:[24]

> In addition to my work teaching at the university and working as a pastor for students, I am now doing something else, which takes up all my time and attention; that is teaching a confirmation class for fifty boys in the northern part of Berlin. Most are children of unemployed fathers. There you see so much suffering and can only help a little. The boys don't get anything from home for Christmas, naturally, so I have to try, with the help of some friends, to give them something that will make them happy.[25]

A letter to Sutz described his practical work with students in the confirmation class. The boys in the class would occasionally act wildly, presenting him with challenging discipline problems. His way of addressing these situations reveals growth in the practical wisdom that guides discernment in ministry, particularly preaching and teaching: "But here, too, one thing helped, namely, just simply telling the boys Bible stories in massive quantity, and especially eschatological passages."[26]

As Bonhoeffer worked with the boys through preaching, teaching, and sharing in their lives, he reflected on what he was doing and why. He was led to rent a small apartment in the neighborhood so the boys would be able to join him for dinner, games, and conversation. He was surprised by their openness to Scripture and catechetical material, which led to profound conversations concerning their life and place in the church. He also learned of the daily pressure placed on the boys by political-party organizations and clubs that made them feel more at home than the church.[27] He described the desperate conditions in which he worked in a letter to Paul Lehmann: "And now to preach the gospel under these circumstances! In confirmation class things sometimes go amazingly well. They really listen, with their mouths open. Then sometimes they are really bratty again."[28]

Bonhoeffer shared similar experiences with Sutz—that he would not prepare for confirmation classes in detail but instead chose to trust his knowledge of the material and understanding of the boys: "I didn't hesitate, quite often, just to preach to the children." He expressed his surprise at the outcome of this approach, its simplicity in getting to the point through conversation: "You just have to start talking." Talking meant working with Scripture, pointing to the church's great hope, to which the boys were attentive, even when he spoke for more than half an hour.[29]

Bonhoeffer's work with the confirmands led him to collaborate with Hans Hildebrant (a friend and fellow pastor) to write a Lutheran catechism, "As You Believe, So You Receive."[30] This project reflects the substance of the authors' academic work made plain and accessible for the church. The purpose was to lead young people to affirm the faith of the church in light of Luther's concise statement: "Tknow what you must do and what has been given to you."[31] The opening question and answer appropriately deal with the gospel: "This is the message that has appeared to us in Jesus Christ and has been conveyed through his Spirit. This is the message of the kingdom of God that is contested in the world and intended for God's righteous. This is the message of God's will, which speaks today and decides over life and death."[32]

Knowledge of the Triune God is given in baptism; God speaks before anyone is able to ask: from the church, which seeks the word of God, and from the Bible, since the church lives by the power of its preaching. God makes himself present in this way because God is Lord and capable of speaking himself wherever he wishes. However, it is "God's loving-kindness that he encounters us in earthly form and that we can know where he is to be found. That is the revelation in Christ and in his church." Regarding the power of the Holy Spirit, the catechism affirms the Holy Spirit as the Spirit of God and Christ, who is present in the church. But without the Spirit there is no knowledge of Christ, and without knowledge of Christ there is no knowledge of God. Under the article that addresses God as Father and Creator, there is a strong theological and ethical statement that addresses war, patriotism, the nations, and the church: "God has arranged it so that all races of humanity of the earth come from one blood (Acts 17:26). Therefore, a defiant ethnic pride . . . in flesh and blood is a sin against the Holy Spirit. Zeal that only blindly asserts itself is brought under control by the state. God has established the state for the service of God, so that we might serve God as Christians."[33]

Bonhoeffer was the preacher for Confirmation Sunday in March 1932.[34] His text was Genesis 32:25-32; 33:10. It is the story of Jacob, who wrestled with a stranger, only to have revealed to him that he had struggled with God and was given a new name and identity, from Jacob to Israel. Bonhoeffer addressed the confirmands directly, stating that his intention was to be pastorally responsive to their request that he offer a serious admonishment for their lives: "That is why today in church we will have to talk more than ever about the hope that we have and that no one can take away from you." He invited the confirmands to see themselves in the story of Jacob, since they too were on a journey toward a land where there is peace and love and justice, where "a wonderful Lord rules." The story illumines the path they must follow; Jacob surely felt what they must have been feeling on Confirmation Sunday: "What is to happen, what should they do, and how will things turn out?" Bonhoeffer offers Jacob as a figure of the new life the confirmands were about to enter. The life of faith cannot be taken up casually; becoming a member of the church is something God guards carefully to keep it holy. On this special day, the confirmands' path to Holy Communion would be their path into the holy.[35]

The question "How should we become holy?" turns the sermon back to Jacob. Bonhoeffer's telling of the story demonstrates God's dealing with sinful humanity, the relentless mercy that pursued and grasped Jacob, allowing him to wrestle until he was blessed. Jacob did not know how to hold on to God—but neither do the confirmands.

The good news for them is that God revealed himself as merciful rather than angry: "He let himself be found." Jacob was not pushed away, nor did God abandon him; rather, God allowed Jacob to enter the promised land and blessed him. The victory belongs to God, who overcame the darkness and let the sun rise upon Jacob: "Now God was there, who made it light around him and inside him." Jacob's broken hip was the key to remembering what God had done by pursuing him and allowing him to find his brother. This is also God's gift to the confirmands: that they should find God and their brother in the church—their home and their promised land. In the darkness of night, in the dark conditions and circumstances of life, in uncertain times for the nation, God lets the light of Christ dawn upon them. God makes a path through the world to the promised land in which God's peace, love, and justice rule.[36]

Learning to Integrate Theology and Practice

Bonhoeffer saw his involvement in practical ministry as essential for his growth as a theologian and preacher. This included serving as a pastor to students at the Berlin Technical College. A winter meditation with students drew from the temptations of Jesus in Luke 4. Bonhoeffer focused on two matters: that of God and bread, insisting these are not mutually exclusive. He challenged the prevalent view that saw the church's primary value as meeting people's needs, relieving their suffering, and giving them bread. Many in Germany believed the church had a responsibility to change the conditions in which people lived, or it would be perceived as unloving.[37]

Rather than arguing with this assumption, Bonhoeffer directed the students' attention to the story of Jesus in the wilderness, to the conditions of his temptation. Jesus was tempted to be God's Son on terms dictated by the tempter—to win people over, to help people, and to look after his own needs: "In this voice of apparently pleading love, Jesus recognizes the voice of the devil. This was a shocking discovery. And Jesus turns the tempter away. This means here, basically, God does not deceive people." The God whom Christians worship is not a god of bread and happiness, but shows himself through the death and resurrection of God's Son.[38] Bonhoeffer continued this meditation a week later, calling attention to the preaching of

Jesus as the beginning of his public ministry. Jesus was tempted to seize glory and honor, to become the powerful and glorious ruler of the world. The problem with this strategy is that Jesus would have surrendered his freedom and obedience, his identity and honor as God's Son. But the way of God to humanity is the way of the cross—a particular obedience that brings misunderstanding, rejection, scorn, and even persecution. To walk in the way of Christ is to be the church under the cross, "hidden from view."[39]

Bonhoeffer offered a brief homily to mark the beginning of the summer semester for the technical-college students. His text was John 8:31-32: "If you continue in my word, you are truly my disciples; and you will know the truth, and the truth will make you free." He begins by reminding the students of a popular German view of religion as corresponding to a particular need of the soul and as satisfying that need: "Something that should lead from restlessness of existence to peace, from hectic activity to calm." The relevance and usefulness of religion is in meeting the needs of people looking for relief from the affairs of daily life; its validity is in making people happy. Bonhoeffer counters this view with the gospel: "But with this we forget the one most important question: whether religion is also something true, whether it is the truth." Religion may be beautiful and attractive, but it may not be true, just a pious illusion. The church's greatest challenge was brought on itself by the subordination of truth to religion, to a vision of life derived from human perspective instead of divine revelation. True judgment is received from Christ—living with him, following him, listening to him, and obeying him. Freedom is found in basing one's life on the truth that is Christ himself.[40]

Bonhoeffer wrote to Sutz about the worsening conditions in Germany: "The situation here really looks desperate. One lives from one day to the next; simply no one can see further ahead. It may be that the day after tomorrow everything turns to chaos, and not because something great and new appears on the horizon, but simply because something rotten breaks down completely." He added that there was almost no one in Berlin with whom he could talk reasonably about theology. The situation seemed quite desolate, while his theology was increasingly seen as suspect. His communication with Barth had made him more aware of his dissatisfaction with academic life. And he continued to struggle with the disjunction of theology and ethics in proclamation that had contributed to the invisibility of the church: "For me the problem is becoming more and more acutely and unbearably critical. Recently, I preached on 2 Chron. 20:12. In that sermon I unloaded all my desperation. But that still didn't help me any further along."[41]

The sermon from 2 Chronicles 20:12—"We do not know what to do, but our eyes are on you"—was addressed to a church whose visibility was severely diminished by its national pride and self-sufficiency.[42] The location of the sermon was important, Berlin's historical Trinity Church, where one hundred years earlier Schleiermacher had drawn large crowds to hear his sermons, and where generations of German government dignitaries had worshiped. Trinity Church was also a place where those who had recently organized themselves as "German Christians" preferred to gather. Bonhoeffer's choice of a preaching text was fitting for the theological and political conditions in Berlin.[43]

The sermon was preached during Easter, on *Exaudi* Sunday, which means "Lord, hear us!" It begins with an assertion that establishes the force of what will follow:

> The world rests on the firm commandment of God. That is God's faithfulness to the world, that he gives permanence to his commandment. It is God's anger that he conceals his commandment from us. It is the mercy of God that he lets us know his commandment. It is the promise of God and our hope that we one day will keep his commandment. Lord, do not conceal your commandment from us. Teach us to keep your commandment. . . . Hear us, Lord, proclaim yourself to us.[44]

Bonhoeffer comments briefly on the prayer of Israel's king, which he characterizes as humble and strong. He then shifts the focus to the present, inquiring how such a statement, spoken by a national leader, would be heard in Germany. He suggests that such a fool would be taken and thrown out of office and that public scorn and ridicule would be heaped upon him. This is not the way things are supposed to be, since plans and programs, fueled by enthusiasm for a just and courageous cause, must proceed prayers.[45]

Bonhoeffer's sermon offers an ironic portrayal of Israel's king as one who speaks words that are heard as pitiful, cowardly, disgraceful, and fully without feeling for his fatherland: "We do not know what to do, but our eyes are on you." These seemingly uninspiring words are juxtaposed with the discourse of contemporary German "Christian" leaders, whose confidence in their plans and programs is expressed by Bonhoeffer in the following manner: "We know what to do, but our eyes are still on you, too." Bonhoeffer sarcastically identifies this as an improvement over the sorry state of Israel depicted in the Bible. He suggests, however, that Germany's modern advancement from the world of the Bible has not come without its costs. The consequences should be acknowledged—the diminishment of the church and disintegration of society—conditions that are hidden in plain sight. Germany's loss of moral vision has been caused by a failure to hear and believe God's word and commandment, "Love your neighbor."[46]

God's command has been violated, displaced by laws derived from human wisdom, from a self-justifying use of the Bible that contradicts its theological purpose. The way will not be found in more programs or plans, since the curse of the law and God's anger are real. The only hope is God, who has acted in Christ to recreate the world through the cross and resurrection, raising up a new humanity in Christ. Bonhoeffer calls the church, a church located at the center of German political power, to turn away from itself to Christ, trusting God as the source of a new world revealed in the cross: "We do not know what to do, but our eyes on are on you. Do not hide your commandment eternally from us. We know that your faithfulness is great. Hear us, Lord."[47]

Bonhoeffer preached a few weeks later, choosing Luke 16:19-31 as the sermon text: the parable of the rich man and Lazarus. His opening comments offer a robust articulation of the church's calling to proclaim the gospel: "We cannot understand and preach the gospel concretely enough." A truly evangelical sermon will be "like holding a pretty red apple in front of a child or a glass of cold water in front of a thirsty person and then asking, do you want it?" Preachers should talk about matters of faith so clearly and concretely that their words are met with the outstretched hands of faith: "People should run to Christ to be healed and not be able to rest when the gospel is talked about, as long ago the sick ran to Christ to be healed when he was going around healing (but Christ, too, healed more than he converted)." This is the way it should be whenever the good news of God is spoken. Bonhoeffer then adds his assessment of preaching in Germany: "But it just isn't that way—we all know that."[48]

The situation in Germany should not be accepted as normal, since preaching is no longer concrete, or "close to life," but has been subjected to "audacious and sanctimonious" spiritualization. The parable of the rich man and Lazarus is an example of how a powerful account of the gospel can be domesticated and reduced to principles. The story is made useful as a moral illustration that serves a particular ideal—that the rich should help the poor. Bonhoeffer saw the story as a means of listening for the concrete proclamation of the good news itself, for the concrete things of Christ, for his word and his deeds. This gospel is good news to the poor, the weak, the broken down and ruined, the lonely and abandoned, the victims of rape and injustice, all who suffer in body and soul. This gospel is preached against all human pride and divisions based on economic status and racial or ethnic identity. The reality of Christ, the crucified Lord, is seen in the figure of Lazarus, the neighbor who calls out to be loved. This gospel is the good news of the dawning of a new world in which rich and poor, all people, races and nations, are judged, forgiven, and reconciled in Christ.[49]

Bonhoeffer preached a few weeks later, choosing Colossians 3:1-4 as his text: "Set your minds on things that are above, not on things that are on the earth."[50] The sermon is divided into two parts, with the second addressing a popular view among the German people: "Stay true to the earth; set your mind on things that are on earth." Bonhoeffer responds to this kind of worldly wisdom with a forceful statement aimed toward faith that lacks concrete visibility in the world:

> Today immensely important things will be decided by whether we Christians have strength enough to show the world that we are not dreamers and are not those who walk with their heads in the clouds, that we don't just let things come and go as they are, that our faith is really not the opium that lets us stay content in the midst of an unjust world, but that we, especially because we set our minds on things that are above, only protest all the more tenaciously and resolutely on this earth. Protest with words and action, in order to lead the way forward at any price. Must it be

that Christianity, which began in such a tremendously revolutionary way long ago, is now conservative for all time? That each
new movement must forge a path for itself without the church,
that time after time the church does not see what has actually
happened until twenty years after the fact? If that really is the
way it must be, we should not be surprised if for our church, too,
times will come again when the blood of the martyrs will be
required. But this blood, if we really still have the courage and
honor and faithfulness to shed it, will not be as innocent and
untarnished as that of the first witnesses.[51]

Bonhoeffer continued this focus on ecclesiology in his teaching,
offering a summer seminar titled "The Nature of the Church."[52] The
material builds on previous academic work, particularly the two
dissertations, but it also addresses the "worldliness" of the church
in light of conditions in Germany: "Our church is here. Christ is
present in the church today. That is no ideal but rather reality." Here
ecclesiology is tied tightly to Christology: "The new, whole humanity is set in Christ. Christ as new humanity, as church; the church
is with Christ on the cross and resurrected with him." The worldliness of the church is real; it has become worldly for service to Christ
and others.[53]

The church is free to become a visible reality in the world, to
stand in the place of God himself, to stand in the place of the present Christ. Paradoxically, the worldliness of the church can only be
taken seriously by taking seriously its divinity—that it exists from
and for the reign of Christ. Significantly, Bonhoeffer adds that the
church is free from the state to serve the state—to proclaim the
lordship of Christ from faith in the word:

Obedience to [the] state exists only when [the] state does not
threaten the word. [The] battle about the boundary must then
be fought out! The decision will be difficult in the development
of our future state. [The] office of the state is neither Christian
nor godless; the office must be carried out in a responsible and
objective way. [The] existence as church depends on whether its
criticism can come from listening to the gospel alone. Criticism
of the state [is] demanded where [it] threatens [the] word. The
church can come [through] difficulties only when it sees to it that

it stands or falls with the word of *Christus praesens* as its Lord alone.[54]

Bonhoeffer continued to struggle with the disjunction of theology and ethics and the necessity of proclaiming the concrete word of Christ. Another summer 1932 seminar was titled "Is There a Christian Ethic?"[55] He was working to establish a "new ethic" on the basis of the gospel rather than philosophy, moral principles, human conscience, or religious experience. The focus on the gospel as the starting point for ethics leads to a discussion of preaching, which is defined in a theological manner: "*[The] preaching office [has the task of] proclaiming forgiveness and* preaching [the] law and judgment. Both [are] revelation of the will of God." Preaching presents Christ as both a gift and an example, as a promise actualized by the Spirit:[56] "If one takes the promise away, then one does not preach God." There is also the matter of listeners who respond in belief or unbelief. The preacher's primary responsibility is to make preaching so concrete, clear, and visibly alluring that listeners will feel compelled to believe the word of Christ. Speaking from and for the church, the pastor preaches the will of God in the concrete form of the gospel, which by faith is heard as the Spirit's work: "As you believe, so you receive."[57]

Bonhoeffer wrote to Paul Lehmann in the summer with news of political developments in Germany. The future was uncertain given the instability of the government, which was in large part influenced by the popular appeal of Hitler's nationalist ideology:

> Yesterday we had elections. We're happy that the Nazis did not get a majority. But it is still bad that the parliament, which has just been elected again, will not be able to form a government. But it has not yet gone so far that one can just turn Germany over to a few adventurers—undoubtedly full of enthusiasm. We first have to wait again to see how the leadership of the Nazis, that means how Hitler, reacts to the election results. I don't actually believe he will initiate something violent on his part. He has always taken a stand more on the principle of legality. It's just a question of whether he can keep the masses, who are waiting to see some action on his part . . . quiet any longer.[58]

Bonhoeffer's disposition toward these political developments was in part affected by his appointment as a German youth representative to ecumenical gatherings. There was strong resistance to internationalism in Germany, and those who participated in ecumenical work were perceived as unpatriotic because of their commitment to peace and resistance to war. Bonhoeffer was eager to take up this task, however, and after a period of time he was introduced to Germany's ecumenical partners and began contributing to their work. He was soon invited to address the International Youth Peace Conference in July 1932. The title of his lecture was "On the Theological Foundation of the Work of the Word Alliance." The lecture was an important opportunity for Bonhoeffer at a time when there was urgent need for a strong theology of the ecumenical movement. He immediately addressed this problem: "There is still no theology of the ecumenical movement. Whenever the church of Christ in its history has come to a new understanding of its nature, it has brought forth a new theology commensurate with this self-understanding."[59] His criticism was directed at those engaged in ecumenical work who viewed the church as an organization that needed to stay in step with the times. This view, however, left the church without a strong anchor against which the "waves of the right and left would batter in vain." A theological foundation for the church is necessary, which requires thinking with clarity, decisiveness, and courage: "And now we only notice in the middle of the lake that the ice upon which we stand is cracking." Bonhoeffer's robust theology of the church reflects an increasing clarity in his thinking about the task of proclamation for the church's visibility, its authority to speak from God's revelation in Christ:

> Under the only authority in which the church is in a position to speak, in the authority of the Christ who is present and living in it. The church is the presence of Christ on earth; the church is *Christus praesens*. This alone gives its word authority. The word of the church is the word of the present Christ; it is gospel and commandment. As the word out of the authority of the present Christ, the word of the church today must be considered as the valid, binding word. I can be spoken to with full authority only when a word from the deepest knowledge of my humanity hits me in my full reality, here and now. . . . For that which is "always"

true is precisely true "today": God is for us "always," God precisely "today."[60]

An equally important part of Bonhoeffer's address was to redefine
the popular, progressive notion of "orders of creation" as orders of
preservation. The proclamation of the gospel that creates faith and
empowers ethical obedience is ordered to God's fulfillment of creation in Christ. Because the fulfillment of God's law has been accomplished in Christ, he is the source of the new creation in which God's
order exists. Nothing, therefore, exists apart from him as its Lord,
source, and goal. God mercifully preserves the fallen creation with
the promise of new creation; the orders of preservation (marriage,
family, the nation, culture, and government) cannot derive their
value from themselves, from human desires, aspirations, origins, or
ethnic or national identities.[61]

Bonhoeffer spoke theologically, identifying the "orders of preservation" as forms of purposeful formation against sin that exist
in the direction of the gospel. Unless these structures are open to
Christ, they cannot serve God's purpose; creation and redemption
are united in Christ: "From this point, the church of Christ must
judge the world."[62] This has significant implications for the church's
ethical responsibility: "God's will is directed not only at the new
creation of humanity but toward the new creation of the conditions
as well. It is not right that only the will could be good. Conditions
can also be good; the creation of God was as such 'very good.' Even
in the fallen world conditions can be good but never through themselves, rather always only in view of the action of God himself."[63]

In Bonhoeffer's opinion, the conference was "mediocre." He
wrote to Surtz of his continuing frustration with the problem of ethics, whether it is possible for the concrete commandment to be proclaimed through the church. Bonhoeffer's comments on sermons
Sutz had shared with him reflect his struggle to discern how to proclaim the gospel in a manner that is concrete and fitting for "today":

> I was moved by the fact that it seems to be for you almost exactly
> as it is for me. But I just can't get past this kind of a sermon in
> which you try to say everything and at the end always have the
> terribly depressing feeling that you have talked right past the
> subject. It's the problem of making preaching concrete that is

bothering me so much at present. It is simply not enough and therefore false to say that the principle of concretion could only be the Holy Spirit itself, as several students in my seminar always insisted. The concrete form of the proclamation of grace is, after all, the sacrament. But what is the sacrament of the ethical, of the commandment?[64]

Bonhoeffer continued his ecumenical work during the summer, addressing the International Youth Conference in Gland, on Lake Geneva. He begins by sharing an anecdote about a man who had informed him, "The church is dead." This startling statement is followed by an invitation for delegates to consider the possibility of the "church's final demise and funeral." He clarifies what he meant; there were many in attendance who truly did feel that "it was too late and all over for Christ's church."[65]

Bonhoeffer counters this sense of hopelessness by pointing to Christ—the church is always dying; it is joined to him in his death and resurrection: "Only with clear eyes on reality, without any illusion about our morality or our culture, can one believe." The reality of Christ calls for neither optimism nor pessimism but the clear vision of faith that sees all things in light of God and God's power. Now is the time to believe in God, who "creates and does the impossible, who brings life out of death, the God who has called the dying church into life against and despite us and through us, the God who alone does this." And how will they know this? He states the answer plainly. Too little time is spent listening to and obeying Scripture, while too much time is given to their own thoughts and desires. His assessment of this problem is startling: "We no longer read the Bible seriously. We read it no longer against ourselves but only for ourselves."[66]

The baptism of a child in October provided a unique occasion to address members of the Berlin congregation in light of the sacrament. Bonhoeffer chose to speak from Ephesians 5:14: "Sleeper, awake! Rise from the dead, and Christ will shine on you." The significance of baptism as an event is more than a symbol, more than the parents' expression of desire and commitment, and more than a Christian tradition: "Only God endures in eternity." Baptism is a sign of God, who is able to break down and build up as he wills, including the church. Moreover, this is not a false God of human wishes, idealism, morality, or religious illusion: "God alone wants to be God for this child in eternity; that is God's mercy, which the church assures to this child today."[67]

"Sleeper, awake! Rise from the dead, and Christ will shine on you" is the message of baptism that the church cries out of God's eternal will, before which all are like children. Bonhoeffer's sermon summons the church to awaken from its slumber, to rise up from the dead, to step out of darkness into the light of the future created by God. Only God can call a person to awaken; only God can raise the church from death to life, just as God called Adam into being. To awaken entails a transformation of one's vision, the renewal of one's capacity to see the truth of reality. Bonhoeffer concludes with an elegant depiction of Christ, the wisdom of God, whose presence illuminates the church to be a visible witness to the message of baptism:

> To be illuminated by Christ means to see through love all the sorrow and suffering that Christ saw, into which he entered completely until his death on a cross. And it means knowing in love of the last hope for all suffering, which comes from the Lord of the world, who alone is no idol and will glorify his works. To be illuminated by Christ means to love God above all things and your neighbor as yourself. That, alone, can be called living. To be called to this life is the grace of God in baptism.[68]

"We Cannot Understand and Preach the Gospel Concretely Enough"

Bonhoeffer's preaching in 1931–1932 can be seen as seeking a truthful homiletical discourse grounded in God's revelation in Christ through the testimony of Scripture interpreted theologically—in and for the church. He found himself preaching to a church that had lost its established place, that was desperately seeking to prove to the German people that Christianity could be useful to the nation as a form of religion or morality. Bonhoeffer's sermons are a strong argument against this strategy and its claims. While the style of the sermons is not always explicitly argumentative, a substantive argument is consistently set forth through Bonhoeffer's attempt to allow the authority of the word and the church to counter prevailing individualistic, nationalistic, and ethnic plans and aspirations that many had simply identified as Christian. Theology and ethics are uniting.

Bonhoeffer's sermons display his courage in exercising the practical wisdom that guides speech and action in leading others to acknowledge the contingent, dependent nature of living by faith in the word of God.[69] The sermons were preached during a time of personal, vocational, and political struggle, which accounts for their intensity and directness, sense of urgency, and, at times, even desperation. But the sermons also demonstrate the conviction and constancy required for proclaiming the hope of the gospel—the good news revealed in the "strange world of the Bible." This meant showing the church how to read Scripture against itself rather than in support of its own desires—as an external word. Bonhoeffer challenged the pervasive narrative of national self-interest and idolatry by his prophetic preaching of Scripture, which creates a community of witnesses to Christ's way of peace in the world.[70] His formation as a homiletical theologian was deepened by the necessity of placing himself and his work in service of the church, which lives from the rule of Christ, rather than national or racial power and superiority. As 1932 drew to a close, Bonhoeffer confided to Sutz that he saw himself as "theologically homeless" in Berlin, a condition for which no relief was in sight.[71]

5

Preaching as Politics
London 1932–1935

The deeply troubled and troubling years of the early 1930s were
arguably the busiest in Bonhoeffer's life.[1] This period in German
history is remembered for Adolf Hitler's stunning rise to power,
a political triumph prompting an extended struggle to determine
how the church in Germany would be structured, relate to, and be
affected by the National Socialist vision proclaimed by the Nazis.
Bonhoeffer is remembered for his role in the church struggle: his
leadership in the opposition that formed the Pastor's Emergency
League in 1933 and that constituted itself as the Confessing Church
in May 1934.[2]

Not as well known, however, is Bonhoeffer's significant role
in the struggle for the church's truthful proclamation of the gospel against a Nazi message of "good news," which was aggressively
proclaimed to promote Hitler's Third Reich, the superiority of the
Aryan race, and the restoration of the German nation to greatness.
Bonhoeffer discerned that the National Socialist message of "good
news" sought nothing less than a totalizing claim on the hearts,
minds, and allegiance of the German people. He believed this could
be countered only by faithful proclamation of the gospel made visible in the concrete obedience, confession, and, if necessary, public
resistance of the church.[3]

At the heart of Bonhoeffer's activity during the early years of
Nazi rule was the urgent task of clarifying and defending the integrity of the church's confession of Christ for faithful preaching,

hearing, and adherence to the gospel. Both Bonhoeffer's theological and homiletical commitments form a major thread during a
significant time of personal and professional change that saw him
eventually leave his academic position in Berlin and move to pastoral ministry with two German-speaking congregations in London. Bonhoeffer's pastoral assignment in London, extending from
October 1933 to April 1935, would be his longest-sustained period
of regular preaching in a congregational setting. His engagement in
the struggle to clarify the nature of preaching as an act of confessing Christ as the Word of God revealed in Scripture deserves more
attention that it has received.[4]

Important events in Bonhoeffer's emergence as a homiletical theologian are the seminar lectures he delivered on the book
of Genesis during the winter semester of late 1932 and early 1933,
coinciding with the time of Hitler's appointment as chancellor of
Germany.[5] Bonhoeffer's lectures on Genesis speak directly from the
text of Scripture and only indirectly to the political circumstances
in Germany. Yet the message he communicated was undoubtedly
heard clearly by those in attendance. That the lectures were delivered in the University of Berlin, rather than to a congregation or
gathering of pastors, is even more remarkable. Bonhoeffer's theological exposition in a university seminar represented a major break
with the longstanding tradition of academic discourse in the study
of the Bible as a historical text and ancient cultural artifact.[6] Thus,
removed from doctrinal and ecclesial convictions, an "academic"
Bible could still be useful for addressing modern social, moral, and
political issues.[7]

Bonhoeffer's lectures on Genesis marked an explicit recovery of
the Bible as holy Scripture—as the church's book. His interpretation
of Genesis approached the Old Testament as part of the Christian
Bible, as a unified whole belonging to the church that is unintelligible outside a divinely revealed economy of meaning. Bonhoeffer's exposition was theological and subordinated to the true subject
of Scripture: the Triune God revealed in Christ. Reading Scripture
in this manner constitutes an awakening that is generated by God
through the illumination of the Spirit. Bonhoeffer's lectures on Genesis thus placed him outside the mainstream of university study of
the Bible as an academic discipline, as had Barth's *Romans* more

than ten years earlier. But the lectures also situated Bonhoeffer within a tradition of interpretation that was confessional and kerygmatic, thus well suited for the proclamation of the word in and for the church.[8]

This "turning" was both personal and professional, moving Bonhoeffer closer to a confessional hermeneutic attentive to the scriptural character of the Bible as inseparable from the faith and practice of the church. Looking back on this time a few years later, he shared his reflections on the change of direction in his life:

> But then something different came, something that has changed and transformed my life to this very day. For the first time, I came to the Bible. That, too, is an awful thing to say. I had often preached, I had seen a great deal of the church, had spoken and written about it—and yet I was not a Christian, but rather in an utterly wild and uncontrolled fashion my own master. . . . The Bible, especially the Sermon on the Mount, freed me from all of this. Since then everything has changed. . . . It became clear to me that the life of a servant of Jesus Christ must belong in the church, and step-by-step it became clear to me how far it must go. Then came the crisis of 1933 [Hitler]. This strengthened me in it.[9]

This "turning," moreover, which was intellectual, moral, and spiritual, was also ecclesial in nature: "The renewal of the church and its ministry became my supreme concern."[10] Bonhoeffer's reading of Genesis is the work of a homiletical theologian, a way of listening to Scripture as a witness to revelation in order to understand and speak the truth about God, humanity, and the world—a gift for the material substance of the church's thought, language, and life.[11]

Bonhoeffer's exposition of Genesis was a theological and public protest in step with the Lutheran tradition of the Protestant Reformation. He did not merely replicate Luther's interpretation of Genesis but engaged in an ongoing dialogue with the Reformer's life and work as a way of testing the present in light of the past, as a necessary step toward a future that is received by attending to God's Word in Scripture.[12] His aim was not to be less than intellectually rigorous, but in a manner similar to how Barth's *Romans* sought to be "postcritical"—moving beyond conventional academic methodology to allowing the Word of God to be heard by the church.[13] Such eschatological and ecclesial convictions would inform Bonhoeffer's preaching: "The church of Christ witnesses the end of all things. It lives from the end, it thinks from the end, it acts from the end, it proclaims its message from the end."[14]

The church thus sees and understands the creation from Christ, the world of the new creation, because it is a creature of the Word, and is founded upon the witness of Holy Scripture: "The world exists from the beginning in the sign of the resurrection of Christ from the dead. Indeed it is because we know of the resurrection that we know of God's creation in the beginning, of God's creating out of nothing."[15] Bonhoeffer thus held together the church, Scripture, and the risen Christ: "The church of Holy Scripture, and there is no other church, lives from the end." This is the presupposition of reading the whole of Scripture as the book of the end, of the new in Christ: "The Bible is the book of the church. It is this in its very essence, or it is nothing. . . . For in the whole of Holy Scripture God is the one and only God . . . ; with this belief the church and theological science stand or fall." Bonhoeffer's concern was to hear the Word of God that had been spoken in the beginning and to hear God speaking in the present. His desire was to listen attentively and reverently, receiving God's address as a Word, the person of Christ, who must be proclaimed.[16]

Bonhoeffer had reached a true turning point in his life and vocation. His theological exposition characterized a shift in his way of perceiving reality, a desire to link more closely the concerns of exegesis and preaching as inseparable practices in service of the church. He was becoming increasingly aware that how Scripture is interpreted determines in large part the content and character of the gospel that is preached and the faith and life of the people who listen. Bonhoeffer's exposition of Genesis was also indicative of a maturing in his preaching—a move toward theological performance in homiletical mode, the self-involving practice of biblical interpretation within preaching that bears witness to Christ. Theology, exegesis, and preaching are thus integrally related, presupposing and affirming the existence of the church.[17]

Bonhoeffer perceived that the church in Germany was involved in more than a political struggle, either internally or externally; it was engaged in a fundamental conflict over the nature of God and the gospel—a clash of competing discourses that offered starkly different visions of the church and mission. The "German Christians," those who enthusiastically supported the Nazi Party's nationalist and racist ideology, believed Hitler's role as Führer, or leader, was a providential opportunity for reviving the church and nation to restored prominence in the name of Christ. The Nazi gospel was supported by a revised interpretation of Luther's doctrine of Two Kingdoms in which the history of the nation was read into theological prominence, equating the policies of the Reich with the kingdom of God on earth.[18] Hitler saw himself in Christian terms, as not only a representative of "true" Christianity, but a theological thinker in his own right. His plans for Germany were based upon a progressive, revolutionary, and scientific fulfillment of the Enlightenment in the tradition of liberal Protestantism, a familiar narrative that attracted the support of mainstream theologians and church leaders.[19]

At the heart of Hitler's Christianity was the will, the expression of self-preservation defined in Darwinian terms, as the reality of Nature's laws. This naturalistic religion considered natural selection, the immanent struggle for life against life, as fundamental to the meaning of history. Hitler's way of thinking, then, was based on a reasoned approach to reality, utilizing scientific knowledge in support of blood and race, the natural laws of racial evolution, to proclaim a prophetic message to the German people. Transcendence was dismissed, however, since it went against the rule of natural life as immanent and violent and as enlightened by anti-Semitism.[20]

Hitler saw himself as serving Christ, the Lord and Savior, who was a fighter in the battle against the Jews and whose materialistic greed was a pestilence in the soul of the nation. In the name of Christ, this fight was to be continued according to a revisionist interpretation of liberal theology that would place the state in a position of ruling over all things in the public realm, while relegating the church to a private realm of personal religious experience or doctrinal purity. Nazi theology thus combined a rationalist, deistic god whose laws worked through the process of natural selection that sought fulfillment in a purified Aryan nation. This was made all the more confusing, or syncretistic, in being framed and communicated in theological terms, presented not only as the climax of Christian history but arguably as its replacement. Many Germans embraced

Nazism, but many Nazis also embraced Christianity, building on established understandings of Protestant identity, national origins, and racism.[21] As the Nazi Party Program stated:

> We demand freedom for all religious confessions in the state, insofar as they do not endanger its existence or conflict with the customs and moral sentiments of the German race. The part as such represents positive Christianity without tying itself to a particular confession. It fights against the spirit of the Jewish materialism within and without us, and is convinced that a lasting recovery of our Volk can only take place from within, on the basis of the principle: "public need comes before private greed."[22]

A majority of Christians in Germany continued to believe that the traditional Lutheran Two Kingdoms doctrine kept the church out of politics, since this was the domain of the state. Bonhoeffer was part of a small minority who saw the theological danger in a church/state position that allowed bishops, pastors, and laity to claim membership in both the church and Nazi Party as separate commitments located within separate realms of life according to the "orders of creation."[23]

The "Aryan Paragraph," which was passed by parliament in April 1933, made it illegal for any non-Aryan to work in German civil service, a move to ensure a racially pure public. The German Christians, however, saw the paragraph as a matter of indifference. They pressured the church to adopt its implementation in compliance with the Nazis' desire to create a unified Protestant Reich Church. This would mean the exclusion of Jewish Christian clergy and laity and a denial of all Jewish elements of Christianity, the Old Testament, the election of Israel, and even the Jewishness of Jesus.[24]

Bonhoeffer found himself in a religious/political environment where Christ was given a central place by many in the Nazi worldview, but a Christ stripped of all scriptural, confessional, and ecclesial authority and substance.[25] The Nazis blamed the clergy and the church for their failure to live up to the standard of Christ, who, as the Son of God, preached the necessity of struggle and who struggled for his beliefs, eventually suffering and dying, which was his triumph. Christ as hero fused Christianity and Nazism, the hero and sufferer standing at the center, as fully divine, "true God," and thus the greatest Aryan leader.[26] The church's handling of the

"Jewish Question" provoked Bonhoeffer to express his assessment of the problem: "Here the most intelligent people have totally lost both their heads and their Bibles."[27]

Preaching was seen by the German Christians as a primary means of spreading a Nazi faith supported by Hitler's *Mein Kampf*, the "Holy Book" of National Socialism. Christian virtues were replaced by Nazi values: strength rather than weakness, domination rather than humility, hatred rather than love, dependence on Hitler rather than Christ, the creed of "blood, soil, and race" rather than word and sacrament. The Nazis also held large "liturgical" celebrations that attracted huge, enthusiastic crowds. Nazi gatherings were revivals, consisting of music, songs, "preaching," uniforms and flags, sacred rites, and an inspiring narrative. This was a story of Germany's resurrection from the deep despair of defeat to triumph, from darkness to light, a chosen people returning from exile, overcoming the shame of World War I. All of this centered on Hitler himself, who had come to Germany in the "fullness of time."[28]

Bonhoeffer had summarized the consequences of liberal Protestantism at the conclusion of his first academic seminar in Berlin, "Who Will Show Us Luther?" Preaching on Reformation Sunday, November 6, 1932, in Berlin, Bonhoeffer attacked what he saw as the foolishness of a church that presumed it still stood within its Lutheran heritage and attacked the pretense of the German Christians who saw the National Socialist program as the completion of Luther's Reformation by a heroic strongman: "Let us lay the dead Luther to rest at long last, and instead listen to the gospel, reading the Bible, hearing God's word in it. God's question will not concern proper celebration of the Reformation, but rather faithfulness to the fundamental principles of the Reformation: 'Have you heard my word and kept it?' "[29]

Bonhoeffer discerned the urgent need of evangelizing and forming the church with and for the gospel, the witness of the Old and New Testaments to the presence of Christ speaking in word and sacrament. Given the aggressive tactics of the German Christians who engaged in their own work of proselytism, Bonhoeffer's preaching of the gospel was bound to be heard as polemical and even subversive speech. However, he would come to see the pastoral task of securing the integrity of the church in the word as the most hopeful way of preparing for the future. Both the evangelical faith of Luther and an ecumenical vision had been abandoned in Germany, demanding a radical reevaluation of the relationship between faith, nationality, and the people of God according to the proclamation of the gospel.[30]

Bonhoeffer's commitment to preaching from 1933 to 1935 can be divided into two periods. The first period was in Berlin during the time following Hitler's appointment as chancellor of Germany in January 1933. The second period was in London from October 1933 to April 1935. Bonhoeffer's sermons in Berlin sought to define the nature of the Christian faith and way of life in an intense struggle with the German Christians, who were most heavily concentrated in Berlin and its surrounding regions, within the Old Prussian Union. In addition, there was a surge in church activity and membership in the months following Hitler's assumption of power, with members of the Nazi Party, the SA, clothed in brown uniforms, prominently in attendance as a show of the party's support for the church. The German Christians enthusiastically supported Hitler as a gift and miracle of God, a divinely given source of hope for a strong, unified German nation that required a strong German church united by a purified form of "Christianity."[31] A new eschatology thus emerged in preaching: a secular "Christian" eschatology of the Volkisch movement, the conflation of Christianity and Germanness as a providential act of God.[32]

The German Christian "gospel" was communicated by sermons that tended to focus on a particular "theme" or topic accompanied by a biblical text, often a single verse, and then proceeded with several points related to the theme. The introduction typically framed the sermon within contemporary circumstances and needs, particularly the desires and anxieties of the German people. Although a certain amount of biblical and theological language was used, a steady diet of political rhetoric was added. The sermon, then, was easily accommodated to church/political goals, utilized as an instrument for persuading church members to embrace the nationalist Protestant agenda. Theme preaching, then, was also "situation" preaching that placed the hearer and his or her concerns at center stage. There was no room for the "external word" of God that was capable of calling into question contemporary German people and their desires, plans, enthusiasms, views, and presuppositions. The theological witness of preaching had been eclipsed—replaced by political, psychological, ethical, and practical concerns and tasks.[33]

Bonhoeffer's sermons in Berlin are oriented from and to the gospel, calling the church to repentance from the sin of idolatry—a return to God, to faith in the incarnate, crucified, and risen Lord as the source and substance of its life. At stake was the church's identity: either German or Christian.[34] Bonhoeffer preached just two weeks after Hitler assumed the office of chancellor, on the first Sunday in Lent. The city of Berlin, including the university and churches, were filled with enthusiastic support for the Nazi promise of national renewal. In a rather bold move, which undoubtedly was not lost on his listeners, Bonhoeffer chose to preach from the book of Judges, from the story of Gideon. He began the sermon by affirming the continuing validity of the text for the church: "This is a passionate story about God's derision for all those who are fearful and have little faith, all those who are much too careful, the worriers, all those who want to be somebody in the eyes of God but are not."[35]

The story reveals how God mocks human might and the fear of human beings but wins them over with love. The action of God extends to the present, to the church in Germany, which finds itself ridiculed by the God of Gideon. Thus, for God, "human beings are not heroes, not heroic, but rather creatures who are meant to do his will and obey him, whom he forces with mockery and with love to be his servants." Gideon is an exemplar of how faith is learned in the "school of hard knocks." Bonhoeffer pressed hard the primary issue of right worship (ortho-doxy): "In the church we have only one altar—the altar of the Most High, the One and only, the Almighty, the Lord, to whom be honor and praise, the Creator before whom even the most powerful are but dust." Right worship requires courage to overcome cowardice, as seen in the story of Gideon.[36]

In addition, the church has only one pulpit from which faith in God and no other is preached, not even with the best of intentions. Gideon's faith is living sermon; his witness was concrete and particular rather than abstract, timeless, or otherworldly. There is a gritty quality of ordinariness about Gideon that speaks to the present: "This church is without influence, powerless, undistinguished in every way. It looks at the helplessness of its proclamation, it looks at the apathy and misery of those who are supposed to be listening

and recognizes that it is not equal to this task." Bonhoeffer acknowledges the craziness of the story, since to have the faith of Gideon is
to be defenseless and foolish. To believe like Gideon is to fight not
with weapons but with faith that trusts in the power of God. The
story of Gideon, then, confronts the church with the scandal of the
cross, the "bitter mockery of all human grandeur and God's bitter
suffering in all human misery, God's lordship over the world." Bonhoeffer concludes by simply calling the church to hear God speaking "today."[37]

Bonhoeffer preached at the end of May, on Ascension Day, at a
time when the German Christians had intensified their efforts for a
national Reich Church. The focus of the sermon was fitting for the
liturgical occasion—as a time for rejoicing in the hope of Christ's
final advent. The text was 1 Peter 1:7-9: "Although you have not seen
him, you love him; and even though you do not see him now, you
believe in him and rejoice with an indescribable and glorious joy."
The hymn prior to the sermon had been "Jesus, My Joy," which Bonhoeffer contrasts with a "mushy enthusiasm" that is not grounded
in the gospel. The sermon is indirectly polemical in nature. Bonhoeffer's primary aim was to call the congregation to rejoice in God,
who became human in Jesus Christ for the sake of humankind, the
companion of sinners, who sat among tax collectors and prostitutes.
The source of such joy is the Lord, who became a common criminal
for the sake of convicts, who rose from the dead for the sake of all—
Jesus Christ, who, for the sake of the church, ascended and returned
to the Father. All of this is the action of God and the source of joy.
Bonhoeffer's rhetoric, aimed indirectly at the ideology of the Nazis,
declared the gospel of joy is not "a mere moral law or an added burden to the burdens people already carry."[38]

The sermon proclaims the gospel as a true and joyful alternative
to the claims of the German Christians. Christ is the ascended Lord,
which means God has not abandoned the church but rather rules as
Lord of the whole world. Christ is present and near with the church,
with the Jews, and even with the heathen. Moreover, Christ is not
bound to the past, as a figure from history. Neither is Christ limited
to any nation, but he still makes himself present in word and sacrament to comfort the abandoned, the estranged, the lost, and the sor-
rowful. The sermon expresses the joy of preaching, while lamenting

its loss when more attention is directed to preachers than to Christ. The effect is that the church is emptied of the joy only Christ himself can give. This eschatological claim is based on the joy of Christ that is received in anticipation of his final advent, for which the church awaits, and without which the whole world is joyless and miserable. Without stating the obvious, Bonhoeffer's sermon had challenged the realized eschatology of a Nazi faith that enthusiastically hailed the coming of Hitler as the "end" of history.[39]

Bonhoeffer preached in late May, on *Exaudi* Sunday. His sermon text was from the Old Testament, from Exodus 32, the story of Moses and Aaron. The narrative provided a means for presenting two antithetical visions of worship, faith, and church. This was a timely matter, since the conflict with the German Christians had escalated over the election of a Reich bishop who would be responsible for unifying the twenty-eight regional churches in Germany into an Aryan Reich Church. The sermon addresses the theological foundation and purpose of the church's existence, thereby raising significant questions in relation to its ethos, beliefs, and governance.[40]

Bonhoeffer begins by highlighting the stark contrast between Moses and Aaron, the prophet and the priest. This contrast can be seen between the church of Aaron and the church of Moses, an eternal conflict in the church that can be resolved only by the action of God. Bonhoeffer provided a figural or imaginative interpretation of the narrative to illumine the Word of God for the church in Germany. The story raises the question of why these two brothers could not serve God together. "Why are the church of Moses and the church of Aaron, the church of the Word and the church of the world, always breaking apart?" Bonhoeffer answers his question by describing Moses and his calling as a prophet, then Aaron and his calling as a priest. Moses went up the mountain on behalf of the people, but the people turned to Aaron in their impatience, assuming Moses must be dead and gone, of no consequence for their future:

> Surely, the church of the Word is once again on Mt. Sinai today, and in fear and trembling, amid the thunder and lightning, stands against the Word of God, waiting, believing, praying, struggling—and for whom? For the church of Aaron, for the church down there in the valley, for the church of the world. When the worldly church gets impatient and cannot wait any

longer, that is the first step on its collision course with the church of the Word. It was always so and will always be so.⁴¹

Bonhoeffer had situated the German church in the story of Moses and Aaron. The church of Aaron, the church of the world, is depicted as the church of priests without the Word, a church that runs ahead to take matters into its own hands, meeting the needs of the people, who cry out for gods and religion. The church of Aaron is a celebrating church but not a sacrificing church, celebrating itself and worshiping its accomplishments.⁴²

The church of Aaron meets its end when Moses comes down the mountain with the word of God: "I am the Lord your God." . . . You shall have no other gods before me! This is a time for remembering, repentance, and conversion, for turning away from the idolization of human ideas and values to become a church of devotion and sacrifice, for the worship of God. Bonhoeffer concludes the sermon by pointing to the greater Moses who went up to the cross to end all idolatry and who by his death judged and pardoned humankind. This is the message and gift of reconciliation. Neither one nor the other—the church of the cross is the church of both Moses and Aaron, the whole people of God.⁴³

Bonhoeffer preached his last sermon in Berlin on July 23, 1933, the day national elections were held to choose representatives to represent the regional churches at a national synod for the selection of a Reich bishop. The German Christians had received open support from the Nazi Party, including a speech by Hitler that was broadcast nationally. Bonhoeffer chose as his preaching text Matthew 16:13-18, Peter's confession of Christ, the Lord who will build the church. Bonhoeffer does not hesitate to acknowledge the difficult decisions faced by the church and that many preferred to avoid having to commit themselves to the process. He then adds, "But with God, we get just what we don't want. We are challenged to come out and make the decision; we can't get out of it."⁴⁴ The sermon calls the congregation to hear the word of God without avoiding the difficulties involved:

> In the midst of the creaking and groaning of church structures, which have been profoundly shaken and are collapsing and crumbling away here and there, we can still hear the promise of

an eternal church, against which the gates of hell shall not prevail, the church on the rock, which Christ has built and continues to build through all the ages.[45]

Rather than attempt to persuade the people of their responsibility for rebuilding the church, the sermon is a call to believe the Word of God in Scripture. Bonhoeffer does this by emphasizing the details of the narrative, giving particular attention to the obscurity of the event: "So it is a church of a little flock, a church far out in a quiet place, a church in the face of death, about which we must be speaking here."[46]

The contrast with the German Christians' vision of a Reich Church is more than obvious. Bonhoeffer thus turns to the center of the story: "Who do you say that I am?" After running through the disciples' answers, he offers a contemporary reading: "Some say you are a great man, others that you are an idealist, others, that you are a religious genius, others, that you are a hero, the greatest of leaders. Opinions, more or less serious opinions—but Christ doesn't want to build his church on opinions." Bonhoeffer then turns to the character of Peter; he was nobody, just a person who recognized Christ standing in his path and who confessed his faith in him. The church in Germany is called to do the same, even as it falters and fails, denies Christ, and is ashamed of him. Even these occasions can be times of weeping that lead to joy: "By the rivers of Babylon—there we sat down and there we wept when we remembered Zion." The sermon concludes with an exhortation to believe it is God who will build the church. Those who try to build the church themselves end up destroying it by making it into a house of idolatry. What must the church do? Bonhoeffer answers, "Confess, preach, and pray while God builds, while God tears down, while God reforms the church as God wills."[47]

The church struggle continued to intensify through the summer of 1933. At stake was the nature of a new German Evangelical Church, a Reich Church, and whether it would enforce the Aryan Paragraph to exclude Jewish Christian pastors and members. Bonhoeffer was part of a radical minority that saw this issue as a threat to the very essence of the church's confession of the gospel, a *status confessionis* (a time or situation calling for the church to offer clear public confession of its faith and public protest). Bonhoeffer was designated as a member of a team with responsibility for drafting an evangelical confession of faith that would serve this need, including addressing the Jewish question.[48]

However, Bonhoeffer was so disappointed with the outcome after the editing of the Bethel Confession that he would not sign it. Discouraged and feeling isolated by the church struggle, he began making plans for accepting a call to serve as pastor of two small German-speaking congregations in London. In a letter to Karl Barth, he described this move as a necessary "retreat into silence, a time to go into the wilderness for a spell, [to] simply work as a pastor, as unobtrusively as possible." He was happy to have this opportunity, hoping the time in England would enable him to gain clarity in his vocation, to continue his ecumenical work, and to discern how he might best support the German church. He added, "We do not know what to do, but . . . (2 Chronicles)."[49]

Preaching in Exile

Bonhoeffer's preaching in London displays a shift from the Berlin sermons. There are less explicit references to the church struggle and an easing of polemic against the German Christians, whose aggressive tactics had caused Hitler to distance himself from them out of fear of international embarrassment or rebuke.[50] In addition, Bonhoeffer was concerned his strong public views in the church struggle may have betrayed an air of overconfidence, arrogance, or dogmatism. These concerns, however, did not prevent Bonhoeffer from sharing his understanding of the church struggle with other pastors of German-speaking congregations in England, the Association of Congregations. At a conference of the Pastor's Association in November 1933, Bonhoeffer provided a summary of the church struggle during the previous six months. He did not describe the conflict as primarily a matter of church politics but spoke in doctrinal terms according to the Lutheran confessions of the Reformation, particularly the central doctrine of justification by grace through faith in Christ. The primary question was whether there is a revelation of God independent of Christ in the Scriptures and the preaching of the church: "Is there an independence with regard to nature, blood, race, and ethnic characteristics? Should these things be questioned? Theologically, it is impossible to say they justify, since their validity is not ultimate."[51]

Bonhoeffer's sermons in London are an attempt to work out the ecclesial import of these theological convictions in homiletical form—a homiletical theology. His primary concern was the renewal of the congregation and its ministry as a local appropriation of the gospel. Bonhoeffer's time in London could be seen as preaching in exile, a time of voluntary silence that was necessary for discerning how to speak of God and the church in a future that was still unknown. The London sermons warrant more attention than they have received, since what is remembered most from this period in Bonhoeffer's life are other important commitments that occupied him on a much larger, public stage: ecumenical work, the viability of the Confessing Church in Germany, the continuing struggle with the Reich Church leadership, and resistance increasing pressure from a controlling Nazi state. Although seemingly less important in relation to Bonhoeffer's visibility in either German or ecumenical church matters, his preaching ministry with two small congregations of expatriates illuminates his importance as a preaching theologian engaged in a struggle for truthful proclamation of the gospel.[52]

Bonhoeffer's first sermon in London is indicative of the manner in which he approached his responsibilities as a preacher. It also reveals his expectations for the congregations as his partners in the ministry of the Word. The sermon text he chose was 2 Corinthians 5:20: "So we are ambassadors for Christ, since God is making his appeal through us; we entreat you on behalf of Christ, be reconciled to God." Bonhoeffer begins with a comment on the change of pastors and that such transitions always affect both a pastor and the people. He spoke briefly of the work of pastoral ministry and the close relationships that bond a pastor and people. There is a sense of loss and sorrow when a beloved pastor leaves, bringing uncertainty about the future.[53]

Bonhoeffer had other important matters on his mind. He shifts the focus by inviting the congregation to see its life in light of the work of God present in Christ: "Between you and your pastor should only be Christ. The important matter between you and your pastor, wherever we meet, whether in serious or joyful moments, is always

Christ." Indeed, the pastor is devoted primarily to Christ and serves the people by his or her devotion to Christ. The congregation also shares in this responsibility by allowing the Lord of the church to lead them, rather than clinging to the pastor. Attention should be directed to the preaching rather than the preacher, aided by these important questions: "Is this truly the gospel of our God? . . . Is the pastor giving us stones or bread?"[54]

Bonhoeffer's introductory sermon aimed to clear a space for the word to be spoken, heard, and believed. There was also a prophetic aim: to call the church to turn to God, to recognize God's truth is to be trusted, to choose the "holy restlessness of God." This leads to a remarkable description of preaching as something unique in all the world and completely different from any other kind of speech:

> When a preacher opens his Bible and interprets the word of God, a mystery takes place, a miracle: the grace of God, who comes down from heaven into our midst and speaks to us, knocks on our door, asks questions, warns us, puts pressure on us, alarms us, threatens us, and makes us joyful again and free and sure. When the Holy Scriptures are brought to life in the church, the Holy Spirit comes down from the eternal throne, into our hearts, while the busy world outside sees nothing and knows nothing about it—that God could actually be found here. Out there they are all running after the after the latest sensations, the excitements of evening in the big city, never knowing that the real sensation, something infinitely more exciting, is happening here.[55]

God was asking something of them that was both strange and astonishing: "Be reconciled to God, receive God's kingdom, take heaven as a gift. . . . This is a strange glory, the glory of this God who comes to us as one who is poor, in order to win our hearts."[56]

The message and ministry of reconciliation mean the church is called to the obedience of faith in Christ, who is himself—instead of the preacher—the source, content, and focus of preaching. To preach this message (God's message of reconciliation in Christ) and to preach in this manner (as an ambassador making an appeal on behalf of Christ) represented a decisive shift from familiar "modern" ways of preaching. The end or purpose of preaching is to build up and form the church in the Word, as an eschatological act that makes Christ's presence visible in the world. Bonhoeffer refused to concede that the conditions in Germany were the "end" or final word in God's work. Returning to 2 Corinthians 5 on Repentance Day, he gave voice to God's urgent appeal to repent: "Turn back, turn back! the whole Bible calls to us joyfully. Turn back—where? To the everlasting mercy of God who never leaves us, whose heart breaks because of us, the God who created and loves us beyond all measure."[57]

The London sermons communicate a strong sense of hope in God's promise and command for the church in an increasingly dark time. On New Year's Day, 1934, Bonhoeffer preached from Luke 9:57-62. The sermon begins with a warning: "The road to hell is paved with good intentions." Bonhoeffer challenged the popular notion that New Year's new beginnings are a matter of good intentions, pointing instead to God's new beginning in Christ that is received as a gift. The gospel shows three individuals approaching Jesus. The first was filled with enthusiasm, the second with grief, and the third with many responsibilities. All three, however, were unable to receive the gift of God's new beginning in Christ. Bonhoeffer concludes, "The coming year will have its share of fear, guilt, and hardship, but let it be, in all our fear, guilt, and hardship, a year spent with Christ."[58]

Bonhoeffer sought to create a vision of God's faithful action in the Word that takes hold of the church in the worst of conditions and circumstances. He preached from the prophet Jeremiah to convey the deep sense of being personally grasped by God. Identifying with the prophet's words, Bonhoeffer described God's action as an external word: foreign, unfamiliar, unexpected, forceful, and overpowering, by which God calls "whosoever and wherever God chooses." Paradoxically, the external word God speaks is the incredibly familiar, near, persuading, captivating, enticing word of the Lord, who yearns for his creation in love. Bonhoeffer likens this to "having a lasso thrown over one's head." God does not let go, even when the church is mocked, humiliated, tortured, brutalized, persecuted, oppressed, and no longer in control of its life. The good news is that Christ himself is the nearness of God who continues to make a way through the world, gathering captives in the wake of his victory.[59]

Bonhoeffer also approached preaching as an act of praise. In April 1934, he preached from Psalm 98: "O sing to the LORD a new song." The occasion was *Cantati* Sunday, a day to celebrate the gift of song and music for the praise of God. Bonhoeffer begins the sermon by commenting on the gift of music to the church, its capacity to evoke awe, wonder, and devotion. But music is also capable of calling attention to itself, of becoming an obstacle to the praise of God. The problem, however, is not music. The problem stems from disordered love for creation that exceeds singular love for God. Rather than being played or sung for God's sake, its enjoyment displaces God, thus drowning out the voice of God, who speaks in the simple beauty of Scripture.[60] Bonhoeffer offers an elegant reflection on the word of God and beauty:

> The word of God, as it comes to us in the Bible and in the proclamation of the gospel, does not need ornamentation. It is clothed in its own glory, its own beauty; that certainly is true. But like exceptional human beauty, even the word of God cannot escape being adorned by those who love it. However, like every adornment of true loveliness, adoring the word of God cannot be anything other than letting its own beauty shine even more gloriously. . . . Nothing that conceals its intrinsic beauty, but rather that which reveals it and makes it visible, should be used to adorn it.[61]

Bonhoeffer's sermon was an act of praise for the beauty of the word that attunes the church to hear, receive, and give voice to God's new song in Christ. The sermon was also an example of adorning the word to allow its beauty to shine. The question is whether the church sings either its own song or the new song given in Christ—whether the human person is its measure and focus, or God and Jesus Christ. As God's new song, Christ is echoed in the lives of men and women who turn to him in praise and loving adoration.

Bonhoeffer's preaching was deeply pastoral and directed to the heart of the church. He was capable of addressing particular events and situations, drawing contemporary concerns and needs into the larger world of the Bible. Rather than accommodating Scripture to the immediate desires of listeners, his sermons invited the congregation into the strange world of the Bible to imagine themselves, the church, and the world in light of God's promises and claims. A serious mining accident in Wales was widely reported in the British newspapers. Bonhoeffer addressed the accident in a December 1933

Advent sermon from Luke's Gospel: "Now when these things begin to take place, look up and raise your heads, because your redemption is drawing near."[62]

The sermon draws an analogy between being trapped in a mining accident and the disposition of Advent: "This is a time of waiting for God to come near, for the coming of salvation, for the arrival of Christ." Bonhoeffer sets the disposition of waiting and of hope against what he described as a "petty, fearful, downtrodden, weak sort of Christianity, as we often see, and which often tempts us to be scornful of Christianity itself." Advent is a time for anticipating new life, preparing for God's coming in Christ, who makes new human beings, and preparing to become new human beings in Christ: "Look up, lift your heads!"[63]

Bonhoeffer's London sermons offered imaginative performances of biblical texts that were both "close to life" and "close to Scripture." His Advent sermon on the Magnificat provides a remarkable rendering of Mary's act of praise that not only speaks from the text but seeks also to draw the congregation to join in Mary's song of praise: "The song of Mary is the oldest Advent hymn. It is also the most passionate, the wildest, and one might say the most revolutionary Advent hymn that has ever been sung." Bonhoeffer places Mary within a story of women who spoke prophetically—Deborah, Judith, and Miriam—each was seized by the Spirit for speaking God's word coming into the world through the advent of Christ. The story is not only revolutionary; it is also offensive and irritating to conventional piety, sensibilities, and expectations. Only the humble believe and rejoice that God is so "gloriously free" to perform such miracles among the lowly and those of no account—to offer praise to God, who loves the unremarkable and chooses those of little value: "This is a God whose throne is a manger, who rules from a cross." Bonhoeffer contemporized the story for his listeners, identifying Mary as the "Mother of God" and Christ as "the poor son of a laborer from the East End of London."[64] The sermon led the congregation to perceive its place with the lowly and to acknowledge that God alone is high.

Bonhoeffer's London sermons demonstrate a maturing as a homiletical theologian who was capable of addressing important theological matters with clarity and insight. For Trinity Sunday, he chose to preach from 1 Corinthians 2:7-10, emphasizing the mystery of God's Triune life, a mystery lost in a world that operates by calculation and exploitation. Bonhoeffer saw the loss of God's mystery as also contributing to the decay and impoverishment of human life. Rather than attempting to explain the Trinity as a doctrinal formula, the sermon aims to evoke a sense of awe and wonder in beholding the glory of God's being in the poverty, weakness, and humiliation of Christ on behalf of humanity: "God became a human being like us, so that we might become divine; because God came to us, . . . we might come to God." The doctrine of the Trinity is a form of worship, a feeble way of praising the "mighty, impetuous love of God." The holy mystery of God's love and nearness is always apprehended and understood as mystery.[65] Bonhoeffer's sermon is a simple homiletic gesture toward the divine mystery revealed in the lowliness of Christ and the gift of the Holy Spirit for the world.

Bonhoeffer worked to unite the theological and pastoral aims of preaching. His sermons could be truthful and encouraging without resorting to platitudes or clichés. An example of how he handled this challenge is demonstrated by a sermon he preached in the summer of 1934 after more than two hundred political rivals of Hitler were murdered by the Nazi Party. Bonhoeffer chose to preach from Luke 13:1-5, a story in which Jesus was questioned about a group of Galileans who were murdered by Pilate. The inquirers were seeking a judgment from Jesus about whether the Galileans were so sinful as to warrant such treatment. The response of Jesus was a call for all present to repent or perish as well. Bonhoeffer is honest about the eerie closeness of the story. He acknowledges many people go to church in order to avoid dealing with such things, even using worship as a means of escaping from the realities of the world.[66]

Bonhoeffer turned the sermon in another direction, defining worship as a means of equipping Christians to overcome the world through faith—as a space for confessing honestly one's feelings of fear, anxiety, shock, and avoidance. He let the gospel story do its work, calling attention to its characters and its plot, pointing out the similarities between the world of Scripture and the contemporary world: "This was the official view [that the Galileans' death was the work of God's wrath], we would say, of the daily press." Bonhoeffer did not offer an explanation or attempt to defend God's honor but instead focused on the sermon of Jesus, who called his inquirers to turn back to God, to submit to the justice of God, who bestows mercy upon sinners. Thus, the long, slow journey of the church through the world is a way of repentance leading to newness of life.[67]

Bonhoeffer decided to preach a series of four sermons from 1 Corinthians 13, with the final sermon falling on Reformation Sunday, November 1934. He began by sharing how the sermons were planned in a way that was both theological and pastoral: (1) there was a need in the congregation just as there was in the Corinthian church; (2) the church struggle, in its intensity and significance for the faith and life of the church, brought temptations for arrogance, pride, overconfidence, and even self-righteousness; and (3) although Protestantism had excelled in preaching the victory and power of faith in Christ, it had not always done very well in making clear that faith in God means God is to be loved above all else.[68]

The sermons place the contemporary situation within the "strange world of the Bible." They invite the church into a conversation mediated by the Word of God spoken in Christ, who is himself the perfect embodiment of the virtue of love—a love that is revealed most fully by the cross.[69] The cross means that the Christian life, the life of the church, is one of love, for "this is what God's success looks like."[70] The cross is the action of God's love through human thinking, speaking, and acting. Bonhoeffer acknowledges the importance of right faith, of orthodox theology, and of loyal confession. However, following the witness of Paul, he was emphatic in insisting that if these are not marks of a church of pure and all-embracing love, then they are good for nothing: "[Speak] the truth in love . . . for truth brings us into God's presence, and God is love."[71] The church's mission, then, is to show the world how to believe again, how to hope again, and how to love again: "Do not deny them."[72] Bonhoeffer's sermons from 1 Corinthians 13 unfold in a manner that clearly sets forth a Christian way of life that is constituted by the virtues of faith, hope, and love. But it is love "that shows mature insight, true knowledge, adulthood."[73]

Bonhoeffer's interpretation of Scripture in preaching was informed by Luther's "theology of the cross."[74] This way of seeing reality is clearly evident in a sermon from 2 Corinthians 12:9: "My strength is made perfect in weakness." The choice of this text was timely, since the Nazi Party had begun targeting handicapped individuals as unworthy of life, a glorification of strength and contempt for weakness. Bonhoeffer did not hesitate to address this matter, inviting the congregation to imagine with him the great mystery presented by the poor, the ill, the insane, those unable to help themselves, the crippled, the hopeless, the socially exploited, and "a colored man in a white country."[75] The question raised by the Scripture is, "What is the meaning of weakness in the world?" Bonhoeffer's concern was that the church had adjusted too easily to the worship of power, thus failing to give any offence or shock to the world.[76] Benevolence was also brought in for criticism, since the strong condescend to help the weak but do so without humility.[77] Bonhoeffer concludes with a startling theological claim that articulates a way of seeing reality in light of the cross:

> Christian love and help for the weak means humiliation of the strong before the weak, of the healthy before the suffering, of the mighty before the exploited. The Christian relation between the strong and the weak is that the strong is to look up to the weak and never to look down. Weakness is holy, therefore we devote ourselves to the weak. . . . Our God is a suffering God. Suffering conforms humanity to God. . . . "My strength is made perfect in weakness," says God.[78]

Bonhoeffer preached in anticipation of a coming time when the Confessing Church would experience "splintering and shattering, and the condition of isolation . . . [and] suffering that overcomes the world." He was hopeful such suffering would lead to a rediscovery of personal witness and discipleship, clarity in confessing the faith, and renewed commitment to lifting high the cross, made visible "in our being as church." He states what this could mean for preaching: "All this is not hope for a new kind of Christian heroism, but it is this alone that will create the ground on which we can stand and credibly proclaim Christ."[79]

6

Preaching as Public Confession
Finkenwalde 1935–1937

Bonhoeffer was compelled to return to Germany in the summer of 1935 to direct one of the five "illegal" seminaries established by the Confessing Church.[1] The "preacher's seminaries" had as their primary purpose the training and formation of pastors for parish ministry. They were independent of state control and support, funded only by free-will offerings and donations. The decision to become a member of the seminary community directed by Bonhoeffer in the remote region of Finkenwalde on the Baltic coast was not easily made. In addition to having illegal status according to the laws of the Nazi state and Reich Church, Bonhoeffer's pastoral candidates lived under constant threat of interrogation, imprisonment, and both physical and psychological punishment. Students entered the community at Finkenwalde without any guarantee of pastoral position or support, fully aware they could by removed or prevented from serving in pastoral ministry.[2]

Aligning themselves with Bonhoeffer situated the seminarians within the radical wing of the Confessing Church in relation to its more moderate members as well as identified them as the primary opposition to the German Christian movement. Theological education at Finkenwalde was not a carefree affair; every aspect of the community's daily life and work together was tempered by Bonhoeffer's conviction that Christianity and Nazism were absolutely incompatible. Preaching without enemies was theologically impossible for a church constituted by confessing the truth of the gospel.[3]

Bonhoeffer believed the church struggle in Germany, and thus his work at Finkenwalde, was not merely for its own sake but was being conducted vicariously for the ecumenical church. The heart of the matter was the proclamation of the gospel that requires confessing against its external enemies. Bonhoeffer defined the nature of church communion in light of the proclamation of Christ, emphasizing the necessity of public confession and decision, not merely theological dialog or tolerance: "Believers group themselves around confessions, not around theologies. One must carefully guard against mistaking the one for the other here. Although theology does indeed supply the entire army with weapons that can be engaged anywhere at any time, the external battle is engaged with the confession, not with theology."[4]

Bonhoeffer was concerned that the timeless "legalism" of orthodoxy and theological abstraction had replaced the decision of faith and confession in concrete, contingent witness.[5] The preacher's seminary at Finkenwalde was established to address the urgent need for congregations whose life was constituted by publically confessing the truth of Christ. Approximately thirty young theologians had initially come together for this purpose, "betting their entire future solely on the cause of Christ": "We depend on only one thing, in the word and the help of God, and our strongest weapon remains our daily prayer."[6]

Confessing the gospel was central to the formation of young pastoral theologians. Bonhoeffer acknowledged there were moderate teachers and pastors in the Reich Church whose theology was more Christian and biblical than others. However, the words and actions of its responsible leaders had clearly proved the Reich Church no longer served Christ but was serving the antichrist. Obedience to Christ as the only Lord continued to be coordinated with National Socialism and subordinated toward worldly masters and powers. Bonhoeffer saw the situation in Germany as illumined by Luther's struggle for the late medieval church to be reformed by the gospel: "Our disruption from the Reich Church would be spurious and godless indeed if ours were not the same strong faith which Martin Luther's once was."[7]

The Synod of Barmen had rejected the teaching of the German Christians as false, while the Synod of Dahlem had declared that, by its actions, the Reich Church government had separated itself from the Confessing Church.[8] In both cases, confessional decisions, based on the proclamation of the gospel, acknowledged actions that had already taken place:[9] "Thereafter the Confessing Church accepted responsibility and commission of being the one, true church of Jesus Christ in Germany. This is a fact of church history."[10] Bonhoeffer insisted the boundaries of the church are not set by political legalities or theological disputes but are the boundaries of salvation that exceed exclusive national and racial loyalties: "Whoever knowingly separates himself from the Confessing Church in Germany separates himself from salvation."[11] One outcome of this confession was that proclaiming the gospel was affirmed as the central mission of the whole church. From Finkenwalde, Bonhoeffer continued working for ecumenical unity in confessing against the "new religion" of National Socialism, a decision for speaking concretely the "No" and "Yes" of the gospel as God's judgment and mercy.[12]

Bonhoeffer confided to his longtime friend Ervin Sutz that, although National Socialism had brought about the end of the German church, this situation should be seen as a reason for gratitude. He viewed the church struggle as a transitional phase that would lead to a very different kind of opposition, a struggle that would mean "resisting to the point of shedding blood" by a people who would be capable of "simply suffering through in faith." Then, perhaps, "God will acknowledge the church with his word, but until then a great deal must be believed, prayed, and suffered."[13]

Bonhoeffer believed Christianity in Europe was so thoroughly Westernized, permeated by "civilized" behavior and values, that it had been lost. He also confessed his doubts regarding the strength and conviction of the Confessing Church to withstand the great temptation to compromise.[14] The supporters of the opposition were a cause for more fear than the German Christians; many who opposed Nazi ideology were still concerned about appearing unpatriotic as citizens of Germany: "Many people . . . still seem incapable of realizing or believing that we are really here purely as Christians. . . . Only the complete truth and complete truthfulness can help us now."[15] Bonhoeffer shared how his views had changed on the matter of preparing pastors for leading the church to become a visible manifestation of Christ in the world:[16]

> I no longer believe in the university, in fact I never really believed in it. The next generation of pastors, these days, ought to be trained entirely in church-monastic schools, where the pure doctrine, the Sermon on the Mount, and worship are taken seriously—which for all three of these things is simply not the case at the university and under present circumstances is impossible. It is also time for a final break with our theologically grounded reserve about whatever is being done by the state—which really only comes down to fear. "Speak out for those who cannot speak"—win the church today still remembers that this is the very least the Bible asks of us in such times as these? And then there's the matter of military service, war, etc., etc.[17]

The restoration of the church required training pastors within a monastic community of uncompromising discipleship. This would entail following Christ according to the Sermon on the Mount, a way of life consisting of speaking and standing publically for "peace and social justice without compromise, and for Christ himself."[18]

Bonhoeffer's last seminar in Berlin, during the summer semester of 1933, was on the subject of Christology.[19] The lectures articulated a robust theological vision that would guide his work at Finkenwalde. Given the substantial background "noise" of Nazi propaganda and German Christian zeal, Bonhoeffer was heard by many as offering a strong challenge to idolatrous definitions of Christ. Bonhoeffer began by announcing the doxological nature of Christian doctrine—"orthodoxy" is not only right confession; it is prayer and praise evoked by wonder in beholding the glory of Christ:

> The silence of the church is silence before the Word. In proclaiming Christ, the church falls on its knees in silence before the inexpressible.... To speak of Christ is to be silent, and to be silent about Christ is to speak. That is obedient affirmation of God's revelation, which takes place through the Word. The church's speech through silence is the right way to proclaim Christ.[20]

Bonhoeffer clarified the meaning of silence: "To pray is to keep silent and at the same time is to cry out, before God in both cases, in the light of God's Word." Because proclaiming Christ is an act of worship, Christology, speaking of Christ, is from and to a person who is the transcendent: "The fact that the logos became flesh, a human being, is the prerequisite, not the proof." Because Christology is the center of the church's knowledge, proclamation begins by asking "Who?" rather than "How?" The question of being—"Who are you, Jesus Christ?"—calls human beings into question and reveals who they truly are in the encounter with Christ. Neither an ideal nor a superhuman, Christ is the God-human person, humiliated by his suffering and death on the cross, exalted by his resurrection from the dead.[21]

Bonhoeffer's work with seminarians focused on the mystery of Christ as confessed in the Christology lectures. He introduced students to the paradoxical nature of preaching as an act and event that is dependent upon God, who is pleased to speak the Word, the person of Christ, in the spoken word of preaching. This is eloquently stated in the Christology lectures:

> His presence is present in the word of the church. His presence is, by nature, his existence as preaching. . . . If this were not so, the sermon would not have the exclusive status that the Reformation gives it. The sermon is the poverty and the riches of our church. The sermon is the form of the present Christ to whom we are committed, whom we are to follow. If Christ is not wholly present in the sermon, the church breaks down. . . . Luther says, "This is the human being to whom you should point and say, this is God!" We say, this is the human word to which you should point and say, this is God![22]

Paradoxically, the human speaking of the Word requires silence. Such silence, which is a gift, is not merely the absence of words but rather a silence appropriate for the glory revealed in the wonder of God's incarnation. Silence, then, is humble recognition of the Word, prayerful attentiveness that waits and listens before speaking. Right speech is therefore dependent upon right silence, and right silence is dependent upon right speech. Preaching is an act of faith in the Word, which, from beginning to end, is dependent upon the freedom and initiative of God.[23]

These christological convictions guided Bonhoeffer's work of training preachers within a daily rhythm of silence and speech. Students' sermons were heard with respect and appropriate reverence for the Word of God without being picked apart by peers. Sermon study was practiced in groups or "circles" that prepared full sermons or sermon drafts that were read aloud and discussed in terms of both content and arrangement in faithfulness to Scripture. Those who listened would then attempt a sermon draft of their own, with Bonhoeffer concluding the exercise by presenting his prepared sermon draft. Students had ample opportunities for preaching through frequent visits with Confessing Church congregations and in services of worship within the Finkenwalde community.[24] Yet a robust theological vision comprised the basis of all homiletical instruction. Preaching was not reduced to theory and application, as was the habit in university seminars, dividing theological substance and homiletical form. Preaching is a theological practice in all aspects, dimensions, and considerations.[25]

During the time Bonhoeffer was lecturing on Christology in Berlin, Karl Barth was conducting a seminar in homiletics, exercises in preaching, at the University of Bonn. Like Bonhoeffer, Barth was alarmed by the way "modern" forms of preaching had so easily become useful as tools, instruments, and weapons in support of the Nazi cause and "positive Christianity." However, the turn to homiletics was an emergency move on his part, since the university faculty already included a professor of practical theology responsible for teaching homiletics. Barth, however, saw this task as essential to his work as a theologian, since preaching is a thoroughly theological matter.[26]

Barth's colleague in practical theology, Emil Pfennigsdorf, was widely known as a strong advocate for the "theme" preaching that conflated Christianity and Aryan identity. Blurring the distinction between faith and ideology, Pfennigsdorf was a conservative nationalist who joined Christianity with love of the fatherland. He saw religion and politics in Germany as the work of God that would transform and unite the nation. To this end, "theme" preaching was directed to specific audiences and their particular concerns, which routinely categorized listeners and framed sermons specifically for them.[27] Barth viewed perceiving people in light of age, class, nationality, race, and so forth as removing preaching from its ecclesial calling to speak the claims of Christ. Preaching had been subordinated to a utilitarian purpose for influencing the direction of German life and demonstrating the relevance and value of the church to the nation.[28]

Barth's lectures addressed the nature and purpose of preaching as well as the criteria and content of sermons. After discussing the strengths and weaknesses of works by several Protestant homileticians, he ventured to offer a new definition of preaching:

- Preaching is the Word of God which he himself speaks, claiming for the purpose the exposition of a biblical text in free human words that are relevant to contemporaries by those who are called to do this in the church that is obedient to its commission.
- Preaching is the attempt enjoined upon the church to serve God's own Word, through one who is called hereto, by expounding a biblical text in human words and making it relevant to contemporaries in intimation of what they have to hear from God himself.[29]

Barth expanded on this definition by discussing nine criteria of the sermon: revelation; church, confession, ministry, heralding, Scripture, originality, congregation, spirituality.[30]

The primary task of preaching is proclaiming the past and future revelation of God—the epiphany and parousia of Jesus Christ. Preaching, as homiletical theology, is always on the "way" from yesterday to tomorrow, from the presence of Christ in the flesh to his coming again in glory to reign: "If preaching sounds this basic eschatological note, it conforms to revelation and is in right relation to the Word of God it is to proclaim." Preaching is thus oriented to baptism, as the sign of grace, and to the Lord's Supper, as the sign of hope, and to Scripture, as the trust that is the basis of the church. Preaching thus builds up and edifies the church by carrying out its commission as a response to what has been accomplished and what is yet to come.[31]

Barth located authority to preach in the divine calling to ministry for God's will and work: "Preaching is always a matter of calling." Preachers are justified in this calling by God, who calls and speaks; it is to God whom preachers are primarily accountable. Preaching is also joined to holiness—the action of sinners that has its law and promise in the command and blessing of God. Preaching is "heralding," comprising the relation between God and humankind as the work of simple obedience: "A human being becomes a hearer of the Word."[32] Proclamation, then, is provisional, the act of "one sent in advance" of the coming Lord, who claims and sanctifies preaching as a "good work."[33]

Preaching is also an exposition of Scripture, "following after" both the substance and the movement of a biblical text. A sermon is "biblical" when both form and content, how and what, are congruent with the biblical witness. The originality or freshness of preaching is the fruit of repentance and gratitude, borne of the freedom realized in the presence of God. Such preaching springs from attentiveness to the testimony of Scripture in personal engagement with the text: "In other words, holy scripture first has to break through to them." The sermon, however, is not the goal of preaching. The end of preaching is the creation of a people who by hearing the word come to faith in Christ as the sole basis and hope of their lives. In preaching, God personally addresses listeners on the "way" between baptism and the Lord's Supper.[34]

Barth believed that the spirituality of the preacher is characterized by humility, "as the prayer of those that realize that God himself must confess their human word if it is to be God's Word." Preachers are incapable of this on their own but are "caught up" by the mystery of grace that empowers the sermon as God's gift. Barth concluded, "Preaching, then, must become prayer." The preacher invokes, calls upon God to be God, acknowledging complete dependence upon God, who hears and answers. Preaching is a liturgical activity from beginning to end, springing from and oriented by prayer: "Our attitude, then, must be controlled from above; nothing from me, all things from God, no independent achievement, only dependence upon God's grace and will."[35]

Coming of Age in Dealing with Scripture

According to student notes, Bonhoeffer's homiletical lectures in Finkenwalde included discussion of Barth's criteria for the sermon. There are many similarities between Barth and Bonhoeffer as homiletical theologians. Bonhoeffer, however, offered a few Lutheran qualifications, citing Luther as an advocate of preaching in accordance with the whole of Scripture, which has the person of Christ as its core.[36] Following Luther, Bonhoeffer situated preaching within the union of Christology and ecclesiology, offering a remarkable theological vision of the "sacramental" nature of preaching:

- The sermon derives from the incarnation of Jesus Christ and is determined by the incarnation of Jesus Christ.
- In the incarnation, God the Son takes on human nature.
- The word of the sermon is in fact this Christ who bears human nature.
- Because the word by nature bears the new humanity, it is by nature always oriented toward the church-community.
- The shape of the preached word is different from that of every other word.
- The spoken word receives the promise that it will be able to take on people and to bear or sustain them.
- Because the world was created and is maintained by the word, God can be recognized only through that word.[37]

Bonhoeffer's stunning vision of preaching affirmed Christ present as the content, purpose, and efficacy of the sermon: "Christ [who] walks through the church-community." As the incarnate Son of God, Christ is present in the act of proclamation, taking on human nature, which has been adopted by God, "being fully flesh of the flesh Christ bore." This is the body of Christ, united in the incarnation and established as the *communio sanctorum*. The word of the sermon is "the incarnate Lord who seeks to take up people to bear sinful human nature." God does not coerce, teach, or improve people through Christ. Rather, as demonstrated by the cross, God speaks a word that takes on a body to create a community borne by Christ himself. The word has become incarnate, it desires to have a body, and thus it inherently moves toward the church by its own initiative.[38]

As God's initiative and gift, the word does not need to be implemented or applied, nor does it need to be shaped to fit the desires or self-interests of listeners. The preacher's calling is to follow after the free and gracious movement of the word in the scriptural witness to Christ. Preaching possesses a unique character, not as mediated truth, a word of expression, a form of communication, or the preacher's goal. The preached word needs no support or enhancement but simply expresses itself, being what it is, rather than searching for something lying behind, above, or beyond the word. The word itself is the content: Christ himself bearing humanity, Christ addressing and challenging humanity, Christ taking up humanity, and humanity bearing Christ in the world. As the first and original word of God, "it supports and sustains the whole world and lays a foundation for a new world in the sermon." Proclamation, then, directs attention to the wonder of Christ made clear, audible, and comprehensible. Amazingly, "in the proclaimed word, Christ steps into the congregation, which is waiting for and calling on Christ, worshiping and celebrating Christ. In the proclaimed word, Christ takes up his congregation."[39]

Bonhoeffer shared Martin Luther's commitment to the oral, sacramental nature of the Word.[40] As a preacher, Luther had devoted himself with single-minded purpose to breaking open the words of Scripture. He believed this was the means by which the gospel, the voice of God speaking through the risen Christ in the power of the Spirit, becomes a shout of praise in the church, penetrating the hearts, minds, and souls of its listeners.[41] In a sermon from the Gospel of John, Luther articulated a profound vision of Christ present with the church assembled for prayer, praise, and proclamation:

> When Christ commands His apostles to proclaim His Word and carry on His work, we hear and see Him Himself, and thus also God the Father; for they publish and proclaim no other Word than that which they heard from His lips, and they point solely to Him. . . . The Word is handed down to us through the agency of true bishops, pastors, and preachers, who received it from the apostles. In this way all sermons delivered in Christendom must proceed from this one Christ. . . . For it is all from God, who condescends to enter the mouth of each Christian or preacher and says: "If you want to see Me or My work, look to Christ; if you want to hear Me, hear this Word." . . . There you may say without hesitation: "Today I beheld God's Word and work. Yes, I saw and heard God Himself preaching and baptizing." To be sure, the tongue, the voice, the hands, etc., are those of a human being; but the Word and the ministry are really the Divine Majesty Himself.[42]

Preaching is situated within a liturgical context of hearing, speaking, and believing in God's presence, *coram Deo*. Preachers announce the "good report" that has been heard—the glad tidings of the risen Lord, who rules in the midst of a battle between God and the devil. Preaching is thus oriented to the action of God in Christ speaking through the whole scriptural witness to continue the work of creation and salvation.[43] Luther was confident the power of the gospel was capable of softening even the most hardened of hearts, thus effecting the Spirit's joy in all who "sing, thank and praise God, and are glad forever, if only they believe firmly and remain steadfast in faith."[44]

Luther's theological and pastoral wisdom demonstrates how Christian practices mediate God's Word to form the church as a people who embody the confession of the gospel. As a "sacrament of salvation," the church is where faith is born, nourished, and lived in communion with the Father through the Son in the Holy Spirit. The church is a people in whom the Spirit makes Christ present through word and sacrament, thus constituting the community as the heart of evangelical witness.[45]

Bonhoeffer's vision for training pastors at Finkenwalde entailed a significant rethinking of Luther's life and work.[46] Luther's influence is reflected in the practical and pastoral direction of Bonhoeffer's instruction with seminarians. Biblical exposition unites the hermeneutical and homiletical task—an intensive form of prayerful, rigorous study that seeks to interpret Scripture as a spoken summons to hear, believe, and obey the gospel of Christ himself. Like Luther, Bonhoeffer began with the presupposition that Scripture is the living Word of God, an active voice whose enlivening power must be let loose in preaching. This requires a disposition of reverent, attentive receptivity toward God, who freely speaks the word of Christ. A preacher, then, is a disciple, one who follows after Christ in the word of Scripture. Exegesis is both a holy calling and a concrete act of obedience to the Word echoed in the sermon and life of the church.[47]

The preacher's seminary was a place where the credibility of proclamation could be strengthened by bringing clarity to Christian faith, life, and ministry: "The goal is not monastic isolation but rather the most intensive concentration for ministry in the world." Bonhoeffer envisioned a community of freely committed pastors, ordered for the "sake of decision and discernment of the Spirit in the present and future struggles of the church, a group prepared for immediate service and proclamation wherever new emergency situations might arise." This ministry would involve them in a sacrificial way of life: "They must be prepared to make themselves available wherever their services are needed, under any circumstances, and without consideration of financial or other privileges otherwise associated with the ministry."[48]

Finkenwalde, then, was a community of preachers formed around the Word of God. Learning was self-involving, a way of formation devoted to doctrinal, ecumenical, exegetical, homiletical, catechetical, pastoral, and liturgical subjects studied and appropriated in close proximity.[49] The community was a context for understanding Christian faith in light of Lutheran confessions, training in discipleship, and preparing for credible Christian witness. Bonhoeffer identified the central focus of the community: "The Bible stands at the center of our work. It has once again become the point of departure and the center of our theological work and of all our Christian activity."[50] Bonhoeffer summarized the significance of Scripture for candidates preparing to assume the pastoral office and commission of preaching: "*The goal of a Protestant pastor is to come of age in dealing with the Holy Scripture.*"[51]

Bonhoeffer placed the highest degree of importance on listening to Scripture as constitutive of a community of preachers. He described this practice in a letter to a friend who had raised questions about how preachers address the questions and concerns of listeners, which was the primary aim of "modern" preaching. Bonhoeffer acknowledged that while preaching cannot provide answers to every question or solutions to every problem, it does engage people in the more important activity of listening to God, who speaks in Scripture:

> I believe that the Bible alone is the answer to all our questions, and that we merely need ask perpetually and with a bit of humility in order to get the answer from it. One cannot simply *read* the Bible like other books. One must be prepared genuinely to query it. Only thus does it reveal itself. Only if we are really expecting an ultimate answer from it will it give us that answer. The reason is that God is speaking to us in the Bible. And one cannot simply reflect on God on one's own; one must ask God. Only if we seek God will God answer.[52]

Bonhoeffer was convinced biblical interpretation that follows the rules of textual/critical methodology cannot get to the real substance of Scripture. Reading Scripture for the church is done best according to the way followed by Mary: "Ponder it in your heart." This means approaching the Bible by presupposing that the one speaking is "the God who loves us and has no intention of abandoning us with our questions."[53]

To presuppose God speaking in the Bible means listening for a word that exceeds what is already known. Searching for God is not an end in itself, a self-serving activity; it is the desire to find God wherever God says he is to be found. Although God does give himself to be found in Christ, God is not determined by prior experience, understanding, or convenience. Moreover, the place where God gives himself most fully is the cross, where God is encountered in the Son. Bonhoeffer's way of reading offered a hermeneutic of Scripture that turns the reader away from the self in order to inquire of the Bible, "What is God saying to us here?" He adds, "God does not speak in universal eternal truths" but instead reveals his will concretely, in ways that are "alien and repugnant to us." God is concealed beneath the sign of the cross, where all human thoughts and desires come to an end.[54]

Bonhoeffer did not see this as a sacrifice of the intellect, failure to seek understanding, or reluctance to do exegesis. However, he acknowledged that the experience of reading as an act of faith had become increasingly miraculous to him. Reading the Bible was indispensable to living and believing and, much to his surprise, had been practiced by Christians for centuries in living a genuine life of faith. He had also come to see the superficiality of modern people who assumed they were different or better than their predecessors: "Christian people continue to be dependent upon God speaking in Scripture." He continues, "Perhaps this is a rather primitive consideration. But you cannot imagine what a joyous thing it is when one finds one's way back to these primitive things after losing one's way along the false paths of so many theologies. And I do believe that in matters of faith we are always consistently primitive."[55]

Bonhoeffer shared with Luther the conviction that reading Scripture requires decision—confident trust in the word of the Bible for sustenance in both life and death. Luther was a member of the Augustinian Friars, a fraternal organization of highly educated preachers who were trained to shepherd souls through the art of pastoral care. He was attracted to the order's strong emphasis on biblical study and biblical spirituality, which united learning and practical ministry. Luther's strong desire for and devotion to God was nurtured by study centered on the Bible that was summarized in the Constitutions of the Augustinian Order: "A friar is to read the Sacred Scripture avidly, listen to it devoutly, and learn it fervently." The order provided the framework for a biblically oriented theology and hermeneutic that Luther embraced instead of philosophical theology. This practice produced a much more direct and prayerful way of reading, without added layers of intellectual categories—an orational rather than rational approach.[56] This meant becoming a student of the Holy Spirit in learning the language of Scripture as a whole, its vocabulary and grammar, in learning to speak the reality of God's revelation, the truth of Christ. The church, as the creation of the Word, lives by hearing God's original testimony spoken in human words.[57]

Luther was formed theologically within a liturgical context of prayer and meditation into which he incorporated the work of linguistic and historical scholarship. Exegesis and edification are not antithetical. The Holy Spirit affects both the intellect and the heart through prayerful study, transforming one's thinking and desiring to impart the knowledge and experience of faith in Christ that is joyfully proclaimed. Because prayer and thinking are united, the monastic and scholastic aspects of theology—theory and practice— are united in human receptivity shaped by God's Word. As an interpreter of Scripture and a preacher, Luther was both a friar and a professor, joining the two aspects of theology that embrace the whole person before God.[58]

Homiletical instruction at Finkenwalde took place within a community of preachers in which Bonhoeffer, as a pastor and professor, served as teacher, exemplar, and mentor. This way of teaching was necessary for cultivating integrity and constancy in preaching.[59] Bonhoeffer's experience had taught him how young pastors suffered from isolation—of their urgent need for help and fellowship with others in grasping both the purpose and the actual way of preaching. He had also observed the desire among young theological students for a more ordered and accountable life in community, since "proclamation that derives from a community that is lived and experienced in a more practical fashion will, in its own turn, be more objective . . . and less likely to run aground." He shared with Barth his concern that young theologians' questions were not being addressed and that, when they were, answers tended to be either abstract or dismissive. The answers they sought could be attained only by living, praying, and reflecting together on the commandment and promise of the gospel. This kind of formation, however, would find its legitimacy and basis only when accompanied and guided by rigorous theological, exegetical, and dogmatic work.[60]

Preaching with "Unclipped Wings"

An example of the serious nature of Bonhoeffer's work with seminarians is his lecture "Contemporizing New Testament Texts," which presupposes preaching as the primary place of biblical interpretation for the church.[61] According to Bonhoeffer, "contemporizing" makes relevant the witness of Scripture to Christ through the work of the Holy Spirit. Relevance in preaching occurs where God is concretely present in the Word with the Spirit as its primary subject. Christ himself is the "relevance" of preaching, addressing his people in the Spirit's power to judge, command, and forgive.[62]

Most pastors and congregations in Germany would have perceived this way of interpreting Scripture for preaching as strange. Bonhoeffer referred to it as "an alien gospel," an external word originating neither in reason nor in experience but as the gift of God, who is pleased to speak.[63] Bonhoeffer's statement was an act of confession, a decision for the gospel, and resistance to the "faith" of the German Christians. The Scriptures, taken as a mythic or symbolic framework, provided a familiar narrative that could be interpreted to fit into a contemporary "Aryan" worldview to justify the German nation against its enemies. Rather than beginning with God, the starting point was the historical context and situation, which was guided by reason and experience and oriented toward the restoration of Germany to greatness.[64]

Bonhoeffer offered two starkly different ways of contemporizing, of making "relevant" the New Testament message. On the one hand, this can mean the biblical message must justify itself to the present. This option was rooted in the Enlightenment, the era of reason that had been set free from faith in declaring its freedom from the claims of God. It was a form of rationalism that continued to shape modern liberal theology, including the ideology of the German Christians.[65]

The German Christians demanded the New Testament justify itself before the forum of their ideology. Bonhoeffer described the forum before which the biblical message must justify itself as changing over time—for example, reason in the eighteenth century, culture in the nineteenth, Nazi Germany in the twentieth. Yet one basic question remained unchanged: "Can Christianity become contemporary for us as we simply—thank God!—are now?" This is the fixed "Archimedean point." The Christian message must change to pass through the sieve of one's knowledge, or it simply will not pass: "Whatever does not pass through is disdained and thrown away, so that one trims and prunes away the Christian message until it fits the fixed framework, until the eagle can no longer rise and escape into its true element and instead is put on display *with clipped wings as a special exhibit among the other domesticated pets.*"[66]

For Bonhoeffer, a domesticated Christianity—with "clipped wings"—is a faith that if scrutinized honestly cannot sustain serious interest: "This contemporizing of the Christian message leads directly to paganism, which means that the only difference between German Christians and so-called neo-pagans is honesty."[67] Such honesty requires courage to raise the question of the actual substance of the Christian message, a matter advocates of contemporizing chose to avoid: "Those who are thirsty have always found *living* water in the Bible itself and in a *substantively* biblical sermon, even when such was quite out of sync with the times."[68] On the other hand, the positive meaning of contemporizing the New Testament message is the justification of the present to the message:[69] "True contemporization is found in the question of substance. . . . The substance here is Christ and Christ's word; wherever Christ is expressed in the word of the New Testament, one has contemporization."[70]

Theological interpretation of Scripture is a practice in which the "present" is determined by the word of Christ as the Word of God. The "present," however, is not a temporal feeling, a set of values, a meaning, or a worldview; the "present" is created by the proclamation of the Word in the Spirit's power: "Wherever God is present in the divine word, there one has the present; there God posits the present."[71] The subject of the present is the Holy Spirit, just as the Spirit is the subject of contemporization. Preaching is an eschatological act in which the present is determined by God's future, by the risen Christ speaking in the Spirit today. To move from the past to the present defines the present as autonomous, as possessing within itself its own criteria. However, the criteria for the authentic present is external to itself, lying in a future revealed by the substance of Scripture as the word of Christ attested there.[72]

Bonhoeffer articulated a surprisingly "alien" and unfamiliar gospel. Contemporizing is an exegesis of Scripture. Moreover, exegesis does not move from Scripture to the present but moves from the present to the word of Scripture, where it is drawn from a false into an authentic present. Bonhoeffer concedes this is incomprehensible for many who seek to bring Scripture before the forum of the present, which is made to yield to familiar forms of knowledge: "They themselves know where the word of God is and where the word of human beings is."[73] Whatever cannot be used because it does not conform to the present is left to the past, judged as neither eternal nor divine. For example, the doctrines of sin and justification were seen by the German Christians as temporally bound and past, while the struggle for the good and pure was seen as eternal. The ethical teachings of Jesus were eternal, while the miracle stories were temporally bound. The fighter Jesus, especially in his death, was an expression of the eternal struggle of light against darkness; but the suffering, defenseless Jesus was of no concern. The doctrine of grace was an eternal principle, while the Decalogue and commandments of the Sermon on the Mount were no longer judged as useful.[74]

Bonhoeffer offered an alternative way of reading Scripture for which the point of every passage is to make the character of this witness available. Substantive exposition of Scripture is the witness of Christ that already possesses the promise of his presence.[75] Not surprisingly, Bonhoeffer considered application to be the work of the Holy Spirit rather than the preacher. Because Christ and the cross make Scripture concrete in the life of the church, contextual work belongs to the Spirit, who speaks Christ's judgment, command, and forgiveness: "Precisely by not taking seriously in any ultimate sense the so-called concrete situation of the congregation, one is able to see the true situation of human beings before God."[76] Preaching is unable to raise itself above the witness of the New Testament; it cannot add something eternal that transcends the New Testament without becoming an abstract word:

> The New Testament is the witness of the promise of the Old Testament as fulfilled in Christ. It is not a book containing eternal truths, teachings, norms, or myths, but the sole witness of the God-human, Jesus Christ. As a whole and in all its parts, it is nothing other than this witness of Christ, Christ's life, death, and resurrection.[77]

All texts, not just a select group, bear witness to his uniqueness and historicity, which is the common witness of the New Testament. Christ himself is the One who performs the miracle, speaks the parable, issues the commandment, and, by speaking, calls and binds human beings to himself: "This Jesus is the Christ . . . a witness to the present Christ, the crucified, resurrected Lord who calls to discipleship. . . . Contemporizing means Christ alone speaks through the Holy Spirit. . . . Christ steps toward us."[78]

Bonhoeffer's concern was the church's calling to live by simple obedience to the word—to "come of age" in dealing with Scripture. The proclamation of Christ is a witness of the whole Christ in the world: the Lord and his body, over which the cross stands visibly. The New Testament witness to Christ creates the church as a community that serves and welcomes people from all places and classes, particularly those who suffer violence, injustice, and abandonment. Witness requires the question of credibility: "The church and the pastor speak differently than they behave; because the existence of the pastor no longer differs from that of the [German] citizen." The credibility of preachers is created by the freedom of the gospel that binds them to the word of Christ. Bonhoeffer ended the lecture on a rather sobering note, concluding that the pastors of the Confessing Church should "ask [themselves] whether through [their] own lives [they] have not already robbed [their] scriptural word of credibility."[79]

Credibility is a matter of practical wisdom and judgment, of discerning the intimate relation of theology, faith, Scripture, and preaching in the concrete witness of the church.[80] Bonhoeffer began with the conviction that the proclamation of the word is a gift of God that creates and builds up the church as the visible body of Christ. This conviction is the basis for discerning what faithful proclamation is and what it is not—what a preacher does and does not do to be a credible witness. Because the primary speaker is Christ, who proclaims himself, the role of the preacher is as a servant of the word for the good of the church. The church is the "wither" and "whence" of the sermon—not the preacher's opinions, feelings, and experience, or contemporary conditions, circumstances, and events:[81] "Discipleship is the place where the proclamation is made present. . . . [This is] its alien character in this world."[82]

Bonhoeffer viewed current circumstances and conditions as ambiguous, since both God and the devil are at work. The condition of people before God in preaching is as sinners for which Christ is God's answer. Preachers should trust the text of Scripture and the Holy Spirit to "[read] the Bible as one reads a love letter." Preachers should also ask questions of the text in relation to God and humankind, God's way of dealing with humankind, and God's work among the congregation. Preaching remains close to Scripture and life through prayerful listening that discerns the center from which the sermon moves and to which it returns. Daily prayer, study, and preparation are essential: "A sermon is born twice, once in the pastor's own study and once *in the pulpit*."[83]

The formation of homiletical wisdom requires humility and respect, a particular disposition that desires the purpose and life of the word: "Everything depends on this humility. It is always a matter of the distress and sin of those called before God." Preaching, then, is both humble speech and humbled speech. It is natural and truthful, spoken with simplicity shaped by service and discipline. Because God is free to speak, preachers are free to follow; there is no rule or law of sermon style. However, style often ends up separating from content to seek its own attention and praise. Bonhoeffer adds, "Indeed, do not try to develop a specific preaching style! *Instead simply interpret the word; style is left to itself*."[84] The preacher's task is to conform the words of the sermon to Christ present in the witness of Scripture.[85]

Bonhoeffer also commented on what a credible sermon is not: an attempt to persuade and educate, a presentation, poetic or pious talk, the language of elevated religiosity, a dogmatic lecture, the popular language of the street. He encouraged the use of natural language informed, enabled, and confirmed by its subject matter.[86] Lastly, the preacher is a person who prays: for the sermon, for freedom from anxiety and vanity, for forgiveness, for colleagues, for the word to work in the congregation, for the gift and joy of preaching.[87]

Bonhoeffer's aim was to form seminarians within a particular ethos appropriate to knowing and confessing Christ for proclaiming the gospel. At the heart of preaching is the inexpressible mystery of Jesus Christ, the incomprehensibility of Christ's person: "To speak of Christ means to keep silent; to keep silent about Christ means to speak." As a practice constituted by the divine-human speech of God, preaching requires cultivating a desire and capacity for careful listening to the biblical witness—a "coming of age" in dealing with Scripture in preaching, teaching, and pastoral care. Arguably, the whole of Bonhoeffer's Finkenwalde experiment as "life together" (lectures, sermon discussions, preaching exercises, biblical meditations, corporate prayer, singing, Bible reading, confession, and celebrations of Holy Communion) was extended practice in attending to God's concrete address in the person of Christ on behalf of the Confessing Church.[88]

Proclaiming the gospel was central to the church struggle. The Confessing Church found itself in a situation that made preaching without enemies a theological impossibility. Faithful preaching of the word of Christ was a matter of truth and falsehood, a case of life and death for a church confronted daily with the decision to believe and live according to the reign of Christ or Hitler. Bonhoeffer's theologically disciplined and prayerfully ordered vision of prayerful engagement with Scripture in preaching was a stark alternative to "modern" homiletical sensibilities and practices. He was convinced this homiletical path was necessary to liberate the church from the idolatry and falsehoods that had rendered invisible the concrete reality of Christ.[89]

III

Consequences

7

A Forced Itinerary
1937–1939

In the fall of 1937, the Gestapo moved to close the preacher's seminaries of the Confessing Church. The action was part of a series of decrees and orders by the official state church against Confessing Church seminarians, pastors, and congregations. Arrests increased, as did the number of ordinands who chose "legalization," placing themselves under the authority of official church committees.[1] Bonhoeffer's greatest concern during this time was the training of the next generation of pastors. He had begun to look beyond the church struggle, toward the establishment of a "free" church in Germany—one no longer under state control—committed to the truth of the gospel proclaimed and lived in light of Lutheran confessions.[2]

There was an urgent need to focus on the Gospels, particularly the call of discipleship, to form preachers in faithful obedience to the word of Christ. Becoming a preacher would require learning to "follow after" Christ—a way of believing, living, and speaking during a time when Nazi propaganda proclaimed the greatness of Germany's Führer and people. A popular song in Germany said as much: "Führer, command and we will follow you." Plans were thus made to continue the work of Finkenwalde in a way that would bring its members together for times of fellowship, instruction, and service. Bonhoeffer thus became an itinerant teacher, dividing his time between several secluded locations in Pomerania for a half week in duration and alternating weekends.[3]

Given the conditions in Germany under Nazi rule, particularly the threatened status of the Confessing Church, Bonhoeffer's direction of the collective pastorates arguably represents his strongest work as a homiletical theologian and teacher of preachers. The "collective pastorates" were conducted at a time when the Confessing Church was at its lowest point. Bonhoeffer's work as a teacher of preachers required much more than introducing them to principles of homiletics. The Confessing Church found itself in circumstances for which any act associated with confessing and proclaiming the truth of the gospel could be seen as an offence and declared illegal, thus bringing harsh consequences. An additional threat to Confessing Church leadership was that "illegal" pastors, and eventually Bonhoeffer himself, were targeted for the draft in support of Hitler's increasingly aggressive military strategy.[4]

Bonhoeffer's work during the post-Finkenwalde years required that he address the relentless temptation to break away from the confessional positions declared at the synods of Barmen and Dahlem. He saw this as a serious matter of confessional truth, a decision for either resistance or compromise, to remain with or depart from the call of concrete witness to the gospel.[5] Bonhoeffer's teaching and leadership, which were conducted more often by means of "paper and ink" rather than "face to face," were themselves acts of prophetic opposition to Nazism and its destructive ways, which exerted crushing pressure on all opposition.[6]

Bonhoeffer's first sermon after the closing of Finkenwalde was in the congregation of Gross-Schlonwitz, the location of one of the collective pastorates. The sermon, which was based on Romans 12:17-21, is a remarkable proclamation of the gospel and addresses the serious nature of the Confessing Church situation. Bonhoeffer oriented the sermon to the words of a hymn that had just been sung by the congregation: "Mercy has befallen me." He elaborated on this claim, offering examples from various situations in life when the mercy of God is real but difficult to understand. He then moved into the Romans text: "Do not claim to be wise." Bonhoeffer found the apostle's claim to be particularly true regarding enemies, the desire for vengeance, and God's mercy, which overcomes enmity to create friends.[7]

The sermon draws from the apostle's words, "Do not claim to be wise," to highlight the wisdom of God and its incomprehensibility:

"Truly, it is foreign and inaccessible, to our wisdom that God sought us, forgave us, that he sacrificed his Son for us, and thereby won over and converted our hearts." Bonhoeffer's exposition traces the story of divine wisdom and human foolishness from the beginning, from Adam and Eve, to show the prideful presumption of humankind in imagining itself to possess whatever is necessary to deal with God and others. The message is, "Do not claim to be wise" but focus instead on God's path to humankind, to God's enemies. This path is identified by Scripture as "foolish," since it is the path of God's love toward enemies, "the love God extends to them all the way to the cross."[8]

The heart of Bonhoeffer's sermon is precisely the claim of divine foolishness: "God loves our enemies."[9] He marveled at what this means for the church: "This is God's vengeance, namely, that he inflicts pain and suffering upon himself but spares and accepts us." God's vengeance is interpreted in light of Christ, who takes the suffering of the world on his shoulders and forgives God's enemies. Bonhoeffer then turned to the astonishing assertion of Paul in Romans: "If your enemies are hungry, feed them; if they are thirsty, give them something to drink; for by doing this you will heap burning coals on their heads."[10]

Bonhoeffer's sermon would undoubtedly have been heard as a surprising word that was startling and challenging more than comforting and assuring, given the tenuous status of the Confessing Church and given the forced termination of the Finkenwalde community: "Do not be overcome by evil, but overcome evil with good. This is what Christ did for us. Who is the enemy? The one for whom Christ died."[11] In Bonhoeffer's view, the real "church struggle" was with neither the German Christians nor the Nazi state but was the struggle to hear and obey the gospel when surrounded by enemies.[12]

Bonhoeffer continued to view the church struggle in light of the gospel rather than competing claims over church law and legal status. The church's confession determined its life and was the source of joy, faith, witness, and authority. Soon after the closing of Finkenwalde, Bonhoeffer sent a circular letter to the members of the Finkenwalde community to reaffirm their shared convictions. The letter provides a perspective on how he continued to see his role as teacher and mentor. It was a sign of continuing fellowship, a means of sharing the fullness of joy comprising their common calling and commitment. Sustaining a community of preachers shaped by the Word included remembering those imprisoned for their faith and ministry, and it was a source of hope in God as they looked ahead to an unknown future.[13]

Bonhoeffer interpreted the closing of Finkenwalde as an opportunity to ground the community more deeply "by listening together to the Word and by prayer. . . . This is a time of testing for us all."[14] Significantly, praying, meditating on the word, and enduring testing were described by Martin Luther as the means by which theologians, as preachers and teachers of the word, are made. For Luther, the path leading to truthful speech requires submission to the pathos of transformation by learning to be attentive to God's word, thus standing under Scripture as one who is interpreted, rather than standing over Scripture as one who is its judge. Luther's "Preface to the Wittenberg Edition of Luther's German Writings" invited students to learn the necessary habits for theological study: "This is the way taught by holy King David (and doubtlessly used by all the patriarchs and prophets) in the one hundred nineteenth Psalm. . . . They are *oratio, meditatio, tentatio*" (prayer, meditation, temptation).[15]

Students of Scripture must humbly pray for the Holy Spirit to give understanding, turning from themselves to wait on God, whose presence is mediated through Christ's promises to the church. David thus prayed, "Teach me, Lord, instruct me, lead me, show me," to allow God as the true teacher of Scripture to speak the work of salvation in his life.[16] Students of theology must prayerfully meditate on Scripture, indwelling the language of the word through the practices that prepare and create space for God's saving presence. Meditation requires constant repetition and careful attention, a patience in reading that allows the Spirit to unite the life of the one who prays with the word.[17]

Lastly, temptation is the touchstone that cultivates knowledge and understanding of the word. It is an external experience that, when suffered, demonstrates the credibility and power of God's word. Although public exposure to the word provokes assaults and afflictions from powers that rage against the reign of Christ, these are the conditions in which God makes true doctors of holy

Scripture. True theologians of the church are those who hear and love God's word and are thereby equipped for the task of preaching. Above all else, preachers must guard against the temptation of pride, against thinking too highly of their own wisdom or seeking the praise of others, since in the book of Scripture only God is worthy of praise. As Luther notes, "God opposes the proud, but gives grace to the humble."[18]

Bonhoeffer's timely letter to young theologians of the Confessing Church in Pomerania echoed Luther's wisdom. Many were undergoing severe testing, particularly the temptation to become "legal" pastors in the official state church, a move that promised jobs, salaries, homes, and pensions. Bonhoeffer emphasized the joy of their fellowship, particularly their willingness to suffer for the gospel and the church. He reminded them of the character of the Confessing Church as "a new life under God's joy-giving word," a word whose presence overcomes fear and anxiety regarding the future: "With this word we were willing to pass through struggle, through suffering, through poverty, through sin, and through death to finally reach God's eternal kingdom."[19]

Pastors find unity, strength, and gladness in the presence of Christ, who builds up his church as a community that "lives solely for the preaching of the pure, unadulterated gospel and by the grace of his sacraments, and which in its actions is obedient solely to him." Bonhoeffer was deeply concerned about the effects of lost confidence in God's word and God's work in the Confessing Church: "And has all of this not had its effects upon our preaching?" He also looked forward, pointing to the path they had been called to follow: "Prayer, theological clarity, and preaching the truth."[20]

Bonhoeffer's circular letters were a means of maintaining the spiritual bonds of the Finkenwalde community and for encouraging its members who felt isolated or abandoned in their ministries. The letters communicate a profound pastoral theology and spirituality, a way of thinking and acting faithfully in the tasks of leadership and ministry within the concrete circumstances of the church.[21] Bonhoeffer's wisdom is theological and pastoral, written in a manner that reflects his Finkenwalde lecture, "Contemporizing New Testament Texts." He does not privilege the "historical" context as ultimate: Hitler's oppressive reign, the German Christians, Nazi ideology, the crushing defeats suffered by the Confessing Church, the temptation to legalization, hardships endured by pastors and congregations, the brutality of the state. Instead, Bonhoeffer "read" the conditions in Hitler's Germany in light of the reality revealed in Scripture's witness to Christ as Lord of all that is.[22]

The mood of Bonhoeffer's letters are neither optimistic nor pessimistic, but they express a hopeful realism rooted in the confession of Christ as the only basis of the church's existence and witness. He thus sought to nurture courage and inspire hope by bringing together Finkenwalde seminarians for retreats, "face to face . . . so that things don't fall apart in the long period in between gatherings." He encouraged pastors to visit one another whenever possible not only to catch up on each other's lives but to remember, "We need someone occasionally to ask us where we stand with our reading of the Scripture, our time for meditation, our prayer, and our work on sermons. . . . We all need this help today."[23] The tasks of pastoral ministry and preaching are carried out by attending daily to the content and form of the gospel—as "theology on the way."[24]

Bonhoeffer interpreted the long-term effects of the church struggle in light of God's providential care, as a means of strengthening and renewing their spiritual life in the midst of troubles that were "unbelievably hard." He wrote of the fierce temptation to focus one's attention on current difficulties and events so as to be captivated by them. His aim was to direct the attention of preachers back to Scripture—to be captivated by the glory of the word, to remember the narrative of God's mighty acts, and to inspire faithful obedience in their ministries: "But we will experience this help only when we take the step of promise and obedience, just as the waves of the Red Sea only parted when Israel set its foot in the water. Thus everything is to stand on faith and obedience."[25]

For Bonhoeffer the call of discipleship informs everything related to the life and work of preachers—the "preaching life." Soon after the closing of Finkenwalde, Bonhoeffer published a book on the way of simple obedience to Christ based on the Sermon on the Mount. *Discipleship*, or *The Cost of Discipleship* as it is widely known, is Bonhoeffer's most popular book and rightly described as a "devotional classic."[26] What is often forgotten, however, are the circumstances of its publication. The content of *Discipleship* is largely derived from Bonhoeffer's lectures to preachers preparing for pastoral ministry in a church that was fighting for survival and struggling to proclaim and obey the claim of Christ in the darkness of National Socialism and its totalizing claim.[27]

Discipleship is a handbook of homiletical wisdom, a manual for preachers that weaves together hearing, proclaiming, and obeying the call of Christ. Based on Bonhoeffer's reading of the Gospel of Matthew, particularly the Sermon on the Mount, *Discipleship* provided preachers with a subversive counternarrative to the "gospel" promoted by National Socialism.[28] There is a profound theology of preaching embedded in Bonhoeffer's exposition of the narrative of Christ's call and commands that begins by recalling Scripture's significance in times of church renewal. Bonhoeffer perceived behind the church struggle a deeper concern for Jesus, a desire to hear him speaking to the church in the present: "When we go to hear a sermon, his own word is what we want to hear." However, Jesus is not heard, and, if he were actually present among churches in their preaching, a quite different group of people would be present, and a different set of people would turn away. Preaching the gospel in Germany had been overwhelmed by many dissonant sounds, conflicting views, false hopes, and deceptive promises that obscured the word of God.[29]

Discipleship addressed challenges to preaching the gospel in Germany. Some preaching was too harsh and difficult, weighted down with incomprehensible concepts and formulations. Bonhoeffer considered such criticism of preaching as valid. He believed many people sincerely desired to hear the word of Jesus but found listening too difficult, in that much preaching consisted of human opinions and institutional defensiveness and was too doctrinaire. There was also the problem of formulaic preaching, excessive repetition, and preaching that was overly contextualized, or too "German." On the other hand, there was preaching that did not speak to life and that was too abstract. The problem went much deeper than homiletical method or style; it was that Christ himself was either crowded out of sermons by preachers' opinions and convictions or displaced by the weight of moralistic rules and principles.[30]

Bonhoeffer's christological interpretation of discipleship conveys a depth of homiletical wisdom. The call of Christ must not be muted by preaching that effectively drives people away but must be proclaimed as a compelling story and attractive way of life that consists of following Jesus. Becoming a preacher entails having one's whole being and life reoriented "to the word and call of Jesus Christ himself." *Discipleship*, then, calls preachers back to the source of their calling: "Away from the poverty and narrowness of our own conviction and questions, here is where we seek the breadth and riches which are bestowed on us in Jesus." To proclaim the call to follow Jesus is not a heavy burden, a set of rules, the inducement of guilt, a "spiritual reign of terror," or the exercise of tyranny and violent abuse of people. Proclaiming the call of Jesus is the announcement of freedom, release, and strength for joyful obedience to him. An essential part of preaching, then, requires reflecting on what the call to follow Jesus means concretely for Christians who live and work in the world.[31]

Bonhoeffer acknowledges that while all people are called by grace, the call to follow Jesus is a path known only by him, "a path full of mercy beyond measure, a path which is joy." To proclaim Christ *is* the joy of preaching. Although following Christ is not an easy way, it is the narrow path that leads to Christ's great love of all people, particularly the weak and godless. The paradox of preaching is that Christ's narrow way opens up to the wideness of God's patience, mercy, and loving-kindness: "May God grant us joy in all seriousness of discipleship, affirmation of the sinners in all rejection of sin, and the overpowering and winning word of the gospel in all defense against our enemies."[32]

Bonhoeffer saw distinguishing between cheap grace and costly grace as the fundamental challenge of preaching. His concern was that preaching must be truthful, that costly grace must be proclaimed and obeyed. Moreover, the life and speech of preachers must too be formed by hearing and believing costly grace: "Cheap grace means grace as doctrine, as principle, as system." Cheap grace means forgiveness of sins as a general truth; it means God's love as merely a Christian idea of God. Cheap grace is an abstraction, creating a church that forfeits concrete, visible witness in the world. On the other hand, Bonhoeffer states, "[Costly grace] is the call of Jesus Christ which causes a disciple to leave his nets and follow him. . . . It is costly, because it calls to discipleship; it is grace, because it thereby makes them live. . . . Thus, it is grace as living word, word of God, which God speaks as God pleases."[33] The powerful lure of cheap grace as a commodity and its enticing rewards evoked Bonhoeffer's biting sarcasm:

> Cheap grace means grace as bargain-basement goods, cut-rate forgiveness . . . grace as the church's inexhaustible pantry, from which it is doled out by careless hands without hesitation or limit. It is grace without a price, without costs. It is said that the essence of grace is that the bill for it is paid in advance for all time. Everything can be had for free, courtesy of that paid bill. The price paid is infinitely great. . . . What would grace be, if it were not cheap grace?[34]

The implications of this charge for preaching are significant: "Cheap grace is denial of God's living word, denial of the incarnation of the word of God."[35] Continuity with Bonhoeffer's Finkenwalde homiletical lectures is also obvious. The incarnate Word, Christ himself walking among the church in the sermon, the living Word heard in the words of the preacher, Christ present with and for the church, is the fullness of costly grace obeyed and visibly embodied in the world.[36]

Discipleship does not communicate timeless truth.[37] The way of discipleship, "following after" Jesus, is both the content and the form of preaching, its message and its application, the unity of doctrine and of life that is realized daily in answering the call of Christ. The end of preaching is the grace of discipleship. And while costly grace is its concrete outcome and visible result, it is not its presupposition. Bonhoeffer points to Luther, who by acknowledging the reality of grace made the radical break from a self-willed life that cannot be justified by grace: "The acknowledgement of grace was his first serious call to discipleship." Grace is not a principle given in advance to validate one's life as it is. Bonhoeffer offers a "confession" that is based on cheap grace: "I can now sin on the basis of this grace; the world is in principle justified by grace. I can thus remain as before in my bourgeois-secular existence. Everything remains . . . and I can be sure that God's grace takes care of me."[38]

Bonhoeffer viewed the calling of preachers to follow and proclaim the word of Christ as something "truly amazing and seemingly inconceivable." To speak of grace, and to speak from grace, is to speak on behalf of people tempted by despair, for whom preaching has become "dishearteningly empty." Bonhoeffer describes this task: "For integrity's sake someone has to speak up for those among us who confess that cheap grace has made them give up on following Christ, and that ceasing to follow Christ has made them give up on costly grace." A pure doctrine of grace is not sufficient, since discipleship requires a community that practices the presence of Christ in hearing and following him, "[living] in the world without losing themselves in it." Central to the work of ministry, and particularly preaching, is the gift and summons of costly grace: "Blessed are they who by simply following Jesus Christ are overcome by this grace, so that with humble spirit they may praise the grace of Christ which alone is effective."[39]

Bonhoeffer lamented the "Christianization" of the world that had contributed to a "secularization" of Christianity.[40] Being Christian in Germany had become a matter of living in the world and being like the world, but with no difference, and presumably for the sake of grace. The church was seen as existing in a separate "spiritual" sphere where "Christian" citizens went to receive the forgiveness of sins. The effect of preaching cheap grace—"You are forgiven," but without the summons "Come, follow me!"—had been to liberate Christians from costly obedience to Jesus. Bonhoeffer viewed cheap grace as the "bitterest" enemy of discipleship in Germany, since it encouraged Christians to hate and despise discipleship in the name of grace.[41]

Grace—as a principle, law, concept, or doctrine—had taken on a life of its own, becoming like a "god." For Bonhoeffer, how grace is proclaimed, not merely that it is proclaimed, makes all the difference: "It is appalling to see what is at stake in the way which a gospel truth is expressed and used." He was convinced the Reformation doctrine of justification by grace could be spoken to enable listeners to hear and obey the summons of Christ. However, grace was too often spoken in a manner that was destructive of the way of Christ. The price of cheap grace was indeed steep; the collapse of organized churches in Germany was a visible consequence of grace acquired without cost:[42] "Christianity without the living Jesus Christ remains necessarily a Christianity without discipleship, and Christianity without discipleship is always a Christianity without Jesus Christ."[43]

An "Extraordinary" Way of Preaching

Costly grace requires costly proclamation. To be called by Jesus as a messenger is to be set apart for communion with his passion, for having one's life and speech shaped and informed by the truthfulness of his love.[44] The call of Jesus creates a visible community of the cross that he appoints as the salt and light of the world: "It would diminish the meaning to equate the disciples' message with salt, as the reformers did. What is meant is their whole existence, to the extent that it is newly grounded in Christ's call to discipleship, that existence of which the Beatitudes speak."[45]

Bonhoeffer discerned from his reading of Matthew 5:47 that "what is Christian is what is peculiar, the extraordinary, irregular, not self-evident." The extraordinary is "the way of self-denial, perfect love, perfect purity, perfect truthfulness, perfect nonviolence." The "extraordinary" is the love of Christ himself, who goes to the cross in suffering and obedience. Like the cross of Christ, the "extraordinary" must become visible in the life of the community of disciples: "In Christ the Crucified and his community, the 'extraordinary' occurs."[46]

The witness of disciples, then, must be seen and heard: "To flee into invisibility is to deny the call. Any community of Jesus which wants to be invisible is no longer a community that follows him. . . . They are a light which is seen. If it were different, then the call would not be revealed in them."[47] On the other hand, the call to discipleship requires recognizing that preaching is a gift that has real limits. Preachers do not have the light but are the light. Preachers, however, are tempted to judge those who do not respond to their preaching, just as they are tempted to offer grace cheaply as a commodity to a hardened, stubborn world.[48]

Bonhoeffer understood the strong temptation to exceed the limits of Christ's call through preaching that harms the credibility of the message and messenger. Preachers may not force words of forgiveness on people, nor are they free to run after them, seeking to proselytize, using whatever means and powers are necessary to accomplish something in them. Such means and measures are in vain; they defile the words of forgiveness by turning listeners into sinners who are opposed to God's holy gifts: "This signifies for the disciples a serious limitation on their work." Because the ministry of preaching is created and held by Jesus, preachers possess no special right or power of their own, no authority to exceed the limits of effectiveness, enthusiasm, and zeal. When preachers refuse to respect the resistance of listeners, they are tempted to confuse the word of the gospel with a "conquering idea" or triumphalist message, adopting forms of preaching that are the work of "fanatics."[49]

Bonhoeffer's comments on the limits of preaching lead into a remarkable discussion of the strength and weakness of the Word: "But the Word of God is so weak that it suffers to be despised and rejected by people. For the Word, there are such things as hardened hearts and locked doors. The Word accepts the resistance it encounters and bears it." In a rather astonishing remark, Bonhoeffer admits this is a "cruel insight; nothing is impossible for the idea, but for the gospel there are impossibilities." The Word is weaker than a big idea, theme, topic, or concept. Abstract preaching avoids the resistance, rejection, and suffering that accompany concrete speech and obedience to Christ. However, because preachers are disciples, witnesses of the living Word that is Christ himself, they will be perceived as weak when compared to the Nazi propagandists who promoted their grand ideas and programs for the German Volk.[50]

Bonhoeffer perceived suffering as a necessary part of proclaiming costly grace that would liberate preachers from self-confident enthusiasm for their own powers and capacities, "the sick restlessness of a fanatic." Such freedom is found only in Christ; it is not a lack of courage but rather the courage to suffer the weakness of the Word: "They [preachers] should not want to be strong when the Word is weak." The Word cannot be forced onto the world, since the strength of the Word is its lowliness, the strength of mercy that is able to move sinners to repentance from the depths of their hearts. Bonhoeffer adds, "But when the Word is misused, it will turn against them." Concern for others leads preachers to prayer; the promise given to their prayers by Jesus is the greatest power they possess.[51]

The Sermon on the Mount has been spoken, embodied, and fulfilled by the divine and human messenger who is the "Word made flesh." Bonhoeffer describes "the harvest" as the fruit of Christ's completed work (Matt 9:35-38). As Lord of the harvest, Jesus proclaims the good news of the kingdom, cures every disease, and heals every sickness. All Christ speaks and does is with great compassion for the many who sought him in their weak, impoverished condition. Thus, the commissioning of workers for the harvest is guided by the gaze of Jesus. The blessings of his presence belong not only to the disciples; the message of God's reign and power to save belongs with the poor and sick, upon whom Jesus looks with great compassion, "like sheep without a shepherd."[52]

The flock of God's people needs shepherds: "What does it matter that the most orthodox preachers and interpreters of the word of God were present, if they were not filled with all of the mercy and of all the grief over the abused and ill-treated people of God." Bonhoeffer continues his criticism: "What use are scholars of Scripture, pious followers of the law, preachers of the word, if the shepherds of the church-community themselves are missing?" The apostles are not only given doctrine and teaching, they are given effective power greater than the power of the rulers of this world. In their work they stand with Jesus, united by his call and commission. Their effectiveness does not lie in themselves—in their knowledge, skill, passion, or ingenuity. The effectiveness of preachers is grounded in the clear commandment of Jesus, whose will determines their work and message: "Blessed are they who have such an authority given them for their office and who are freed from their own discretion and calculations!"[53]

The commission of Christ is a gift rather than a possession. Love for Christ impels proclamation, where God's promises rest and God's word is found: "The message and effectiveness of the messengers are exactly the same as Jesus Christ's own message and work." The announcement of God's reign is accompanied by signs that authenticate its truth: forgiveness of sins, justification of sinners by faith, destruction of demonic power, healing of the sick, and raising of the dead. The power of the Word is thus experienced as deed, event, and miracle. Bonhoeffer marveled at the astonishing event of Christ going out through his messengers, equipping them with "royal grace" for speaking the life-giving word of the gospel.[54]

The commission to preach has no honor or power in itself. Even university-trained professional pastors are not exempt, since Christ's commission does not consist of social privilege. Sent by

Christ, the disciples discover a peculiar kind of freedom in the poverty that is the credibility of their message: "They may receive their daily wages without shame, and without shame they should remain poor for the sake of their ministry."[55]

Peace is the content of the message proclaimed by Jesus. Because the kingdom of God has dawned in him, the call to repentance and faith is the most urgent of all matters. Nothing is more merciful than the summons to repent and believe, because the kingdom has drawn near. Bonhoeffer adds, "That is gospel preaching." God's language is clear enough; the matter of who hears or does not hear cannot be controlled by those who preach. The word of salvation will be accepted and rejected, but God alone knows "who are worthy." When confronted by the mystery of unbelief, messengers are free to leave for another place: "In fear and astonishment, they have to recognize the simultaneous power and weakness of the word of God." The commission of Jesus, then, does not consist of heroic struggle and success; even lack of success or fierce opposition cannot dissuade preachers from the fact they have been sent by Jesus:[56] "Discipleship should never invest their trust in numbers . . . The disciples are few and will always be a only few."[57]

The vocation of preaching consists of standing by the word of God.[58] Preaching is an eschatological activity, oriented by hope in the fullness of God's reign as both a certainty and a mystery. The consolation of preachers is that, because Jesus is always with them, they will also be like him as bearers of his presence wherever they preach. When they are honored, Christ is honored; when they are received, Christ is received; when they are served, Christ is served. Preaching is the divine-human communication of costly grace that generates and empowers the visible obedience of the church.[59]

Life Together:
The Means and End of Preaching

The visibility of the church is the body of Christ taking up physical space on earth. Bonhoeffer cites Luther's dictum, "To this human being you shall point and say: 'Here is God.'" Christianity is not a religion, a truth, or a doctrine that is bodiless or discarnate, since such "beliefs" do not go beyond "being heard, learned, and understood." The incarnate Son of God, however, needs actual living human beings who follow him, thus raising the critical question of how the body of Christ becomes visible.[60] Bonhoeffer offered a robust depiction of the church as a visible community created and enlivened by the movement of the Word in the power of the Spirit:

> First is the preaching of the Word. . . . It exists mainly within the community. It moves on its own into the community. It has an inherent impulse toward community. It is wrong to assume that on the one hand there is a word, or a truth, and on the other hand there is a community existing as two separate entities, and that it would then be the task of the preacher to manipulate and enliven it, in order to bring it within and apply it to the community. Rather, the Word moves along this path of its own accord. The preacher should and can do nothing more than be a servant of this movement inherent in the Word itself, and refrain from placing obstacles in its path. . . . The Holy Spirit bestows faith on the hearers, enabling them to believe that, in the word of preaching, Jesus Christ himself has come to be present in our midst in the power of his body. . . . The space claimed by the church on earth is for worship, order, and daily life.[61]

In the fall 1938, Bonhoeffer assembled his reflections on the experiment in Christian community at Finkenwalde. While *Discipleship* provides a narrative framework for the vocation of preaching as "following after" Christ, *Life Together* identifies the practices of Christian community in which preachers are formed to believe, obey, and speak the truth of Christ.[62] Bonhoeffer insisted the community depicted in *Life Together* was not a cloistered existence set apart from the world but rather a demonstration of concrete Christian living "in the midst of enemies."[63] The call to discipleship turns the church to answer the call of Christ as the living Word who comes from outside itself. Christ is the Word of God placed in preachers' mouths for speaking sermons; the same Word is manifested in the experience of Christians through mutual love and service that springs from faithful obedience to Christ.[64]

Christian community is shaped by truthful worship of God, which requires refusing to worship false gods and renouncing false ways of living. Worship is not a "religious" activity that occurs in a separate sphere of life. Worship is a whole way of life sustained by the word of Scripture, the hymns of the church, and the prayers of the community—essential practices for Christian existence.[65] Preachers, too, are members of the community and thus dependent upon the faith and gifts of others: "It is by God's grace that a congregation is permitted to gather visibly around God's word and sacrament in the world. . . . The physical presence of other Christians is a source of joy and strength to the believer."[66]

As a "community through Jesus Christ and in Jesus Christ," the church is not built around preachers. Preachers are charged with responsibility for directing the community's attention to the truth of God's word in Christ: "God put this Word into the mouths of human beings so that it may be passed on to others." However, without the Word as its basis, the church is vulnerable to emotional, self-centered ways, subject to the desires of individuals possessing exceptional powers, personalities, experiences, and persuasive abilities. A community not grounded in the Word is thus easily swayed and manipulated by methods or techniques that treat others in seeking, calculating ways. The church is malformed when controlled by human bonds, suggestive influences, and dependencies that allow "self-centered, strong persons [to] enjoy life to the full, securing for themselves admiration, the love, or the fear of the weak."[67]

Bonhoeffer's prophetic vision of community was set against the pervasive presence of Nazi propaganda, manipulation, and violence, a program that sought the exclusion of Jews, the disabled, and all others who were perceived as "enemies" of Hitler's vision of "glory." He offered this theological assessment: "The exclusion of the weak and insignificant, the seemingly useless people, from everyday Christian life in community may actually mean the exclusion of Christ: for in the poor sister or brother, Christ is knocking at the door. We must, therefore, be very careful on this point."[68]

Life Together depicts a way of interpreting Scripture as a community called to receive and embody God's presence in Christ. Bonhoeffer emphasized the importance of attending to the whole of Scripture, reading canonically, and not merely focusing on discrete passages or sayings. Scripture must be read according to its deep connections and interrelatedness, the full witness to Christ in the Old and New Testaments: promise and fulfillment, law and gospel, sacrifice and law, cross and resurrection, faith and obedience, having and hoping. Scripture is therefore a corpus, a body, a living whole that warrants the "so called *lectio continua*," or consecutive reading of the various genres and biblical books "which puts the listening community in the midst of the wonderful revelatory world of the people of Israel, with the prophets, judges, kings, and priests, with their wars, festivals, sacrifices, and sufferings."[69]

Life Together depicts the remarkable experience of a people for whom hearing the Word entails being drawn into the story of Christ—his birth, baptism, miracles, and teaching; his suffering, dying, and rising. Through the revelatory word in Scripture, the church participates in the story of the gospel in receiving Christ's life and salvation in the present: "Following after" the story of God and the world brings the words of Scripture to life through a self-forgetfulness that prepares the church to be drawn into God's mighty acts. The listening community thus passes through the Red Sea, through the desert, and over the Jordan into the promised land. Bonhoeffer comments, "All this is not mere reverie, but holy, divine reality." What God did in the past, God does today. Whether God is a participant or a spectator is not what matters. What matters is that the community is attentive to participating in God's action in the sacred story, the story of Christ on earth: "Our salvation is from outside ourselves (*extra nos*). Salvation is not found in my story, but only in the story of Jesus Christ."[70]

Bonhoeffer called for a great reversal in reading Scripture that places the story of God's action in Israel and Christ at the center of reality. The powerful story of the self and the German nation, Aryan identity and Nazi supremacy, do not determine what God must do and where God must be present:[71] "Only those who allow themselves to be found in Jesus Christ—in the incarnation, cross, and resurrection—are with God and God with them." Understandings of the "present" do not exhaust the meaning of Scripture. All is there, since it pleased God to act there, but it is only there that the whole story is known: "The God of Abraham, Isaac, and Jacob is the God and Father of our Lord Jesus Christ."[72]

Bonhoeffer's description of the Word as the center of reality was not a romantic ideal. To read, hear, and speak in this manner is liturgical, the "work of the people" that orients the whole of life to the worship and service of God.[73] *Life Together* thus provides homiletical wisdom related to the place of Scripture in preaching for a community assembled around the Word in worship. *Discipleship* depicts a narrative "way of the preacher" as following after Jesus, while *Life Together* describes preaching as serving a community of disciples that participates in the narrative character of revelation through the witness of Scripture.[74] *Discipleship* and *Life Together* articulate a prophetic form of Christian faith, community, worship, and ministry that Bonhoeffer hoped would be capable of resisting the powers of an idolatrous Nazi state and its totalizing claim on the soul of the German people.[75]

In December 1939, with Germany at war, Bonhoeffer wrote the first of several theological supplements to the monthly newsletters that went out to Confessing Church seminarians in Pomerania. Bonhoeffer's "Theological Letter on Christmas" offers a beautiful interpretation of the mystery of Christ against the background of Nazi military power and conquest: the origin of all Christian theology is the "miracle of miracles, that God became human." Thus, for Bonhoeffer, the origin of "sacred theology," as opposed to ideology, is "prayerful kneeling before the mystery of the divine child in the stable." Without the birth of Christ there is no theology: "The God-human Jesus Christ, that is the holy mystery, which theology was instituted to preserve and protect."[76]

The mystery of Christ, the God-human person, is set against the foolishness of professional theologians in Germany. Academics had attempted to decode God's mystery, thus reducing it to "commonplace miracle-less words of wisdom" based on human experience and reason—but without the wonder of divine revelation. Bonhoeffer's concern was that the proper task of theology—which was necessary for the vocation of preaching-defending, comprehending, and exalting the mystery of God—had been disparaged by superficiality and thoughtlessness. The mystery of God in the flesh—the birth of Jesus Christ, the God-human Savior—had not been depicted or taught. The loss of God's mystery raised a critical question for pastors: "Where do we hear it preached?"[77]

Bonhoeffer's hope was that the celebration of Christmas as the sacred, unfathomable mystery of God would rekindle in preachers renewed love for theology, "captured and overcome by the miracle of the cradle of the Son of God." He hoped preachers would "devoutly ponder the mysteries of God" to discover "the fire of the divine mysteries was not extinguished and dead in their hearts." He warned against reducing the mystery of Christ to either feeling and experience or logical deduction that subjects it to egocentricity. He encouraged preachers to remember the rich, paradoxical Christology of the early church as declaring and glorifying the mystery of Christ as a true mystery: "So during the time of Christmas, let us take a lesson once again from the early church and try to understand devoutly what it thought and taught about the glorification and defense of the faith in Christ."[78]

Bonhoeffer's Christmas letter addressed the homiletical challenges faced by Confessing Church preachers in Nazi Germany. The value of remembering the splendor of Christmas, the mystery of Christ, is to "place our thinking and our recognition as preachers of the word in the light of that holy night." Preachers must reflect theologically on the subject of preaching so they may "read and contemplate the biblical testimony to the mystery of God's becoming human with more reverence and adoration, and perhaps even to sing Luther's Christmas hymns more thoughtfully and joyously."[79]

Bonhoeffer encouraged Confessing Church pastors to remain faithful to proclaiming the presence of Christ in word and sacrament: "If the Son of God has become truly human, the divine nature is certainly present in all its majesty, otherwise Christ would not be true God. In fact, if Christ is not true God, how could he help us? If Christ is not true human, how could he help us?" He cites Luther to show the significance of this christological formulation: "With Luther it can now be said, 'Wherever you can say, Here is God, there you must also say, Then Christ the man is also there'. . . . 'It is the honor of our God . . . in giving the divine self for our sake in deepest condescension, entering into the flesh.'"[80] Bonhoeffer's reflections on Christmas affirmed the visible form of the church that is created by the Word spoken in the sermon and consumed in the Lord's Supper: "The end of the ways of God is bodiliness."[81]

The collective pastorates were forced to close down in early 1940. Bonhoeffer's last circular letter speaks of the terrible effects of the war that had made the church struggle seem secondary. He adds, "We have the vocation to be preachers of the gospel and shepherds of the church-community. . . . We may still preach, and so let us continue to preach as we have done until now, with a good, free conscience, and to be faithful pastors who do not deny their church even in times of need."[82] He saw the church's mission in wartime as engaging Christian people with the question "Where is your God?" (Ps 42). "Is it true God is silent? Is it only true for those whose God is God of their ideas and thoughts?" Bonhoeffer followed these questions with an astonishing claim for the continued importance of preaching: "The biblical message of the power and terrible might of the Creator and Lord of the whole world must be brought to this people." The truth of the gospel must be seen, felt, and heard: "Preachers are called, in the midst of strife and death, to witness to God's love and peace through their thoughts, words, and deeds."[83] As Hitler's war plans accelerated, Bonhoeffer continued to articulate a concrete vision of the church as a necessary condition for proclaiming and hearing the gospel where Christianity was no longer privileged.[84]

8

Preaching without Words
1940–1945

Bonhoeffer's work with the Confessing Church reached a low point in 1939.[1] He was deeply discouraged by the failure of pastors and congregations to live what they confessed as the truth of the gospel at a time when Hitler was resolutely leading Germany into war. With the encouragement of friends, Bonhoeffer accepted an invitation to return to Union Seminary in New York for a visit that would last only a few months. His brief stay, however, was not without its benefits.

Eight years had passed since his first visit to New York, but he found the church environment in America had changed very little. However, Bonhoeffer's diary from this time in New York shows his approach to the return visit differed markedly from the perspective he brought during his first trip in 1930.[2] He was now resolved to assess Christianity in America in light of the mercy of Christ: "Render true judgments." He understood this as a compelling warning and directive for his task, one that forbade all overconfidence, which made his task even greater. He desired to see others as brothers in Christ who also stood under Christ's judgment, but who had a right to a brotherly word, "without glossing over, without prejudice, without arrogance, and full of merciful love."[3]

Bonhoeffer returned to New York with only one certainty—the call of discipleship in the love of God the Father and Jesus Christ as Savior: "Great programs always lead us only to where we ourselves are; we, however, should be found only where God is." He began to see there was much that connected the churches of America and Germany in spite of their different opinions. Bonhoeffer, however, had not lost a critical eye and ear for preaching despite his more temperate attitude. After worshiping in the famous Riverside Church of New York, the center of liberal Protestantism in America, he described the experience as "simply unbearable." The sermon was based on a saying from philosopher William James: "Accepting the horizon." The preacher was Hal Luccock of Yale Divinity School, whose sermon Bonhoeffer characterized as "a discreet, opulent, self-satisfied celebration of religion." He saw this as a form of religious idolatry that, without the word of God, cannot be held in check: "Such preaching renders people libertine, egotistic, and indifferent. Do the people really know that one can do as well or better with 'religion'—if only it weren't for God himself and his word?"[4]

Bonhoeffer judged that much "religion" in American was not necessarily "Christian." He saw it instead as a kind of "religious hand-out," and he had no doubts a strong storm would someday easily knock it down. Soon after, Bonhoeffer worshiped at Broadway Presbyterian Church, where the preacher was Dr. John McComb. He noted, "The sermon was astounding . . . about our 'likeness with Christ.' A completely biblical sermon—particularly good the sections,: 'we are blameless like Christ,' 'we are tempted like Christ.' " He judged this kind of preaching as capable of enduring the test of temptation and time: "Later this will eventually be a center of resistance long after Riverside Church will have become a temple of idolatry. I was pleased about this sermon. . . . With this sermon, an America heretofore unknown to me has been opened up."[5]

He also observed that nothing seemed to have changed regarding the treatment and inclusion of blacks in America, and he noted what he perceived as an increase in anti-Semitism.[6] He found himself reflecting upon whether America was a land "without Reformation," a thought that he qualified: "If Reformation is the God-given recognition of the failure of all paths to the building of the kingdom of God on earth, then this is accurate." A visit for worship with a Lutheran congregation brought similar disappointment. He noted the sermon topic or theme was about overcoming fear, while serious exegetical engagement with the text was lacking; there was much in the way of analysis but very little gospel: "It is very pathetic."[7]

Bonhoeffer continued to practice daily prayer and meditation on Scripture as the path of discernment during this time of testing. When reading 2 Timothy 4:21 ("Come before winter"), he heard God addressing him, "not as something pious, but vital . . . if God gives me the grace for that." An important part of his discernment was comparing the American experience with the churches of the Reformation. He surmised that Americans left Europe to live faith "freely on their own" and had thereby cultivated what he observed as "dogmatic indifference." The church was a religious province for meeting religious needs but "a waste of the word and the sacraments."[8] This conclusion was reinforced by another visit to a prominent New York church, where he heard well-known preacher Ralph Sockman: "The sermon was about 'today is ours'—without a text, and not the faintest echo of Christian proclamation." The experience prompted a time of somber reflection that revealed a deep longing for the Confessing Church community.[9]

Bonhoeffer observed how American preachers spoke much about freedom; yet he found freedom as a possession, especially for the church, to be a dubious thing. Freedom must be won under the constraint of necessity, and the freedom of the church arise from the necessity of God's Word; otherwise, it becomes arbitrary and ends in many a new bondage. He questioned whether the church in America was truly free, since only the Word is able to create true community: "These are lonely Sundays over here. I yearn for a good devotional service in community in my own language. The news [from Germany] is not good. Will we come in time?" (Isa 35:10). He estimated the study of theology in America stood where it had been in Germany approximately fifteen years earlier. While he enjoyed theological conversations with members of the Union Seminary community, he was careful to note, "I must watch myself, that I don't become neglectful in reading the Bible and in prayer."[10]

Bonhoeffer was invited to remain in New York to serve as a pastor with German refugees and as a lecturer at Union Seminary. There he would be protected from being conscripted for the German war effort as well as positioned to return after the war to provide leadership for a reconstructed church. He was convinced, however, his calling was in Germany, with the Confessing Church and the German people.[11] Soon after his return to Germany in July 1939, he wrote a circular letter to the Finkenwalde seminarians, describing the terrible effects of war and acknowledging how the struggles of the church often seemed so secondary. He then offered words of encouragement:

> We have the vocation to be preachers of the gospel and shepherds of the church-community. . . . We may still preach, and so let us continue to preach as we have done until now, with a good, free conscience, and to be faithful pastors who do not deny their church even in times of need. We know that God demands this service of us today, and that we thereby perform the greatest service to human beings that can be done for them.[12]

Bonhoeffer's comments addressed the content of preaching, which presumably was a response to his experience of preaching in America—a kind of preaching he had assessed as "Christianity without Reformation."[13] He asserted, "We are preachers of justification through grace alone." He exhorted his preachers to consider what this meant for them, that God's ways and goals cannot be equated with human ways and goals—that the judgment of God is a matter of life or death. God's judgment, however, is for the sake of mercy; God humbles in order to lift up. Moreover, God thwarts rather than confirms human action to redirect the gaze of humankind to himself. Bonhoeffer's summary was prophetic: "The word God speaks is the cross which is planted on the earth, where God is at work and calls the church 'to serve those who live, struggle, suffer, and die.' "[14]

The collective pastors were dissolved by the Gestapo in March 1940. Bonhoeffer continued to reach out to the seminarians in conditions that eventually spelled the end of the church struggle. There remained in Germany a committed core of Confessing Church pastors and parishes, with Bonhoeffer a leading voice in support of both the Barmen and the Dahlem confessions. The steadfastness of the Confessing Church in the face of overwhelming external pressure and internal conflicts had served as an obstacle to the German Christians' aim of creating an official pro-Nazi Reich Church. However, Bonhoeffer continued to be disappointed with the Confessing Church as a whole, particularly its failure to resist the oppressive claims of National Socialism. In the early 1940s, he saw the challenge as more than mere survival; he saw it as an urgent need for a church living in a manner truthful to the gospel, a church willing to bear costly witness in serving those whose lives were crushed by the weight of Hitler's idolatrous Reich.[15]

Bonhoeffer's work to sustain the Confessing Church during the early war years is remarkable, given the paralyzing effect of what many Germans accepted as the eventuality of the Third Reich and given the day-to-day preoccupation with mere survival. The consequences of the Confessing Church's witness could be severe. Even those pastors and seminarians who tried to distinguish their loyalties to Germany from allegiance to Hitler faced conscription and the reality of war. For some, this dilemma was partially resolved by choosing to fight for Germany but not for Hitler. Arguably, Bonhoeffer's greatest challenge was providing theological guidance to a church that struggled daily with the contradiction of privately held Christian convictions, the totalizing claims of Nazism, and loyalty to Germany. The call to discipleship and confessing the gospel had to be proclaimed to people who sought to be at once Christian, patriotic, and anti-Nazi.[16]

As Nazi authorities gradually lost interest in winning the support of the churches for an official Reich Church, the Confessing Church was faced with the daunting task of standing up to the oppressive claims of a National Socialist regime. Any resistance by Confessing Churches—preaching, praying, worshiping, helping Jews, and challenging the influence of Nazis and German Christians in churches or communities—was seen as an exceptional, and even desperate, attempt to preserve integrity while helping those "under the wheel." Bonhoeffer's biblical meditations, theological essays, circular letters, and secret visitations during the early war years, when he was banned from speaking publically, continued to call the church to seek more than its survival and self-preservation. A constant refrain in his writings was the necessity of resistance as *status confessiones*, for the sake of confessing the gospel, which entailed great sacrifice and risk. He had grown weary with a church that placed personal "religion" and institutional integrity ahead of public witness and responsible service in all of life.[17]

Bonhoeffer's occasional writings exemplify his work as a homiletical theologian who sought to serve the church as a community that exists to proclaim the Word for and with the world. His persistent desire was to allow the gospel to address the conditions in which Confessing Church pastors and seminarians struggled to live, think, and speak faithfully in the shadow of the Third Reich. During the war, most Protestant clergy, as well as almost 98 percent of seminarians, were eventually drafted into military service.[18] In addition, approximately half of the seminarians taught by Bonhoeffer would lose their lives on the front. For Bonhoeffer the war years were a time of "homelessness," during which he was prevented from all public speaking, publishing, and traveling. In spite of increasingly limited opportunities, Bonhoeffer's persistent attempts to instruct and encourage a weakened Confessing Church are impressive. His occasional writings reflect unwavering commitment to Christ as the center of reality—the Lord whose word and work embraces faith, theology, preaching, and the church for the sake of the world.[19]

During the war years, Bonhoeffer assumed what was essentially a "double life." While he continued to provide leadership for a struggling and divided Confessing Church, he also became involved in a conspiracy against Hitler. As a highly secretive operation, the conspiracy required that Bonhoeffer not disclose his involvement to the church, since there was no precedent for a Protestant pastor in Germany to participate in such activity. Bonhoeffer's active involvement in the conspiracy also coincided with the reality of military service. His involvement in the plot against Hitler gave him access to the Office of Military Intelligence, which classified him as indispensable, working in a civilian occupation as a courier for military intelligence.

Bonhoeffer's value to the conspiracy was in the many international contacts he had through ecumenical activities. From 1940 to 1943, he was able to travel abroad in assisting the work of the conspiracy. In April 1943, after an assassination attempt against Hitler failed, Bonhoeffer was arrested along with other coconspirators. He remained a prisoner until his execution for treason on April 9, 1945, following another failed coup and assassination attempt to rid Germany of Hitler and National Socialism, a desire he held until his death for both theological and political reasons.[20]

Preaching as "Theology on the Way"

Bonhoeffer's constancy in reading Scripture theologically, as God speaking in the present, refused to privilege the historical situation of Nazi Germany, a modern hermeneutic that had relegated the Bible to an ancient text that needed to be "contemporized."[21] His interpretation of Scripture in preaching was served by doctrine and Lutheran confessions, offering a vision of reality that was not limited to a separate realm identified as "religion." Bonhoeffer's work with preachers remained focused on the reign of God as established in the weakness and lowliness of Christ.[22]

An important work by Bonhoeffer during the war years is *Prayerbook of the Bible*, the last book published in his lifetime.[23] Bonhoeffer's short primer on prayer as central to the life and work of preachers is often overlooked, or even dismissed, as the product of an earlier stage in his thought that was surpassed by his later works. Compared with the depth of historical, philosophical, and theological reflection that comprises *Ethics*, and the provocative reflections of *Letters and Papers from Prison*, *Prayerbook of the Bible* is too easily categorized as a "devotional" or "spiritual" piece of writing. However, *Prayerbook of the Bible* is best read as a prophetic work, written to assist Confessing Church pastors in perceiving and proclaiming the "way" of God revealed in Scripture and embodied in following after Christ.[24]

The "way" is revealed, discerned, and entered into through prayer, "finding the way to and speaking with God. . . . No one can do that on one's own. For that one needs Jesus Christ." Bonhoeffer did not assume prayer is a natural activity but rather assumed that it is learned by hearing and speaking God's Word. The way that is from God is Jesus Christ, and the way that is to God is also Jesus Christ: "So we learn to speak to God because has spoken and speaks to us. . . . We ought to speak to God, and God wishes to hear us, not in the false and confused language of our heart but in the clear and pure language that God has spoken to us in Jesus Christ: God's speech in Jesus Christ meets us in the Holy Scriptures."[25]

Bonhoeffer compared learning the language of prayer, God's speech, with a child learning to speak by listening to her parents. Christian people learn God's speech, the language of faith that names the reality of God and the world, by learning to pray with Christ, who is the Word of the Father. The true teacher of prayer, God's speech, is Christ the Son of God, "who has brought before God every need, every joy, every thanksgiving, and every hope of humankind."

Prayer is nothing less than Jesus Christ, the incarnate Word, who prays in, with, and for God's people: "In Jesus' mouth the human word becomes God's Word. When we pray along with the prayer of Christ, God's Word becomes again a human word."[26] Bonhoeffer's reflection on prayer as central to Christian faith, life, and ministry is consistent with his insistence that Christ and the church cannot be divided. Prayer, particularly the Psalms, the "prayerbook of the Bible," is first and foremost about Christ; the Psalms are God's Word spoken by Christ, and only then God's Word spoken by the church.[27]

Praying the Psalms in the name of Christ is a way of standing by the Word. Moreover, the Word of God, Jesus Christ, stands by the church in its fears, weaknesses, sufferings, and even death. Praying the Psalms is to follow the path that God has made in Christ, who is present with the church—alive, enjoying blessings, suffering, and even crucified anew. The Psalms, then, provide a mirror of the church's life in being joined to Christ for the sake of the world: "Therefore it is the prayer of the human nature assumed by Christ that comes before God here. It is really our prayer. But since the Son of God knows us better than we know ourselves, and was truly human for our sake, it is also really the Son's prayer. It can become our prayer only because it is his prayer."[28]

The language of preaching is tested and purified by the language of prayer, since learning to speak to God is necessary in order to speak of God.[29] Bonhoeffer's reading of the Psalms is a primer for preachers, a "grammar" of the language of faith, and a way of perceiving reality within the communion of the Father and the Son.[30] Just as prayer does not come naturally, neither does preaching come naturally; it must be learned by acquiring the clear, pure language that God speaks in Christ to reveal the truth of all that is. Preaching, which is inseparable from praying, is an act of worship that is given theological meaning in light of God the Creator and Redeemer. Prayer and proclamation are thus inseparably bound in Christ; the Word of God is the way from God and to God, the path completed by the incarnate, crucified, and risen Lord.[31] *Prayerbook of the Bible* thus sets forth the cosmic scope of the Word in describing the various types of Psalms: creation, the law, the history of salvation, the Messiah, the church, life, suffering, guilt, enemies, and the end.[32]

Bonhoeffer's study of the Psalms depicts a journey of faith in which Christians follow Christ in the whole of life. The whole of Christian life is prayer—the way to God provided in Christ and the church's answer to God in Christ that it "speaks" with both words and actions. Bonhoeffer emphasized the repetitious nature of praying the Psalms that is highlighted by Psalm 119: "To such a degree that it seems so simple that it is virtually impervious to our exegetical analysis, is there not a suggestion that every word of prayer must penetrate to a depth of the heart which can be reached only by unceasing repetition?" The repetition of Psalm 119 is a way of praying that forms one for hearing and speaking the word of God, "an unbroken, indeed, continuous, process of learning, appropriating and impressing God's will in Jesus Christ on the mind."[33]

The Psalms occupy a significant place in Bonhoeffer's homiletical theology. The anti-Semitism of National Socialism had sought to remove all vestiges of Israel as God's elect people and of the Scriptures of Israel as God's revelation. This was a theological and political decision that helped prepare the way for the "Nazi fiction" of the Bible, preaching, and the church. Bonhoeffer's use of the Psalter sought to counter idolatry and falsehood that was more German than Christian. Moreover, his exemplary integrity of practice and teaching invited preachers into a way of formation that he hoped would be manifested in homiletical commitment to Christ and the church's embodiment of the gospel.[34]

Bonhoeffer's interpretation of Psalm 119 articulates a vision that draws together prayer, reading Scripture, preaching, and the witness of the church in the world.[35] His reading of Psalm 119 is congruent with the message of the psalm: that God provides a "way" for his people to become a visible sign of Christ's presence and action in the world. In late 1939, Bonhoeffer wrote a liturgy for Christmas that has been preserved in fragmentary form. This brief act of prayer points to the christological vision that guided Bonhoeffer's interpretation of the Psalms within the relation of worship, doctrine, and preaching:

Lord, God of all peace and all love, you have come to us, so that we should come to you. You became human, so that we would become godly. In grace, you took on our flesh and blood, so that we might partake of you. Through your most holy birth, may we

be born anew in peace and love, and turn us poor sinners into
children of your mercy.[36]

Bonhoeffer thus began his meditation on Psalm 119 with a theological conviction: that the "beginning" has already occurred. The life
of the church is not continually remade or begun anew, but rather
it is a path followed within God's forgiving and renewing word in
Christ, which is the gracious work of God in baptism, rebirth, and
conversion. There is a "joyful certainty of faith" in which the church
is called to walk the path of God, who continually seeks his people.[37]

Bonhoeffer saw the Confessing Church, its pastors, and its
preachers as following the path of the psalmist as the way of God's
grace and faith. The church is always tempted to return to the
beginning, to search for something new, which is the same as turning back to itself and choosing to live under the weight of the law.
To do so is to deny the gift of God, who has given the law, decrees,
statutes, and commandments as God's act of redemption and
promise that the narrative of salvation confirms: "We were Pha-
raoh's slaves in Egypt, but the Lord brought us out of Egypt with a
mighty hand. . . . Whoever asks about the law will be reminded of
Jesus Christ and the redemption from servitude in sin and death
that in him has been accomplished for all human beings and will
be reminded of the new beginning set by God in Jesus Christ for all
human beings."[38]

The way of God's law leads to God himself and God alone. The
testimonies of those who seek God with all their hearts are sign-
posts and reminders lest God's people lose their way. The way has
been tried before, since it is a path God has walked and prepared
himself. Bonhoeffer affirmed the surpassing value of this journey,
as not merely "marking time," but as a movement led by God who
knows the entire way, while the church knows only the next step
and the final goal.[39] Moreover, the reality of God's faithful action
and guidance has profound implications for preaching: "The entire
gospel message of salvation can be called simply 'the way' . . . or the
'way of God.' In this way it becomes clear that the gospel and faith
are not a timeless idea but an action of God and of the human being
in history."[40]

God's path is made visible by those who follow the way of God to
human beings, which is the way of human beings to God: "The way

of God is not abstract doctrine; a plan, program, or principle; it has a name, Jesus Christ (John 14:6)." The way of God in Christ requires diligence in keeping God's commandments, which point to the One who commands. The commands of God, then, offer direction, purpose, and a goal; they are not ends in themselves or obeyed for themselves, but rather for God, "who wants to enter us deeply and wants to be held fast in every condition of life." The focus of proclaiming God's way is neither the self nor one's plans, intentions, failures, or wanderings. Bonhoeffer viewed such self-referential preaching as an obstacle preventing the church from perceiving the sure, clear path provided by God. He notes that, too often, "our prayer begins with ourselves." The challenge in preaching is not to seek a better way or straighter path, since God's statutes already contain the way of all that is: "The course of heaven, earth, and humankind has been irrevocably prescribed by these statutes. The call is to enter God's firmness and faithfulness."[41]

The necessity of preaching is the way of the Psalter, since there is no situation in which God's word does not provide direction: "But serious attention, tireless asking, and learning are necessary to recognize the right commandment and to recognize the inexhaustible kindness of God in all his commandments." Gratitude is a sign of such attentiveness; thus, listening and learning, thankful praise and obedience, are united in the proclamation of the word. The psalm offers a "hermeneutic of thankful praise," which is the way of learning God's commands "with an upright heart."[42] Thankfulness is a way of looking back to the God who gives as well as a looking forward to the God who commands—a way of living out of the past and into the future that seeks to discern God's righteousness in the present. Because God speaks from divine abundance to human poverty, preaching is a way of speaking precluding prideful arrogance that presumes upon God's goodness and gifts.[43]

The Holy Spirit instructs and transforms the heart to desire God's way. Bonhoeffer notes, "We need to unlearn completely saying: 'I want.'" The greatest obstacle is piety, personal pious longings, and religious desires that focus on one's own ego. The grace of God, however, works a transformation of the heart, creating a new beginning that comes in Christ through word and sacrament. The Holy Spirit grants faith that gladly acknowledges, "I want in a quite new and different way." Filled with the power of the Spirit, the church desires God's will and cooperates with God's way. To live by faith in the Spirit's power, then, is to acknowledge one's weakness, a kind of "blamelessness" that does not consist of good intentions, ideals, hard work, or fulfilling one's duties. Such blamelessness is the fruit of God's forgiveness rather than bourgeois satisfaction with the self.[44] The word of God is therefore spoken as a gift and not a possession.[45] Bonhoeffer offers a beautiful summary of this homiletical truth:

> The clearer and deeper God's word shows itself to us, the more vivid the desire in us becomes for the consummate clarity and inexhaustible depth of God. Through the gift of his word, God drives us to seek ever richer knowledge and an ever more glorious gift. He does not like false contentment. The more we receive, the more we have to seek God, and the more we seek, the more we will receive from him. God wants to be fully glorified in us and be revealed in all his abundance. Certainly, we can never seek God anywhere else but in his word, but this word is alive and inexhaustible, for God himself lives in it.[46]

Bonhoeffer's astonishing affirmation of God's living word challenged the idolatrous use of Scripture by the church in Germany. His meditation on Psalm 119 was decidedly liturgical—an act of worship that directs the gaze to God, who has completed the path from which the church must not go astray:[47] "When God's word has struck us, we may say: 'I seek you with my whole heart.' For we would seek an idol half-heartedly, but never God himself. God needs the whole heart. God wants nothing (not something) from us; rather he wants us ourselves, entirely. God's word has told us."[48]

The commands of God pass from the mouth of God to the lips of human speakers. Bonhoeffer acknowledged the ease with which the word can be received in the heart but still be difficult to speak. However, the word is not a private matter but must be proclaimed as public witness to the world. Moreover, speaking the word cannot be "empty lip service" but must be a voicing that fills the heart and engages the entire self: "Do our lips not often seem locked, in the face of great woe, because we fear a pious formula will take the place of the divine word?" There is also a kind of thoughtlessness in speaking that lacks discernment of the right word and remains silent. The result is that warnings and admonitions are glossed over, while needed consolations and encouragement are left unspoken. There may also be false reticence or fear of people. Christ is preached but is often forced and spoken with anxiety instead of faith.[49] Bonhoeffer offers a compelling description of the practice of prayerful study and conversion of the self that are required for the ministry of the word:[50]

> It demands a great measure of spiritual experience and practice as well as childlike faith and confidence to be able to speak all demands of God with one's lips without succumbing to a spiritual routine, without becoming a moralizer or an obtrusive babbler. The whole heart must belong to the word of God before we learn to place our lips also entirely into the service of Jesus Christ.[51]

Bonhoeffer adds that joy is the "grand word" without which there is no walking in the way of the Lord: "God's word creates joy in the one who takes it in." The word proclaimed to the church is full of God's joy, which breaks forth in the lives of those who speak and listen. Wherever the whole story of the gospel is told, there is great joy: "Complete joy is the gift of the word of God to its listeners." God's word is the source of all joy; and the paths of God's witnesses are full of joy, because they are the paths that God himself has walked and still walks. The refusal of God's way is itself a reason for sorrow, the loss of great joy.[52]

Bonhoeffer summarized the wisdom of Psalm 119 for preaching. Hearing God's word takes time and maturity, pondering and reflecting, silence and contemplation: "God's word claims my time; God's word entered time and wants me to give him my time." Discerning God's will is a daily task, since God's new word is received and expounded as a never-ending wealth of interpretation. Bonhoeffer was opposed to abstract principles and rules derived from Scripture that were applied without prayerful consideration, without taking Scripture into the heart, without involving one's whole self. Preaching moral rules and values prevents the work of exegesis that recognizes God's Word in Scripture as God's speech. Preachers who do not practice meditation and exegesis deny their office and calling, since prayerful reading and thoughtful study require each other.[53]

Scripture does not need to be made relevant for contemporary contexts, since "the past becomes the present for the one who grasps

the 'for me' in faith." Preachers are like blind Bartimaeus in the
Gospel of Mark, who cried out to Jesus for help, "My teacher, let me
see again." Walking in God's way, hearing and obeying the word
that is proclaimed by human lips, is given in gradual, step-by-step
recognition and seeing: "One whose eyes God has opened to his
word will see into a world of wonders." What once appeared dead
is full of life; contradictions are resolved into a higher unity; harsh
demands become gracious commands. The human words of Scripture become a medium for hearing God's eternal Word, by which
God is recognized as present—working salvation, making new
claims, and lightening burdens.[54] The word of God's commands
that is received through prayerful study is Christ himself, in whom
the fullness of reality—God and the world reconciled in Christ—is
revealed. Bonhoeffer's meditation ends with a challenge: "Can we
speak this word without knowing that it is directed to us?"[55]

Bonhoeffer's meditation on Psalm 119 provides a picture of his
commitment to listening to, speaking from, and living by the Bible
in the concrete reality of the world. Preachers must stay close to both
Scripture and life, allowing neither one to command full attention
to the exclusion of the other. The importance of meditation is not
merely hearing and obeying God's command but rather hearing
and obeying the present Christ, who fulfills God's law and speaks
God's commandment to the church. Bonhoeffer's meditation offered
a model of moral discernment for hearing the voice of Christ and
responding in faithful and fitting ways. Reading Scripture, then,
is a spiritual exercise by which one is conformed to the person of
Christ and attuned to hearing God's word in Christ. Although prayer
is central, it cannot be separated from the intellect. Meditation and
exegesis are equally important for the work of preaching that seeks to
perceive and articulate the way of God in the present.[56] Bonhoeffer's
commentary on Psalm 119 exemplifies a particular "ethos" or character of preaching—a way of being, thinking, and speaking generated
by prayerful attentiveness to and reflection on the word of God.[57]

The Ethics of Preaching

Bonhoeffer's meditation on Psalm 119 plays an important transitional role from *Discipleship* to *Ethics*.[58] His concern in both works is
to direct preaching away from abstract language, since discipleship

and ethics are concrete practices that aim toward conformation to Christ in all of life. *Ethics* also marks Bonhoeffer's turn to the future, as an "explication of a concrete Protestant ethic" for the postwar work of peace and reconstruction. Although *Ethics* is arguably Bonhoeffer's most significant work, his thinking on church and state, moral discernment, and God's command to responsible action in the world are too often considered apart from the importance of preaching.

Bonhoeffer's meditation on Psalm 119 establishes an exegetical framework for understanding the ethos or character of preaching as "theology on the way." He opposes the reduction of Christianity to principles, programs, ideals, moral values, and propaganda since the end of preaching is conformation to Christ. Preachers are disciples called to participate in the justifying and sanctifying work of God, while preaching summons the church to follow the way that leads to integrity and unity in discerning and doing God's will.[59]

The words and work of a preacher are therefore those of a human being participating in Christ. *Ethics* offers a rich, christological vision of humankind, a "Christian humanism" that sets forth Christ as the true form of real humanity in relation to God and others.[60] Preaching, then, cannot be reduced to the communication of religious truths and moral instruction, to either offering spiritual advice or making apologetic arguments. Preachers proclaim the whole narrative of the gospel—the astonishing reality of a new humanity in Christ becoming visible in the form of the church.[61] As Bonhoeffer summarizes,

> *Ecce homo*—behold the human being, accepted by God, judged by God, awakened by God to a new life—see the Risen One! God's "Yes" to this human being has found its goal through judgment and death. God's love for this human being was stronger than death. A new human being, a new life, a new creature has been created by God's miracle. "Life has gained the victory; it has conquered death." The love of God became the death of death and the life of this human being. In Jesus Christ, the one who became human was crucified and is risen; humanity has become new. The new human being has been created.[62]

Preaching communicates God's affirming, judging, and reconciling grace in the form of Christ, who is present in the human words of preaching. Proclaiming Christ is a divine and human activity through which the Holy Spirit illumines the preacher's perception of reality for discerning rightly the relation between Christ and the context of the church in which preaching takes place.[63]

Preaching requires simplicity and wisdom—the daily practice of receiving and reflecting on the word of Scripture. An undivided heart is necessary—a way of seeing reality fixed on the simple truth of God proceeding from God: "Because of knowing and having God, this person clings to the commandment, the judgment, and the mercy of God that proceed each day from the mouth of God." The wise person sees into the depths of things: "Only the person who is wise sees reality in God." A preacher's gaze will be directed to Christ, since to look at him is to see "in fact God and the world in one. 'Ecce homo—behold, what a human being!' "[64] *Ethics*, then, does not offer advice on homiletical method and technique, on "how to preach." *Ethics* offers instead a description of the ethos or character of preaching.[65] Attentiveness to Christ revealed in Scripture guides and directs preachers through daily habits of meditation, study, reflection, moral discernment, and deliberation for speaking truthfully, in accordance with reality for particular times, places, and circumstances: "The truthfulness of our words that is owed to God must assume a concrete form in the world. Our word should not be in principle but concretely in accordance with the truth. Something not concretely in accordance with truth is, before God, not at all in accordance with the truth."[66]

Bonhoeffer's "ethic of preaching" provided a stark contrast to familiar forms of preaching in German churches. His understanding of preaching required a concrete rather than abstract way of speaking that was shaped by his vision of the church as "nothing but that piece of humanity where Christ has taken form."[67] He was suspicious of the language of formation because of the German Christian agenda that had aggressively sought to coordinate all of life, including the church, with the ideology of National Socialism.[68] His comments on this are particularly insightful for preaching:

> We are tired of Christian agendas. We are tired of the thoughtless, superficial slogan of a so-called practical Christianity to replace a so-called dogmatic Christianity. We have seen that the forces which form the world come from entirely other sources

than Christianity, and that so-called practical Christianity has failed in the world just as much as so-called dogmatic Christianity. Hence we must understand by "formation" something quite different from what we are accustomed to mean, and in fact the Holy Scripture speaks of formation in a sense that at first sounds quite strange. It is not primarily concerned with formation of the world by planning and programs, but in all formation it is concerned only with the one form that has overcome the world, the form of Jesus Christ. . . . This does not mean that the teachings of Christ or so-called Christian principles should be applied directly to the world in order to form the world according to them. Formation occurs only by being drawn into the form of Jesus Christ, by *being conformed to the unique form of the one who became human, was crucified, and is risen* . . . as the form of Jesus Christ himself so works on us that it molds us, conforming our form to Christ's own (Gal. 4:9).[69]

Bohnoeffer's chapter entitled "On the Possibility of the Church's Message to the World" begins by asking, "What is behind the desire, which is awakening in Christendom throughout the world, to hear a message from the church that offers solutions?" He viewed this kind of pragmatic preaching as a failure of the church which hindered people from believing its message. Theologically correct proclamations and moral principles were not enough, since there was an urgent need for a "concrete directive in the concrete situation."[70]

Bonhoeffer challenged a popular view in Germany that assumed the church's mission was to offer solutions for the world's problems, answers for its social questions, and advice on how to put its life back in order. He was convinced the church had much to say to the world about "worldly things." However, the church does not have solutions and answers in advance that need only be applied. Bonhoeffer turned to the gospel to expose the arrogance of this view; Jesus did not solve the problems of the world; Jesus did not answer every question; nor did Jesus implement a program that would make the world a better place. The word of Jesus is the divine answer to the divine question addressed to humankind. The word is not an answer or a solution but the redemptive word of God that unites human beings in the Son with the will of the Father, so that "all these things will be given."[71]

Bonhoeffer judged preaching that begins with human problems and seeks useful solutions as "unbiblical." The way of Jesus Christ, and thus the way of all Christian thinking, is not the way from the world to God, but it is the way from God to the world: "The message of the church can be none other than the word of God to the world. This word is Jesus Christ, and salvation in his name." The church's responsibility to the world begins with hearing and believing its own message. It is the church's witness to the world, as offensive as it may be, which makes room for the gospel in the world.[72]

The church does not have a double message, a double ethic, or religious and nonreligious ways of living; God's word extends to wherever Christians find themselves. Because God became fully human in Christ, proclamation is both Christian and worldly. Everything created is for the sake of Christ and sustained in Christ (Col 1:16-17). There is no room for Christian triumphalism in preaching. Proclamation requires a patience and humility that are shaped by its message, by faith in the One whom it announces—the divine Word taking human form and expression as concrete service and responsibility.[73]

God is determined to speak to the world in person through the proclamation of the church. The church's specific mandate, then, is that "God wants a place at which, until the end of time, God's word is again and again spoken, pronounced, delivered, expounded and spread." The word of the church's preaching is Jesus Christ, who came from heaven, and who wants to come again in the form of human speech. Significantly, the church's mandate is the divine Word and not itself or its life and mission—its needs, survival, or self-preservation.[74]

"God is determined to speak to the world in person" is a concise summary of Bonhoeffer's mature homiletical theology. He believed the moment of the Word in preaching is the "advent" of Christ's presence. The sermon is determined by neither the preacher's choice nor the peoples' will but rather "through God's will and mercy descends on human beings from heaven, a word commanded and instituted by Jesus Christ." Only Christ can legitimize preaching as "Christian." As Bonhoeffer claims, "On the basis of Holy Scripture the preaching office proclaims Jesus Christ as the Lord and Savior of the world . . . so that any other message is just 'empty chatter.'"[75]

Proclamation cannot be both "Christian" and "non-Christian." The church proclaims the one commandment of God revealed in

Christ for the world, which includes challenging the state to fulfill its mandate as given for the service of Christ. Bonhoeffer saw the proclamation of Christ, the incarnate, crucified, and risen Lord, as capable of overcoming the creation/redemption, private/public, spiritual/political divisions that had severely compromised the church's witness in Germany. His explication of the church's commission to proclaim Christ is remarkable, a homiletical theology that witnesses Christ as the "eternal Son with the Father in eternity." All that has been created can be conceived and essentially understood in relation to Christ as the mediator of creation: "Everything has been created through Christ and toward Christ, and everything has its existence only in Christ (Col. 1:15ff.)." God's will with creation cannot be understood apart from Christ. The commandment of Jesus Christ as proclaimed by the church is neither a law foreign to human life nor permission for autonomous existence apart from Christ. The commandment of Christ, the living Lord, sets created being to fulfill its own law. the "law inherent in it from its origin, essence, and goal in Christ."[76]

Bonhoeffer concluded *Ethics* with a description of the church's "double divine purpose" as standing with the Word and standing with the world for the world's sake. The church does not rule the world but proclaims the liberating word of Christ to all humankind in the respective functions of church, government, marriage, family, and culture: "Jesus Christ can always only be proclaimed and witnessed as the one in whom God has taken on humanity. Jesus Christ is the one in whom there is a new humanity, the community of God." Preaching and discipleship are inseparable—following after the one "who was the Christ precisely in being there completely for the world and not for himself." On the one hand, the church, gathered around Christ, is a means to the end of proclaiming Christ to the world. On the other hand, the church, as inseparable from Christ, is an end in itself, the concrete manifestation of the goal and center of all God is doing in the world, which is the message it proclaims.[77]

A Prisoner for the Gospel

For many readers, Bonhoeffer's part in the conspiracy and his imprisonment represent the most fascinating part of his life and career. *Letters and Papers from Prison*, collected and edited by Eberhard Bethge, Bonhoeffer's closest friend and biographer, is rightly viewed as a theological classic that embraces life in all its dimensions from the perspective of discipleship, "following after" Jesus Christ.[78] Bonhoeffer's prison correspondence offers little in the way of constructive statements concerning the nature and practice of preaching, but rather it offers deeply probing questions and daring proposals that draw from his previous work and experience to discern a concrete direction for preaching in a radically changing world. His homiletical wisdom is expressed in fragments, written in the day-to-day uncertainty of his legal status, under the weight and duress of existence as a prisoner of the Nazi state.[79]

Bonhoeffer's "theological letters" from prison, which were written in 1944 after a final plot to assassinate Hitler had failed, reflect his sharpened focus on the future in hopeful anticipation of a reconstructed church in Germany and Europe. Bonhoeffer's correspondence offers concrete reflections on a repentant church, restored and reoriented toward serving in the world and renewed in its commitment to confessing and proclaiming authentic faith in Jesus Christ. Bonhoeffer also expresses his emerging insights on the church's ministry in a "world come of age" that he perceives will require proclaiming and living a form of Christianity that is "religionless." As he writes, "What keeps gnawing at me is the question, what is Christianity, or who is Christ actually for us today? The age when we could tell people that with words—whether with theological or pious words—is past, as is the age of inwardness and of conscience, and that means the age of religion altogether."[80]

Bonhoeffer continued with this line of thinking, acknowledging how nineteen hundred years of Christian preaching and theology were built on the "religious a priori" in human beings. By this he means that people were conditioned for the need to be "religious," for its necessity as a form of human and cultural expression. Is it necessary for a person to become "spiritual" or "religious" in order to be Christian? Can Christian and fully human be one and the same existence? Can there be such a thing as a "religionless" Christian?[81] He struggled with such questions, asking, "What does a church, a congregation, a sermon, a liturgy, a Christian life, mean in a religionless world? How do we talk about God—without religion, that is, without the temporally conditioned presuppositions of metaphysics, the inner life, and so on? How do we speak (or perhaps we can no longer even 'speak' the way we used to) in a 'worldly' way about 'God'?"[82]

The prologue to the prison writings does not answer these questions, but instead it offers important glimpses into the theological perspective from which Bonhoeffer had come to view the past, present, and future of the church in Germany and the West:

> Who stands firm? Only the one whose ultimate standard is not his reason, his principles, conscience, freedom, or virtue; only the one who is prepared to sacrifice all of these when, in faith and in relationship to God alone, he is called to obedient and responsible action. Such a person is the responsible one, whose life is to be nothing but a response to God's question and call. Where are the responsible ones?[83]

Bonhoeffer continued with a discussion of success as guiding the course of history and the possibility of assuming a "heroic" stance in the face of defeat at the hands of evil. He notes, "The ultimate responsible question is not how I extricate myself heroically from a situation, but how a coming generation is to go on living. In short, it is much easier to see a situation through on the basis of principle than in concrete responsibility." He acknowledged the younger generation is able to sense when decisions are made on principle rather than from living responsibly, since "their future is at stake." His reflection echoes what he had written in *Ethics*: that the church's commission to proclaim Christ cannot resort to abstract ways of thinking and speaking but rather must offer "concrete direction in the concrete situation."

Bonhoeffer perceived that the church was decisively lacking "a greatness of heart." He recalled the vicarious ministry of Christ, who "experienced in his body the whole suffering of humanity as his own—an incomprehensibly lofty thought!" Bonhoeffer considered the reality of Christ's sufferings as providing a truthful perspective on the church's proclamation and service:

> Certainly, we are not Christ, nor are we called to redeem the world through our own deed and our own suffering. . . . We are not Christ, but if we want to be Christians it means that we are to

take part in Christ's greatness of heart, in the responsible action that in freedom lays hold of the hour and faces the danger, and in the true sympathy that springs forth not from fear but from Christ's freeing and redeeming love for all who suffer.[84]

In a telling commentary on how his way of perceiving the world, and thus the gospel, had been changed, he writes,

> It remains an experience of incomparable value that we have for once learned to see the great events of world history from below, from the perspective of the outcasts, the suspects, the maltreated, the powerless, the oppressed and reviled, in short from the perspective of the suffering. If only during this time, bitterness and envy have not corroded the heart; that we come to see matters great and small, happiness and misfortune, strength and weakness with new eyes; that our sense for greatness, humanness, justice, and mercy has grown clearer, freer, more incorruptible; that we learn, indeed, that personal suffering is a more useful key, a more fruitful principal than personal happiness for exploring the meaning of the world in contemplation and action.[85]

In May 1944, Bonhoeffer wrote a deeply personal but theological letter for the baptism of Bethge's infant son, Dietrich Wilhelm Rudiger Bethge, for whom he was named as godparent. He began by looking forward, identifying the infant Dietrich as one who would "lead the procession of the next generation." He would take his place within a span of generations reaching back to the eighteenth century and forward beyond the year 2000, thus making his baptism an occasion for reflecting "on how times change, and for trying to discern the outlines of the future."[86] Bonhoeffer expressed his confidence and joyful hope for the child's future, encouraging him to find the deep roots of his life in the soil of the past—a disposition that he perceived as making life "harder, but also richer and more rigorous." He shared his thoughts on how the changes of history had diminished the quality and character of life—that the shape of Christian faith and living had become "formless or even fragmentary."[87]

He lamented that planning for life had been in vain, how so much that had been built up was destroyed overnight. He found the words of the prophet Jeremiah quite fitting: "Thus says the Lord: I am going to break down what I have built, and pluck up what I have planted. . . . And you, do you seek great things for yourself? Do not seek them, for I am going to bring disaster upon all flesh, says the Lord; but I will give you your life as a prize of war in every place to which you may go (chap. 45)." Bonhoeffer's comments are striking: "It will be the task of our generation not to seek 'great things,' but to save and preserve our souls out of the chaos, and to realize this is the only thing we can carry as 'booty' out of the burning house." His hope was to do so for young Dietrich's generation—that they would be empowered "to plan and build up and give shape to a new and better life."[88]

He surmised that thinking had been too much of a preoccupation, a waste of time and energy which could instead have been given to responsible action. He perceived there was need for a new way of relating thought and action that would be truer to reality, but also more painful and sacrificial, since "thought must serve action and not stand in its way." He turned to the gospel: "Not everyone who *says* to me, 'Lord, Lord,' will enter the kingdom of heaven, but only one who *does* the will of my Father in heaven (Matt. 7:21)." Christians cannot evade God's judgment, and "we shall prove ourselves worthy to survive by identifying ourselves generously and selflessly with the whole community and the suffering of our fellow human beings."[89]

Bonhoeffer perceived how the baptism of an infant child reveals the true condition of the church as a creature of the Word. In baptism, "all those past and ancient words of the Christian proclamation will be pronounced over you, and the command of Jesus Christ will be carried out, without your understanding it." The church is thrown back all the way to the "beginnings of our understanding." Baptism, then, addresses the church and its commission to proclaim Jesus Christ to the world. Bonhoeffer, however, judged that the truth of the gospel had become so difficult and remote that there were only a few who dared to speak it anymore. The mystery of God's revelation, "what redemption and reconciliation mean, rebirth and the Holy Spirit, love for one's enemies, cross and resurrection, what it means to live in Christ and follow Christ," had eluded the church's grasp. What they had sensed was new and revolutionary in these words and actions, as a way of life before God, had not been expressed in the world. This failure prompted a confession: "This is our fault. Our church has been fighting during these years only for its self-preservation, as if that were an end in itself."[90]

The church's preoccupation with its own survival had obscured its vision of the reality of God and the world reconciled in Christ, and was therefore incapable of the work that was the purpose of its existence: "Bringing the word of redemption and reconciliation to humankind and the world." The failure of responsibility, to both Christ and the world, calls for repentance, a change of mind and direction. Bonhoeffer did not envision such change coming from new plans or programs, but rather from prayer and silence that listen and are obedient to the Word. Familiar words and established ways of speaking must lose their power and control. Repentance therefore means "all Christian thinking, talking, and organizing must be born anew, out of . . . prayer and action [doing justice among human beings]." The church must regain its visibility, which requires a way of life shaped by receiving, reflecting upon, and responding to the word of God. Until this happens the church's proclamation cannot be heard as credible.[91]

Bonhoeffer looked forward to a church that would be re-formed and re-molded by prayer and action—renewed as "Christian" in the depth of its soul. He discerned that working to reestablish the church as a powerful organization in a reconstructed Germany would "only delay its conversion and purification." At the same time, he looked forward to a day, without knowing the time of its advent, when "people would once more be called to speak the word of God in such a way that the world is changed and renewed." Bonhoeffer perceived that this language would be a new language, perhaps quite "non-religious," yet language spoken with power that liberates and redeems in the name of the words spoken by Jesus. Proclamation of such depth, character, and wisdom will indeed be alarming and overcoming, capable of awakening and captivating those who hear and believe by its power.[92]

Bonhoeffer expressed his deep longing for a language of preaching that would communicate a new righteousness and truth, "a language that makes peace with humankind and that God's kingdom is drawing near." However, the language of God is a gift that comes in its own time and its own way. He discerned that, for the time being, the Christian cause would need to be quiet and hidden, sustained by word and sacrament, by prayer and catechesis, by mutual love and service, thus preserving the "mysteries" of the faith. There will be people who continue to pray and do justice and wait upon God. Bonhoeffer concludes with a blessing upon young Dietrich: "May you be one of them, and may it be said of you one day: 'The path of the righteous is like the light of dawn, which shines brighter until full day' (Prov. 4:18)."[93]

Conclusion

Dietrich Bonhoeffer was a preaching theologian, a "homiletical theologian" who was convinced the visibility of the church was a necessary condition for proclaiming the gospel to the world. The visibility of the church means the body of Christ takes up physical space on earth since, by becoming human, Christ claims a place in the world. The whole narrative of the gospel provides the basis for this "evangelical" conviction. Christ was born in a manger and was crucified on a cross. Bonhoeffer thus followed the lead of Martin Luther, who exclaimed, "To this human being you shall point and say: 'Here is God.'"

Christianity is not a set of doctrines, an inward religious experience, or a list of moral rules and principles. These are "bodiless." When Christianity is reduced to abstract topics, ideals, or values and communicated on the basis of its practical, personal, or political utility, it fails to go beyond being heard, thought, felt, and understood. Concrete confession of and witness to the gospel is rendered invisible, a "Christianity without Christ." "Christianity without Christ" is Christianity without the present reality of Christ, without Christ's call and claim to discipleship, without Christ's costly grace that cost him his life for the life of the world. Preaching Christ does more than inform the mind or move the heart. The end of proclamation is to call, form, and build up a community of human beings into the great joy and humbling risk of concretely following the costly way God has made in the world through the life, death, and resurrection of Christ. As Bonhoeffer stated eloquently, "God is determined to speak in person."

The body of the incarnate, crucified, and risen Lord is made visible in taking the form of the church in the world. In the proclamation of Christ, the word of Scripture binds the church in the present with the earliest Christian communities, as the apostolic witness speaks God's Word in human words today. The Word of God is a living and life-giving word that has its own inherent movement toward and with a visible church, as "theology on the way."[1] There is no division between the Word and community as two separate entities existing in separate spheres of life—spiritual and secular, religious and worldly. Because Christ is present in proclamation, there is no need for preachers to use, manipulate, or improve upon the word to make it practically relevant and applicable for those who listen. The Word of God freely moves along a path of its own accord—the path God makes in "Christ existing as community" with the sinful, the weak, the suffering, the poor, the sick, the oppressed, the despised and disenfranchised.

The Word of God in Christ is thus spoken most credibly by those who share the humble way of the cross. Preachers must be formed as servants of the Word and not its masters. Paradoxically, the strength of preaching is found in the "weakness" of the Word. Those called to preach engage their whole selves in listening and "following after" the movement of the word of Scripture through daily habits of prayer, meditation, and exegesis to discern the will of God in Christ for today. Moreover, the efficacy of preaching, the work of the Word in the present, is accomplished by the Holy Spirit—rather than by a preacher's skill, method, style, personality, and persuasiveness. Faith that comes by hearing is a gift of the Spirit that enables listeners to believe that, in the words of the sermon, Jesus Christ himself comes to be present in the congregation, mercifully gathering and bearing its life in compassionate service with the world.

The whole of Bonhoeffer's career, as a preacher and teacher of preachers, demonstrates an increasingly courageous commitment to proclaiming the gospel that he understood theologically, as a "homiletical theologian." Homiletical theology unites doctrine, historical confessions, scriptural meditation, and moral reflection in the proclamation of Christ, who summons the church to faithful obedience in the world. Preachers are thus called to test both the church's confession and the practice of the gospel against the Word of God revealed in the whole of Scripture. Truthful preaching cannot be practiced in principle, but it is spoken concretely in accord with the reality of God and the world as loved, judged, and reconciled in Christ.

Notes

Preface and Acknowledgments

1 I have attempted to address the topic of "homiletic theology" in Michael Pasquarello III, *Sacred Rhetoric: Preaching as a Theological and Pastoral Practice of the Church* (2005; repr., Eugene, Ore.: Wipf & Stock, 2012); *Christian Preaching: A Trinitarian Theology of Proclamation* (2006; repr., Eugene, Ore.: Wipf & Stock, 2011); *We Speak Because We Have First Been Spoken: A "Grammar" of the Preaching Life* (Grand Rapids: Eerdmans, 2009).

2 See Isabel Best's editor's Introduction in *The Collected Sermons of Dietrich Bonhoeffer*, ed. Isabel Best, trans. Douglas W. Stott et al. (Minneapolis: Fortress, 2012), xiii–xxvi. I was also encouraged by several earlier works that called attention to Bonhoeffer's sermons and thinking about preaching, particularly Clyde E. Fant, ed., *Bonhoeffer: Worldly Preaching* (Nashville: Thomas Nelson, 1975); Edwin Robertson, *The Shame and the Sacrifice: The Life and Martyrdom of Dietrich Bonhoeffer* (New York: Scribner, 1988); Frits de Lange, *Waiting for the Word: Dietrich Bonhoeffer on Speaking about God*, trans. Martin N. Walton (Grand Rapids: Eerdmans, 1995).

3 Randi Rashkover, "The Future of the Word and the Liturgical Turn," in *Liturgy, Time, and the Politics of Redemption*, ed. Randi Rashkover and C. C. Pecknold (Grand Rapids: Eerdmans, 2006), 3–4.

4 Charles Marsh writes, "Bonhoeffer did not become a practical theologian as such, at least in the sense in which that term is sometimes used to describe a theological field separate from systematic or philosophical theology; although I would say that the kind of writing he forged in the crucible of the church struggle points us toward a style of theological writing beyond conventional types, or perhaps one that moves us closer to the truth of things: a theology that confesses, that preaches, that prays, that rejoices, that proclaims the Amen and the Yes, that encourages and

sustains the redemptive practices of the church; a theology, which even should the church fall into ruins, cleaves to the mysteries of Christ's presence in the world." Marsh, "Bonhoeffer on the Road to King: 'Turning from the Phraseological to the Real,'" in *Bonhoeffer and King: Their Legacies and Import for Christian Social Thought*, ed. Willis Jenkins and Jennifer M. McBride (Minneapolis: Fortress, 2010), 137.

Introduction

1   Eberhard Bethge, *Dietrich Bonhoeffer: Theologian, Christian, Contemporary* (London: Collins, 1970), 174.

2   Stephen R. Haynes' study includes "the radical Bonhoeffer," "the liberal Bonhoeffer," "the conservative Bonhoeffer," and "the universal Bonhoeffer." Haynes, *The Bonhoeffer Phenomenon: Portraits of a Protestant Saint* (Minneapolis: Fortress, 2004).

3   This argument has been made by Haynes in *The Bonhoeffer Phenomenon*.

4   John W. de Gruchy, "The Reception of Bonhoeffer's Theology," in *The Cambridge Companion to Dietrich Bonhoeffer*, ed. John W. de Gruchy, Cambridge Companions to Religion (Cambridge: Cambridge University Press, 1999), 93–94 (emphasis in original).

5   On the chronology of Bonhoeffer's writings in relation to his theological development, see Wayne Whitson Floyd Jr., "Bonhoeffer's Literary Legacy," in de Gruchy, *Cambridge Companion*, 71–92.

6   A recent example of this approach is Andrew Root, *Bonhoeffer as Youth Worker: A Theological Vision for Discipleship and Life Together* (Grand Rapids: Baker Academic, 2014).

7   See Keith L. Johnson, "Bonhoeffer and the End of the Christian Academy," in *Bonhoeffer, Christ, and Culture*, ed. Keith L. Johnson and Timothy Larsen (Downers Grove, Ill.: IVP Academic, 2013), 153–74.

8   Rashkover, "Future of the Word," 3–4.

9   This argument has been made by Haynes in *The Bonhoeffer Phenomenon*.

10   See Best's editor's introduction in *Collected Sermons of Dietrich Bonhoeffer*, xiii–xxvi. For an older, but still informative, introduction to Bonhoeffer's thought on preaching, especially his homiletical lectures, see Fant, *Bonhoeffer*. It is interesting to note that the *Cambridge Companion to Dietrich Bonhoeffer* does not include a chapter on Bonhoeffer's homiletical work.

11   A good example is the best-selling biography by Eric Metaxas that portrays Bonhoeffer as an "evangelical" but contains no references to preaching in its index. Metaxas, *Bonhoeffer: Pastor, Martyr, Prophet, Spy* (Nashville: Thomas Nelson, 2010). For a historical survey of evangelical appropriations of Bonhoeffer, see Timothy Larsen, "The Evangelical Reception of Dietrich Bonhoeffer," in *Bonhoeffer, Christ and Culture*, ed. Keith L. Johnson and Timothy Larsen (Downers Grove, Ill.: IVP Academic, 2013), 39–57.

12   *Dietrich Bonhoeffer Works: Act and Being; Transcendental Philosophy and Ontology in Systematic Theology*, ed. Wayne Whitson Floyd Jr., trans. H. Martin Rumscheidt, Dietrich Bonhoeffer Works (English) 2 (Minneapolis: Fortress, 1996), 133. Hereafter the volume information will be abbreviated as DBWE. DBWE volumes are cited in the notes and bibliography by editor and volume title.

13   Charles Marsh writes, "Bonhoeffer did not become a practical theologian as such, at least in the sense in which that term is sometimes used to describe a theological field separate from systematic or philosophical theology; although I would say that the kind of writing he forged in the crucible of the church struggle points us toward a style of theological writing beyond the conventional types, or perhaps moves us closer to the truth of things: a theology that confesses, that preaches, that prays, that rejoices, that proclaims the Amen and the Yes, that encourages and sustains the redemptive practices of the church; a theology, which even should the church fall into ruins, cleaves to the mysteries of Christ's presence in the world." Marsh, "Bonhoeffer on the Road to King: 'Turning from the Phraseological to the Real,'" in Jenkins and McBride, *Bonhoeffer and King*, 137.

14   I have attempted to address the topic of "homiletic theology" in *Sacred Rhetoric*; *Christian Preaching*; and *We Speak Because We Have First Been Spoken*.

15   *Dietrich Bonhoeffer Works: Barcelona, Berlin, New York, 1928–1931*, ed. Clifford J. Green, trans. Douglas W. Stott, DBWE 10 (Minneapolis: Fortress, 2008), 128.

16   I am indebted to David Schnasa Jacobsen for the term "theology on the way." See Jacobsen's introduction to *Homiletical Theology: Preaching as Doing Theology*, ed. Jacobsen, The Promise of Homiletical Theology 1 (Eugene, Ore.: Cascade, 2015), 5.

17   Robert W. Jenson writes of the Trinitarian nature of the conversation: "As the church speaks and hears the gospel and as the church responds in prayer and confession, the church's life is a great conversation, and this conversation is our anticipatory participation in the converse of the Father and the Son in the Spirit; as the church is enlivened and empowered by this hearing and answering, the inspiration is by none other than the Spirit who is the life between the Father and the Son." Jenson, *Systematic Theology*, vol. 1, *The Triune God* (Oxford: Oxford University Press, 1997), 228.

18   I have discussed the participatory nature of the homiletic tradition in *Sacred Rhetoric*. Joseph Dunne follows Alasdair MacIntyre in demonstrating the importance of tradition, language, and ethos for learning, participating in, and teaching a practice. Dunne, *Back to the Rough Ground: Practical Judgment and the Lure of Technique* (Notre Dame, Ind.: University of Notre Dame Press, 1993), 370–78; from a theological perspective on tradition, see Stephen R. Holmes, *Listening to the Past: The Pace of Tradition in Theology*

(Grand Rapids: Baker Academic, 2002); and Rowan Williams, *Why Study the Past? The Quest for the Historical Church* (Grand Rapids: Eerdmans, 2005).

19   *Dietrich Bonhoeffer Works: Ecumenical, Academic, and Pastoral Work, 1931–1932*, ed. Victoria J. Barnett, Mark S. Brocker, and Michael B. Lukens, trans. Douglas W. Stott, DBWE 11 (Minneapolis: Fortress, 2012), 443.

20   This aspect of Bonhoeffer's work is given extensive attention in Joshua Kaiser, *Becoming Simple and Wise: Moral Discernment in Dietrich Bonhoeffer's Vision of Christian Ethics* (Eugene, Ore.: Pickwick, 2015).

21   *Dietrich Bonhoeffer Works*: Sanctorum Communio; *A Theological Study of the Sociology of the Church*, ed. Clifford J. Green, trans. Reinhard Krauss and Nancy Lukens, DBWE 1 (Minneapolis: Fortress, 1998), 122.

22   DBWE 11:316.

23   See the recent biography of Bonhoeffer by Charles Marsh, *Strange Glory: A Life of Dietrich Bonhoeffer* (New York: Alfred A. Knopf, 2014).

24   *Dietrich Bonhoeffer Works: London, 1933–1935*, ed. Keith Clements, trans. Isabel Best, DBWE 13 (Minneapolis: Fortress, 2007).

25   Kaiser, *Becoming Simple and Wise*, 88–91; see the discussion of Bonhoeffer's incarnational/theological hermeneutic in Jen Zimmerman, *Recovering Theological Hermeneutics: An Incarnational-Trinitarian Theory of Interpretation* (Grand Rapids: Baker Academic, 2004), 274–84; idem, *Incarnational Humanism: A Philosophy of Culture for the Church in the World* (Downers Grove, Ill.: IVP Academic, 2012), 267–320. On Bonhoeffer's hermeneutical way of thinking, see Michael P. DeJonge, "Bonhoeffer from the Perspective of Intellectual History," in *Interpreting Bonhoeffer: Historical Perspectives, Emerging Issues*, ed. Clifford J. Green and Guy C. Carter (Minneapolis: Fortress, 2013), 197–204.

26   *Dietrich Bonhoeffer Works: Theological Education at Finkenwalde, 1935–1937*, ed. H. Gaylon Barker and Mark S. Brocker, trans. Douglas W. Stott, DBWE 14 (Minneapolis: Fortress, 2013), 509–10. Here I find it illuminating to read Bonhoeffer's incarnational/theological vision of preaching and the church in relation to the work of philosopher Charles Taylor, who describes at length the uneasiness of late modern people with being in the flesh and thereby dependent, vulnerable, and destined to die. Taylor names this condition "ex-carnation" and states, "We have to struggle to recover a sense of what the Incarnation can mean." See Taylor, *A Secular Age* (Cambridge, Mass.: Harvard University Press, 2007), 753.

27   An insightful discussion of Bonhoeffer's interpretation of Scripture as a "path" and "way" is provided by Brian Brock, *Singing the Ethos of God: On the Place of Christian Ethics in Scripture* (Grand Rapids: Eerdmans, 2007), 71–95. Brock comments on Bonhoeffer's reading of the Psalms: "The whole Bible claims our whole being, or rather, God uses the space and diversity of the scriptural commands to make us aware that we exist only within the sphere of his rule. We come to possess Scripture as we develop knowledge of Christ in the form of lived certainty." Brock, *Singing the Ethos of God*,

85. I agree with John Webster's assessment of Bonhoeffer's interpretation of Scripture: that it became increasingly theological and practical, oriented by the place of the Bible as the church's book as generated by God's revelation in Christ. See Webster, *Word and Church: Essays in Christian Dogmatics* (New York: T&T Clark, 2001), 87–110.

28 DBWE 13:323.

29 One of the primary translators of the English edition of *Dietrich Bonhoeffer Works* writes, "Even at the height of his most abstract thinking, Bonhoeffer never makes a separation between academic theology and the practice of the church. Bonhoeffer's theological program is at once intellectually demanding, spiritually challenging, and eminently practical. At its very core, Bonhoeffer's theology presses toward the practice of the church as the embodied and worldly presence of Christ." Reinhard Krauss, "Discovering Bonhoeffer in Translation: New Insights from the Bonhoeffer Works, English Edition," in Green and Carter, *Interpreting Bonhoeffer*, 77.

30 Stanley Hauerwas has written about the form of theology and its need for concreteness, which was certainly a concern for Bonhoeffer. Hauerwas asserts, "There is no method that can free theology of the necessity to respond to the challenges of trying to discern what being a Christian entails in this place and at this time. There is no prolegomena for all future theology. Indeed there is no prolegomena period. It is performance all the way down. Thus my presumption that letters, sermons, and essays may well be the central genres for theological reflection." Hauerwas, *The Work of Theology* (Grand Rapids: Eerdmans, 2015), 24.

31 *Dietrich Bonhoeffer Works: Ethics*, ed. Clifford J. Green, trans. Reinhard Krauss, Charles C. West, and Douglas W. Stott, DBWE 6 (Minneapolis: Fortress, 2009), 92–93.

32 David Jacobsen draws from Luke 24, the narrative of two disciples conversing with the risen Christ on the road to Emmaus, to show the nature of preaching as "theology on the way." Jacobsen, introduction to *Homiletical Theology*, 4–5.

33 Dunne follows Alasdair MacIntyre in demonstrating the importance of tradition, language, and ethos for learning, participating in, and teaching a practice. Dunne, *Back to the Rough Ground*, 370–78; from a theological perspective on tradition, Holmes, *Listening to the Past*; and Williams, *Why Study the Past?*

34 DBWE 2:129.

35 See Holmes' discussion on the importance of acknowledging historical place and human limitations in God's providential ordering of history, including the handing on of Scripture in Christian tradition. Holmes, *Listening to the Past*, 12–13. Stanley Hauerwas writes, "Of course the story that is Dietrich Bonhoeffer is complex. Bonhoeffer's agency is to be found in how he negotiated [the] complex narratives that made him Dietrich Bonhoeffer. That 'agency' is surely to be found in the story that came to him

through the church." Hauerwas, *Work of Theology*, 88. An encouraging development in Bonhoeffer research is the growing interest in his intellectual formation and the influence of theologians and philosophers, both past and contemporary, on his thought. See Peter Frick, ed., *Bonhoeffer's Intellectual Formation: Theology and Philosophy in His Thought*, Religion in Philosophy and Theology 29 (Tubingen: Mohr Siebeck, 2008).

36 See Rowan Williams' description of church history as a "spiritual discipline." Williams, *Why Study the Past?* 110–13.

37 DBWE 10:385.

38 I am indebted for my understanding of this matter to Stanley Hauerwas, *Performing the Faith: Bonhoeffer and the Practice of Nonviolence* (Grand Rapids: Brazos, 2004), 34.

39 *Dietrich Bonhoeffer Works: Letters and Papers from Prison*, ed. John W. de Gruchy, trans. Reinhard Krauss, Nancy Lukens, Lisa E. Dahill, and Isabel Best, DBWE 8 (Minneapolis: Fortress, 2010), 389. The poet Wendell Berry calls such integrity of language and life "standing by words." He writes, "We are speaking where we stand, and we shall stand afterwards in the presence of what we have said." Berry, *Standing by Words: Essays by Wendell Berry* (Washington, D.C.: Shoemaker & Howard, 1983), 62.

1: Learning a Theology of Preaching from Luther and Barth

1 Eberhard Bethge, *Dietrich Bonhoeffer: A Biography*, rev. and ed. Victoria J. Barnett (Minneapolis: Fortress, 2000), 66: "At the onset of his studies in Berlin, his impetuous thirst for knowledge still lacked direction. The broad horizon of Berlin's liberal and 'positivist' school of theology, embodied by its great teachers, opened before him. At the end of this period, Bonhoeffer had proven himself through his own considerable scholarly achievement, and he had completed an incredible amount of work. The decisive turning point occurred in midyear, when he succumbed to the fascination of dialectical theology; he arrived at this by way of literary detour. He was eighteen at the time." I have also drawn from the following biographical accounts: Ferdinand Schlingensiepen, *Dietrich Bonhoeffer 1906–1945: Martyr, Thinker, Man of Resistance* (New York: T&T Clark, 2010), 18–37; Marsh, *Strange Glory*, 41–61.

2 I am indebted to Stanley Hauerwas for this description of Bonhoeffer's persistent theological and ecclesial concerns. He writes, "Bonhoeffer's work from beginning to end was the attempt to reclaim the visibility of the church as the necessary condition for the proclamation of the gospel in a world that no longer privileged Christianity." Hauerwas, *Performing the Faith*, 34.

3 On the University of Berlin, see the following: Thomas Albert Howard, *Protestant Theology and the Making of the Modern German University* (Oxford: Oxford University Press, 2006); Hans W. Frei, *Types of Christian*

Theology, ed. George Hunsinger and William C. Placher (New Haven: Yale University Press, 1992), 95–132; Gavin D'Costa, *Theology in the Public Square: Church, Academy, and Nation* (Oxford: Blackwell, 2005), 15–20. D'Costa describes the place of theology in the modern university as "theology's Babylonian captivity." He suggests that if theology is to escape from the captivity, from the market and the nation state, it will be only as theologians "learn to pray as part of their vocation" (112). See the discussion below of Bonhoeffer's turn to Luther, who claimed his vocation was constituted by "prayer and the dear word of God."

4   Howard, *Protestant Theology*, 16–28.

5   John A. Moses, "Bonhoeffer's Germany: The Political Context," in de Gruchy, *Cambridge Companion*, 13–14.

6   See Frei's discussion of Harnack and Barth in *Types of Christian Theology*, 116–18. Frei suggests the heart of the argument focused on whether figures such as Paul or Luther could be studied only as objects of historical research or as speaking, acting subjects. Like Barth, Bonhoeffer pursued the latter option.

7   Cited in Howard, *Protestant Theology*, 405–15. For an excellent discussion of the conflict, see George Hunsinger, "The Harnack/Barth Correspondence: A Paraphrase with Comments," in *Disruptive Grace: Studies in the Theology of Karl Barth* (Grand Rapids: Eerdmans, 2000), 319–37. Hunsinger concludes, "It seems fair to suggest that Harnack was incapable of recognizing Barth's theological proposals as legitimate, ultimately because what Barth was proposing vis-à-vis Harnack was a revolutionary theological paradigm. . . . Barth's arose in an attempt to explain certain anomalies and to avoid them. The anomalies were basically two: theologians who defended a war of aggression; a theological method which eviscerated the content of the gospel. The radical explanation was that both depended at bottom on making anthropological phenomena the condition for the possibility of talking about God" (336–37). I want to argue that what I am calling Bonhoeffer's developing "homiletical theology" follows the same path as Barth with important Lutheran distinctions.

8   Bethge, *Dietrich Bonhoeffer: A Biography*, 74–75: "It was only now that he found genuine joy in theology. It was like a real liberation. The mere fact that the new theology took its start from a task as unmistakable as preaching . . . tore him away from the games of speculation. Bonhoeffer was arrested by the fact that Barth pulled attention away from the facts of humanity that had been laid bare so disastrously in that generation." For a concise summary of Barth's influence on Bonhoeffer, see Andreas Pangritz, "Dietrich Bonhoeffer: 'Within, Not outside the Barthian Movement,'" in Frick, *Bonhoeffer's Intellectual Formation*, 245–82. The next chapter will take up the Barth/Bonhoeffer relation more extensively.

9   Hauerwas, *Performing the Faith*, 38; Martin Rumscheidt, "The Formation of Bonhoeffer's Theology," in de Gruchy, *Cambridge Companion*, 61–64;

Michael P. DeJonge, *Bonhoeffer's Theological Formation: Berlin, Barth, &*
Protestant Theology (Oxford: Oxford University Press, 2012), 36–68; Wolf
Krötke writes, "An examination of Dietrich Bonhoeffer's theology in relation to that of Martin Luther . . . entails an appreciation of all of Bonhoeffer's theology. For Luther is present more than anyone else at every stage
of his path and in every dimension of his thought." See Krötke, "Dietrich
Bonhoeffer and Martin Luther," in Frick, *Bonhoeffer's Intellectual Forma-*
tion, 53–82.

10   *Dietrich Bonhoeffer Works: The Young Bonhoeffer, 1918–1927*, ed. Paul
Duane Matheny, Clifford J. Green, and Marshall D. Johnson, trans. Mary
C. Nebelsick, DBWE 9 (Minneapolis: Fortress, 2003), 451–55.

11   DBWE 9:452–53.

12   DBWE 9:453.

13   DBWE 9:454–56.

14   DBWE 9:453.

15   DBWE 9:454–56.

16   Krötke, "Dietrich Bonhoeffer and Martin Luther," 60–63: "To 'return to
the real Luther' was his objective in studying the Reformer and guided his
lifelong theological orientation towards him."

17   DBWE 9:451.

18   In the following discussion of preaching in Germany, I am indebted to
the work of Angela Dienhart Hancock, *Karl Barth's Emergency Homiletic,*
1932–1933: A Summons to Prophetic Witness at the Dawn of the Third Reich
(Grand Rapids: Eerdmans, 2013), 139–65.

19   Stanley Hauerwas comments on the role of the university in serving the
state: "The university is the institution of legitimation in modernity whose
task is to convince us that the way things are is the way things have to
be. The specialization, what some would describe as fragmentation, of
the knowledges that constitute the curriculums of the modern university
is critical for the formation of people to be faithful servants of the status
quo and, in particular, the modern nation state." Hauerwas, *The State of*
the University: Academic Knowledges and the Knowledge of God (London:
Blackwell, 2007), 8. Given the state of things in Germany during Bonhoeffer's student years, his theological and homiletical turn was even more
remarkable.

20   As Hancock states, the preacher was seen as "a species of virtuoso, akin to
an artist or poet." Hancock, *Karl Barth's Emergency Homiletic*, 139–43. L.
Roger Owens explains, "Religious feeling presupposes communicability,
first expressed in the immediacy of gestures and expression, but receiving
in time enough cultivation to be expressed verbally. . . . Doctrine for Schleiermacher is the cultivated outward expression of these religious emotions;
and preaching as the re-presentation of these doctrines in a rhetorical
mode that endeavors to elicit religious emotion, the highest of which is a
feeling of dependence." Owens, *The Shape of Participation: A Theology of*

Church Practices (Eugene, Ore.: Cascade, 2010), 68–69. Owens argues that this method of preaching, emphasizing an "inner/outer" dualism, continues to be very influential in North American churches. The problem, however, is that making the task of preaching anthropological rather than theological "robs us of any way to understand how the church's practice of preaching implicates the church in the life of God. Insufficiently corporate and insufficiently christological, these accounts of preaching, which focus on rousing the religious emotion of the individual, make it impossible to see the church's practice of preaching as a practice of participation in the life of God and a practice by which the church practices its own identity, its own existence in the world" (73). See the extensive theological critique of modern homiletics that give central place to human experience in Charles L. Campbell, *Preaching Jesus: The New Directions for Homiletics in Hans Frei's Postliberal Theology* (Grand Rapids: Eerdmans, 1997), 117–88.

21 Cited in Owens, *Shape of Participation*, 70. Frei considers the implication for biblical interpretation that flows from Schleiermacher's theology. He sees the latter's correlation of Christian language and Christian experience as reducing the Bible to a historical and textual representation or illustration of pious God consciousness and experience that does not allow for the mediation of an external word. See Frei, *Types of Christian Theology*, 82–84.

22 Hancock, *Karl Barth's Emergency Homiletic*, 165: "[The decade] of the 1920's began with a Protestant church in crisis. More than ever it needed to assert its relevance, slow the tide of church defections, and preach Christian values to the nation even as it worked to bind up the wounds of those mourning fallen sons, the lost monarchy, and the now distant spirit of 1914. Many Protestant preachers undertook these tasks using the homiletical ethos that came with 'modern preaching.' . . . Indeed, in many ways it was well suited to the needs of the day."

23 Hancock, *Karl Barth's Emergency Homiletic*, 164–65.

24 "The most consequential among these structures and emphases were the sequestration of theology, a commitment to research, an emphasis on the self, and a reliance on the state. . . . The quarantining of theology institutionalized Kant's argument in his *Conflict of the Faculties* (1798) that philosophy—as the expression of autonomous reason and human freedom—should be liberated from the confining constraints of dogmatic theology." Brad S. Gregory, *The Unintended Reformation: How a Religious Revolution Secularized Society* (Cambridge, Mass.: Belknap Press of Harvard University Press, 2012), 348–49.

25 See the excellent discussion, "What Karl Barth Learned from Martin Luther," in Hunsinger, *Disruptive Grace*, 293–304. Eberhard Busch comments that the early Barth "rediscovered" Luther through his study of Romans. Busch, *The Great Passion: An Introduction to Karl Barth's Theology*, ed. Darrell L. Guder and Judith J. Guder, trans. Geoffrey W. Bromiley (Grand Rapids: Eerdmans, 2004), 22. See also the recent argument

concerning Barth's ambivalence toward Luther in Rustin E. Brian, *Covering Up Luther: How Barth's Christology Challenged the* Deus Absconditus *that Haunts Modernity* (Eugene, Ore.: Cascade, 2015).

26 Cited in Hunsinger, *Disruptive Grace*, 293.

27 Hunsinger notes, "Perhaps one way to appreciate the powerful impact on Barth of the primacy Luther assigned to God's Word would be to say that it led Barth, almost alone among modern theologians, to grant uncompromising precedence to the Reformation over modernity itself. Barth took Luther extremely seriously that, apart from God's Word, ultimate reality cannot possibly be known, and that it can be apprehended by faith alone. Barth by no means rejected modernity, but he accepted it only on Luther's grounds." Hunsinger, *Disruptive Grace*, 293. I am suggesting Bonhoeffer's discovery of Barth during his student years was deeply influential for the way he approached his study of Luther, particularly in relation to the interpretations of Luther by his teachers Karl Holl and Reinhold Seeberg.

28 DBWE 1. For the influence of Holl and Seeberg on Bonhoeffer's study of Luther, see Rumscheidt, "Formation of Bonhoeffer's Theology," 55–61; DeJonge, *Bonhoeffer's Theological Formation*, 83–128; see also Martin Rumscheidt, "The Significance of Adolf von Harnack and Reinhold Seeberg for Dietrich Bonhoeffer," in Frick, *Bonhoeffer's Intellectual Formation*, 202–9. Rumscheidt's essay shows that Seeberg's interest in Bonhoeffer's work was significant, as was his example of constant engagement with philosophy and sociology. Rumscheidt also comments on why Bonhoeffer was unable to follow Seeberg's optimistic views in theology and anthropology.

29 DBWE 9:257–84.

30 DBWE 9:300.

31 DBWE 9:276.

32 DBWE 9:262–63. Here, Bonhoeffer may be alluding to Luther's "Preface to the Wittenberg Edition of Luther's German Writings": "I want to point out to you the correct way of studying theology. . . . This is the way taught by holy King David . . . in the one hundred nineteenth Psalm. There you will find three rules, amply presented through the whole Psalm. They are *oratio, meditatio, tentatio* (prayer, meditation, temptation)." Timothy F. Lull, "Preface to the Wittenberg Edition of Luther's German Writings (1539)," in *Martin Luther's Basic Theological Writings*, ed. Lull (Minneapolis: Fortress, 1989), 68. This topic will be treated more thoroughly in subsequent chapters.

33 DBWE 9:268.

34 DBWE 9:284.

35 See the insightful discussion of Harnack's academic and personal influence on Bonhoeffer in Rumscheidt, "Significance of Adolf von Harnack," 209–24.

36 DBWE 9:285.

37 DBWE 9:286.

38 Michael C. Legaspi, *The Death of Scripture and the Rise of Biblical Studies* (Oxford: Oxford University Press, 2010), 25: "The chief characteristics of modern biblical scholarship . . . were preoccupation with the textuality of the Bible, qualification of its authority, a turn to referential theories of meaning, and a focus on the world *of* the Bible (rather than the world as seen *through* the Bible)" (emphasis in original).

39 DBWE 9:287.

40 DBWE 9:292–93.

41 Lull, *Martin Luther's Basic Theological Writings*, 113.

42 See Fred W. Meuser, "Luther as Preacher of the Word of God," in *The Cambridge Companion to Martin Luther*, ed. Donald K. McKim, Cambridge Companions to Religion (Cambridge: Cambridge University Press, 2003), 136–48. See also Jaroslav Pelikan, *Luther the Expositor: Introduction to the Reformer's Exegetical Writings*, Companion Volume in Luther's Works (St. Louis: Concordia, 1959); the American edition of Martin Luther, *Luther's Works*, ed. Jaroslav J. Pelikan and Helmut T. Lehmann, 55 vols. (St. Louis: Concordia, 1955–1986). "Luther lived by the Word of God; he lived for the Word of God. It is no mistake then, when interpreters of Luther take the doctrine of the Word of God as one of the most important single keys to his theology." Pelikan, *Luther the Expositor*, 48, cited in Zimmerman, *Recovering Theological Hermeneutics*. Zimmerman adds, "The proclamation's motivation is love and its message is redemption and life for fallen humankind, the creation of a new humanity. Luther's concept of the Word, then, progresses from the inner conversation of God with its creative power outward to the redemptive incarnated Word which God converses in the flesh, face to face, as it were, with his creature." *Recovering Theological Hermeneutics*, 54, 47–77.

43 DBWE 9:293–94.

44 DBWE 9:297–98.

45 DBWE 9:325–69.

46 DBWE 9:336.

47 DBWE 9:336–38.

48 DBWE 9:358.

49 DBWE 9:338–39.

50 DBWE 9:363–65.

51 DBWE 9:367–68.

52 Bernd Wannenwetsch, *Political Worship: Ethics for Christian Citizens*, trans. Margaret Kohl (Oxford: Oxford University Press, 2004), 67–68. See also Wannenwetsch's discussion of Luther on language and worship in the Spirit as a "form of life." Language is guided by the "grammar of the Spirit" (33–41).

53 DBWE 1.

54 DBWE 1:21.

55 DBWE 1:134.

56 Stanley Hauerwas writes, "From Bonhoeffer's perspective Troeltsch is but one of the most powerful representatives of the Protestant liberal presumption that the gospel is purely religious, encompassing the outlook of the individual, but is indifferent and unconcerned with worldly institutions." Hauerwas, *Performing the Faith*, 40.

57 DBWE 1:24–26. See Clifford J. Green, "Human Sociality and Christian Community," in de Gruchy, *Cambridge Companion*, 113–23. For a good discussion of the importance of this work, see Green's editor's introduction and Joachim von Soosten's editor's afterword in DBWE 1:1–20, 290–306.

58 DBWE 1:144.

59 Hauerwas, *Performing the Faith*, 34.

60 DBWE 1:146–52.

61 DBWE 1:157–58.

62 DBWE 1:199.

63 "The Blessed Sacrament of the Holy and True Body and Blood of Christ and the Brotherhoods," in Lull, *Martin Luther's Basic Theological Writings*, 245, 251.

64 Wannenwetsch, *Political Worship*, 54–55.

65 *The Large Catechism of Martin Luther*, trans. Robert H. Fischer (Philadelphia: Fortress, 1959), 61.

66 DBWE 1:227 (emphasis in original).

67 DBWE 1:208, 216.

68 DBWE 1:227–37. Following the work of Alasdair MacIntyre on practices, Stanley Hauerwas argues for the practice of preaching as a social activity. "Preaching, I believe, is such a practice since it is essential to the church's very being. The church preaches because by its very nature it cannot do otherwise. Preaching is not an activity done for some other purpose, some other reason, that is not already intrinsic to preaching itself. . . . Preaching is not what a preacher does, but rather is the activity of the whole community. Preaching as practice is the activity of the church that requires the church to be able listeners, as well-schooled and well-crafted hearers, as the preacher is the proclaimer." Hauerwas, *Sanctify Them in the Truth: Holiness Exemplified* (Nashville: Abingdon, 1998), 236–37. See also Dunne, *Back to the Rough Ground*, 357–92.

69 DBWE 1:265–69.

70 DBWE 9:540–51.

71 DBWE 9:544–45.

72 DBWE 9:546–47.

73 DBWE 9:547.

74 DBWE 9:549.

75 DBWE 9:548.

76 DBWE 9:550–51.

77   DBWE 9:551. Hauerwas comments, "For preaching to be a practice intrinsic to the worship of God requires that the preacher, as well as the congregation, stand under the authority of the Word. . . . The exercise of the ministry of proclamation requires the minister to make clear that the Word preached is as painful to him/her as it is to the congregation. Such an acknowledgment makes clear that preaching is not just another speech but rather the way this people here, including the preacher, is formed into the Word of God." Hauerwas, *Sanctify Them*, 237. It is by this manner of speaking that Bonhoeffer's sermon might be described as "prophetic."

78   DBWE 9:185.

79   Alasdair MacIntyre describes growing into a historical practice as learning to make judgments or distinctions regarding what is truly good for a particular practice in the present: "It is the possession and transmission of this kind of ability to recognize in the past what is and what is not a guide to the future which is at the core of any adequately embodied tradition. A craft [such as preaching] in good order has to be embodied in a tradition in good order. And to be adequately initiated into a craft is to be adequately initiated into a tradition." MacIntyre, *Three Rival Versions of Moral Enquiry: Encyclopedia, Genealogy, and Tradition* (Notre Dame, Ind.: University of Notre Dame Press, 1990), 127–28.

2: Reconciling Pastoral Ministry with Preaching

1   Karl Barth, *Church Dogmatics*, ed. G. W. Bromiley and T. F. Torrance, trans. G. T. Thompson (Edinburgh: T&T Clark, 1956–1977), IV/2, 641.

2   Eberhard Bethge writes of this time: "Bonhoeffer's year as an assistant pastor took him to a completely new environment. He felt he was 'starting from the beginning.' . . . His new position brought him into contact with a kind of person unfamiliar to him. In [Berlin], he had no contact with the type represented by these Germans living abroad: businesspeople with a petit bourgeois outlook. . . . Until then, Bonhoeffer had lived in an academic world, where every week he could choose from what the worlds of the theater, music, and literature had to offer. Daily meals had been accompanied by well-informed conversation about political or philosophical matters. Now he was suddenly cut off from all this, and had little time even to keep up correspondence with the world he knew." Bethge, *Dietrich Bonhoeffer: A Biography*, 97.

3   DBWE 10:57.

4   DBWE 10:58. Clifford J. Green has pointed to the relative neglect of Bonhoeffer's early years in interpretations of his theology, noting that Bonhoeffer is largely read and remembered in light of his later works from the last years of his life, particularly the time of imprisonment: "First, this period has a professional and vocational unity. It can be described as Bonhoeffer's academic period. The period of his early theology covers his

years as a university theologian, first as a student and then as a professor.
By 'academic' I do not suggest that Bonhoeffer was an ivory tower intellectual whose thought was quite unrelated to personal and social concerns; indeed the opposite is the case. . . . I mean rather to emphasize that
his primary professional activity was academic—as a graduate student,
a post-doctoral scholar at Union Theological Seminary, and a teacher at
the University of Berlin." Green contends that attending to Bonhoeffer's
early years in academic work, which cannot be separated from his practical training and preaching, is necessary for understanding Bonhoeffer's
theological pilgrimage as a whole. I would add that understanding Bonhoeffer's formation as a preaching theologian and teacher of preachers, or
homiletical theologian, which increasingly characterized his work from
1933 forward, requires careful attention to his experience of seeking to
integrate theology and practice during the years 1927–1933. See Green,
Bonhoeffer: A Theology of Sociality, rev. ed. (Grand Rapids: Eerdmans,
1999), 4–5.

5   DBWE 10:63–64. On the importance of Bonhoeffer's work with children
and young people, see Root, *Bonhoeffer as Youth Worker*: "For these three
years [1925–1927] it was his ministerial responsibility to not only teach
(preach to) the children but to also help others prepare their lessons. Bonhoeffer met every Friday night at Pastor Karl Meumann's home to craft the
Sunday school lessons. On Sunday mornings Bonhoeffer led the catechism
classes, becoming known for his energetic children's sermons, in which
he never failed to tell stories with drama and flair, blending the Bible with
analogies and imaginative hooks" (57). Root's study of Bonhoeffer's work
in youth ministry points to an important element in learning to preach:
that of practical wisdom that is borne out of engagement with others for
particular ends.

6   Root discusses the war and its effects on the Bonhoeffer family, especially
the death of Bonhoeffer's elder brother, Walter. Root, *Bonhoeffer as Youth
Worker*, 33–35.

7   DBWE 10:64.

8   Edward Farley describes this as "practical theology" and "theology stirred
into existence as believers struggle for clarity and understanding." He offers
a historical overview of this way of making sense of faith in the church and
its subsequent loss: "Throughout the medieval period and the early centuries of Protestantism, theology meant simply the knowledge of God and
the things of God. Because that knowledge had to do with salvation, it was
a practical knowledge, a 'habit' (habitus) of wisdom: that is, a fundamental
way of being disposed toward things. . . . In the European Enlightenment,
especially in Germany, a new kind of university arose and with it came
the notion that a university is organized by 'sciences'; that is, by discrete,
corporate bodies of knowledge and inquiry, each with its jargon, methods of research, and distinctive subject matter. . . . After this narrowing,

academics and clergy, not believers, were the theologians." Farley, *Practicing Gospel: Unconventional Thoughts on the Church's Ministry* (Louisville, Ky.: Westminster John Knox, 2003), 3–4. Bonhoeffer's year in Barcelona, which he perceived as effecting a "humanistic" turn in his theology, was the beginning of a theological reorientation that occurred through his immersion in the social relations of congregational faith as practiced and understood by nonprofessional believers without the benefit of academic training. Put in Farley's terms, Bonhoeffer was invited to become a "practical theologian" through his involvement with others, which included but was not limited to his preaching responsibilities.

9   DBWE 10:72–75.

10 DBWE 10:77.

11 DBWE 10:174. Bonhoeffer's characterization of Olbricht's preaching— "uninspired" and "boring"—may also reflect a desire to be known as a preacher who was inspired and engaging.

12 DBWE 10:175. Dunne, in an important study of Aristotle's category of *phronesis*, or practical wisdom, argues for the importance of experiential knowledge and practical judgment that are embodied in one's self and conduct and that are not merely a matter of one's logical or intellectual capacities. Dunne cites John Henry Newman, nineteenth-century leader of the Oxford movement, who wrote, "Instead of trusting logical science, we must trust persons, namely those who by long acquaintance with their subject have a right to judge. And if we wish ourselves to share in their convictions and the grounds of them, we must follow their history, and learn as they have learned. We must . . . depend on practice and experience more than on reasoning. . . . By following this we may . . . rightly lean upon ourselves, directing ourselves by our own moral and intellectual judgment, not by our skill in argumentation." Dunne, *Back to the Rough Ground*, 35. Although Olbricht does not appear to have been an exemplary preacher from whom Bonhoeffer might learn and even emulate, he did display a particular kind of character in his daily conduct that caught Bonhoeffer's attention, perhaps even more so since, as a pastor, he did not share Bonhoeffer's academic interests and background.

13 DBWE 10:77. For a good discussion of German pietism and the probable influence of Karl Barth on Bonhoeffer's opinion of it as a popular form of religious expression, see Eberhard Busch, *Karl Barth & the Pietists: The Young Karl Barth's Critique of Pietism*, trans. Daniel W. Bloesch (Downers Grove, Ill.: InterVarsity, 2004).

14 DBWE 10:87. Bonhoeffer's comments refer to the "preacher's seminaries" that served the Evangelical Church of the Old Prussian Union. His obvious contempt for them is indicative of how theological education in Germany had sharply divided theory and practice, a separation that was formalized in two different approaches to preparing pastors for ministry. See the excellent discussion in Frei, *Types of Christian Theology*, 95–132. In

1935 Bonhoeffer would be appointed as director of the Confessing Church's preacher's seminary in Finkewalde.

15 DBWE 10:97. For a good summary of Bonhoeffer's introduction to Spanish culture, see Marsh, *Strange Glory*, 62–87.

16 DBWE 10:104.

17 DBWE 10:116.

18 DBWE 10:116. Marsh writes, "At the same time, the year in Barcelona inevitably broadened his social awareness. . . . As his society became more capacious and broad, he also discovered a larger and more varied inner world." Marsh, *Strange Glory*, 82, 78–82.

19 DBWE 10:120. Here, Bonhoeffer again addresses matters related to the kind of character he sees displayed by members of the Barcelona church in contrast to the intellectual pride and elitism he perceived in Germany. Stanley Hauerwas writes concerning the character required for pastoral ministry: "If we are to think about 'ministerial ethics,' we must think about the kind of persons who are capable of sustaining the practice of ministry for a lifetime. Questions of talent and intelligence are not unimportant, but only when talent and intelligence are shaped or embodied in character can we have the confidence that a person is ready to meet the demands of service to God through being an official of God's church." Hauerwas, *Christian Existence Today: Essays on Church, World and Living In Between* (Durham, N.C.: Labyrinth Press, 1988), 142.

20 DBWE 10:139–40. Bonhoeffer's struggle to understand this text in light of the church's life is a good example of the formation that is required for the practice of ministry, for a particular kind of character and judgment that are fitting for the nature and purpose of the church. Charles M. Wood writes of a need for vision and discernment, that theological education is the cultivation of theological judgment: "Activities such as the imaginative grasp of the Christian witness in its unity, the assessment of one's own distinctive situation as a context for witness, and the testing of actual or potential efforts to convey the gospel. . . . Vision and discernment are not merely routine performances. They require intelligence, sensibility, imagination, and a readiness to deal with the unforeseen. It is precisely this *habitus* which is the primary and indispensable qualification for church leadership, if "church leadership" itself means anything more than the routine performance of established functions." Wood, *Vision and Discernment: An Orientation in Theological Study* (Atlanta: Scholars Press, 1985), 93–94.

21 This is a good example of Bonhoeffer seeking to exercise practical reason or wisdom. Oliver O'Donovan has described this as being about not what we are to do but rather what we think about what we are to do. This requires a kind of knowing that entails learning convictions and descriptions that shape understanding of the way things are—that is, of reality. See O'Donovan, *Self, World, and Time*, vol. 1 of *Ethics as Theology* (Grand Rapids: Eerdmans, 2013).

I am indebted to Stanley Hauerwas for calling my attention to O'Donovan's work. That Bonhoeffer was struggling with such questions should be no surprise. Hauerwas comments on Aristotle's view of practical wisdom: "Aristotle thinks it very unlikely that practical wisdom will be found in the young because they have not developed the capacity to perceive or deliberate about particulars. People of practical wisdom must have the understanding that gives them the capacity of last things, and judgments about ends are judgments about particulars. Such judgments Aristotle identifies as judgments of understanding, because even though they are about matters that can be otherwise they make possible the identification of universals through particulars." Hauerwas, *Work of Theology*, 15.

22   DBWE 10:140. By "eudaemonistic," Bonhoeffer is referring to a view of Christian life oriented to the goal or end of human flourishing, beginning in this life and completed in the life to come. He is inquiring about the possibility of human happiness, or the good life, for historical creatures who have been deeply corrupted by human sin. He presumably mentions Barth because his questions point to a vision of salvation that implies moral progress and change through time, something Barth opposed in liberal theology because it was easily transposed into a vision of human progress without need of God. On "eudaemonism," see Dunne, *Back to the Rough Ground*, 238–42.

23   DBWE 10:480–81.

24   DBWE 10:481.

25   Augustine, *The Confessions*, ed. John E. Rotelle, O.S.A., trans. Edmund Hill, O.P. (New York: New City Press, 1996), 1.1.

26   DBWE 10:481.

27   DBWE 10:482. On Barth's critique of religion, which Bonhoeffer read as a student in Berlin, see Karl Barth, *The Epistle to the Romans*, trans. from the sixth edition by Edwyn C. Hoskyns (Oxford: Oxford University Press, 1968), "God is God" (p. 11), "the great disruption" (p. 424). On the Tower of Babel, see Barth, *The Word of God and the Word of Man*, trans. Douglas Horton (London: Hodder & Stoughton, 1928).

28   DBWE 10:483. Barth writes, "Grace is the gift of Christ who exposes the gulf which separates God and man, and, by exposing it, bridges it. . . . Where the grace of God is, the very existence of the world and the very existence of God become a question and a hope with which and for which men must wrestle." Barth, *Epistle to the Romans*, 31.

29   DBWE 10:485.

30   DBWE 10:490.

31   DBWE 10:491.

32   DBWE 10:492.

33   DBWE 10:494 (emphasis in original).

34   DBWE 10:495. Bethge writes of Bonhoeffer's reading of Scripture at this point in his formation. "Revelation is contained in Scripture because God speaks in it; that is undemonstrable—not a conclusion but a premise.

Divine revelation enables people to recognize divine revelation, that is, the Holy Spirit. Bonhoeffer adopted Barth's conclusion that things can be known only by their like. 'God can only be known by God. Hence it follows that the consistent idea of revelation must be thought of not substantially, but functionally, that is, it is not so much Being as decision, the will of God expressed in scripture.'" Bethge, *Dietrich Bonhoeffer: A Biography*, 80.

35 DBWE 10:495.

36 DBWE 10:104.

37 DBWE 10:500.

38 DBWE 10:503.

39 DBWE 10:504. Bethge describes Bonhoeffer's growing passion for preaching: "He wanted to say something important, and he believed he had something important to say. People were to be confronted and excited, shaken out of their complacency and won over. He approached this goal using his skills and the text boldly, and not very accurately." Bethge, *Dietrich Bonhoeffer: A Biography*, 111.

40 DBWE 10:505. It may be that, for Bonhoeffer, the primary issue was not accurate use of Scripture, although this is certainly a good thing, but more a matter of moral formation. Bonhoeffer's sermon speaks to what in contemporary terms is described as "spirituality." However, as Stanley Hauerwas notes, "The current interest in 'spirituality' in so many Protestant seminaries, I think, reflects more the disease from which we suffer than its cure. For spirituality so understood still stands too much in discontinuity with what is done in the classroom. Courses in spirituality will be of little help if we continue to assume study of the New Testament or theology to be simply a means to make students capable of service in the ministry." Hauerwas, *Christian Existence Today*, 146.

41 DBWE 10:127 (emphasis in original).

42 DBWE 10:127.

43 DBWE 10:127. Here, Bonhoeffer is acknowledging the tension that exists between calling and office—preaching as a commitment and preaching as an activity of the church. Hauerwas writes about preaching as a Christian practice, a social and shared activity that is essential to the church's very being: "The church preaches because by its very nature the church cannot do otherwise. Preaching is not an activity done for some other purpose, some other reason, that is not already intrinsic to preaching itself." Hauerwas, *Sanctify Them*, 236.

44 DBWE 10:127–28. Bonhoeffer appears to be sharing his reflections on an important homiletical question: Who does what in preaching? He admits to having questions about the place of human agency in preaching and about whether it is more important than God's initiative. His concern was that his desire to make sermons relevant in relation to the context and sociological makeup of listeners tended to overlook their identity as members of the church, united by the word in the body of Christ. Here, one of

the main themes of his dissertation, *Sanctorum Communio*, is brought into play in thinking about the practice of preaching.

45 DBWE 10:128. Edward Farley has raised the question of whether preaching can be taught. He concludes that preaching, as a practice of the gospel, is more than skill and technique: preaching is a theological task that requires preachers who are formed to think, live, and speak theologically—that is, in a manner that is shaped by the gospel. Farley, "Can Preaching Be Taught?" *Theology Today* 62 (2005): 171–80.

46 DBWE 10:505.

47 DBWE 10:505–6.

48 DBWE 10:506.

49 DBWE 10:508. Paul R. Hinlicky helpfully points to Luther's "forgotten ecclesiology" and its catholicity. Hinlicky sums this up thusly: "*Sanctorum Communio*—I believe in the Holy Spirit's creatures, those called out from the *civitas terrena* and assembled around holy things, as the new and holy people, the body of Christ, the temple of the Holy Spirit, the foretaste of the Messianic banquet, the anticipation in faith, hope, and love of the Beloved Community that comes down from heaven, the end of all things. So the creedal faith instructs." Hinlicky argues that Luther's "catholic" understanding of the church as *communio* has been obscured by Lutheran scholarship, thus losing sight of Luther's rich account of the church as the "concrete, external, public act of Jesus Christ." See Hinlicky, *Luther and the Beloved Community: A Path for Christian Theology after Christendom* (Grand Rapids: Eerdmans, 2010), 258–300, 290. Bonhoeffer is clearly attempting to define the church in a manner that is congruent with classic Protestant teaching. Given the focus of *Sanctorum Communio*, Luther's christological vision of the church may be his primary inspiration.

50 DBWE 10:509.

51 Here, Bonhoeffer cites Luther's early treatise, "The Freedom of a Christian," which gives some indication of the vision of church he has in mind. Luther writes, "Look here! This should be the rule: that the good things we have from God may flow from one person to the other and become common property. In this way each person may 'put on' his [or her] neighbor and conduct oneself toward him [or her] as if in the neighbor's place. These good things flowed and flow into us from Christ, who put us on and acted for us, as if he himself were what we are. . . . Therefore, we conclude that Christian individuals do not live in themselves but in Christ and their neighbor, or else they are not Christian. They live in Christ through faith and in the neighbor through love." Martin Luther, "The Freedom of a Christian," in *The Roots of Reform*, ed. Timothy J. Wengert, vol. 1 of *The Annotated Luther*, ed. Hans J. Hillerbrand, Kirsi I. Stjerna, and Timothy J. Wengert (Minneapolis: Fortress, 2015), 531.

52 DBWE 10:509–10.

53 DBWE 10:512.

54   DBWE 10:513–14.

55   DBWE 10:514–15. This sermon is significant since it represents Bonhoeffer's initial engagement with the Sermon on the Mount. He emphasizes the importance of transformed vision, a way of seeing more truly in relation to learning the church's language, the act of confession, and the gift of prayer. Hauerwas writes of the intimate relation of language and seeing, "You can only act in the world you can see, and you can only see what you have learned to say." He continues, "If you can only act in the world you can say, then the 'saying' has to come from a determinative community with the habits of speech necessary for the discernment of difference." Hauerwas, *Work of Theology*, 28–29.

56   DBWE 10:152.

57   DBWE 10:155.

58   DBWE 10:542–43.

59   DBWE 10:543.

60   DBWE 10:545–46.

61   DBWE 10:547.

62   DBWE 10:548–49.

63   DBWE 10:550–51.

64   DBWE 10:342–43.

65   DBWE 10:343–44. See Frei's extensive discussion of academic theology in Berlin. Frei, *Types of Christian Theology*, 131.

66   DBWE 10:346–47. Frei provides an excellent summary of how arguments over christological definition and verifiability shaped the German academic study of Jesus. Frei, *Types of Christian Theology*, 133–46. This is Bonhoeffer's first mention of discipleship in a sermon. The academic study of Jesus as a historical figure and teacher was for the purpose of underwriting German religion and culture. Discipleship was not a factor.

67   DBWE 10:352–53.

68   H. Gaylon Barker summarizes Bonhoeffer's Barcelona sermons as stating, "Christianity is God's way to us. In contrast, religion is our way to God. This is alternative language to describe the difference Luther made between a theology of the cross and a theology of glory. Translated into Luther's terminology, religion (a theology of glory) is any theological attempt or justification that seeks to emphasize our goodness, piety, or some such achievement that brings us up to the level of God." Barker cites a passage from Luther on the true Christian religion: "It does not begin at the top as all other religions do; it begins at the bottom." See Barker, *The Cross of Reality: Luther's Theologica Crucis and Bonhoeffer's Christology* (Minneapolis: Fortress), 178.

69   Bonhoeffer was primarily oriented by theological concerns and interests. He had not yet found a way to speak in a manner joining doctrinal integrity and the obedience of faith: the integration of theology and ethics. This requires the cultivation of practical reason or wisdom. Oliver O'Donovan

writes, "Here there is a delicate but important division of labor between a theological Ethics and a doctrinal theology. Doctrine rests in truth. It has to struggle hard for it, and can never perfect its articulation of it once and for all, but the truth of the matter and nothing else is its term, and to that extent it sets the activities of time in the light of eternity. This means Ethics has neither the first nor the last word in Theology. Those words belong to a doctrine that speaks of God's purposes, acts, and ultimate ends. But because God's purposes are alive and active, there is place for a word in between first and last words, a word that speaks reflectively on the Spirit's aid in our present weakness, which discerns the present converse of the Spirit in guiding the human spirit to the service of God's further ends." O'Donovan, *Finding and Seeking*, vol. 2 of *Ethics as Theology* (Grand Rapids: Eerdmans, 2014), 4–5.

70 DBWE 10:357–58. Reggie L. Williams writes of this period, "At this point in his theological career, Bonhoeffer did not refer to the Bible for Christian discipleship. As a result of that glaring omission, it was easy to blend the way of Jesus with German nationalism and to consider patriotism an element of Christian discipleship. With the Bible omitted as a source of concrete guidance for Christian moral living, the popular Lutheran language of the Two Kingdoms, replete with the nationalist notion of orders of creation, filled the void." Williams, *Bonhoeffer's Black Jesus: Harlem Renaissance Theology and an Ethic of Resistance* (Waco, Tex.: Baylor University Press, 2014), 11.

71 Hauerwas addresses the matter of homiletical form by calling attention to Barth as a "performer" of the Word: "For theology, truth is to be found in the worship of God and in particular the sermon, which is an action that enables the church to serve the Word of God so that the world may hear time and again the Word in this particular time and place." Hauerwas, *Work of Theology*, 261. On the particular kind of teaching and learning preaching entails, see Thomas G. Long, "A New Focus for Teaching Preaching," in *Teaching Preaching as a Christian Practice*, ed. Thomas G. Long and Leonora Tubbs Tisdale (Loiusville, Ky.: Westminster John Knox, 2008). Farley writes, "To proclaim means to bring to bear a certain past event on the present in such a way as to open the future. Since the present is always specific and situational, the way that the past, the event of Christ, is brought to bear so as to elicit hope will never be captured in some timeless phrase, some ideality of language. Preaching the good tidings is a new task whenever and wherever it takes place." Farley, *Practicing Gospel*, 80.

72 Joseph Dunne differentiates between a technicist approach that focuses on the skill and technique of the designer or producer (which creates the illusion of control in both the process and its outcomes) and the nature of practice (which requires a particular kind of humility, a willing submission to the tradition, norms, wisdom, and exemplars of a particular practice). This requires initiation into the practice, "a way of articulating and

reflecting upon its nature and purpose, its circumstances and challenges, its present reality in light of both the past and future." Dunne, *Back to the Rough Ground*, 368–69.

73 William Mallard, *Language and Love: Introducing Augustine's Religious Thought through the Confessions Story* (University Park: Penn State University Press, 1994); see also Helen Charry, *By the Renewing of Your Minds: The Pastoral Function of Christian Doctrine* (New York: Oxford University Press, 1997), 120–52.

74 Augustine, *Teaching Christianity (De Doctrina Christiana)*, ed. John E. Rotelle, O.S.A., trans. William P. Hill, O.P. (New York: New City Press, 1996), 1:12–14.

75 See the discussion of this transformation in Christopher J. Thompson, *Christian Doctrine, Christian Identity: Augustine and the Narratives of Character* (New York: University Press of America, 1999).

76 DBWE 10:164.

77 Bethge comments on the long-term importance of the Barcelona sermons: "In several ways, these first sermons revealed the full scope of his theological work and perspective." Bethge, *Dietrich Bonhoeffer: A Biography*, 112.

78 In February 1929, Bonhoeffer gave a public lecture to the congregation, "Basic Questions of a Christian Ethic." In addressing the matter of war, he stated, "God gave me my mother, my people [Volk]. For what I have, I thank my people; what I am, I am through my people, and so what I have should also belong to my people; that is in the divine order of things, for God created the peoples. If for a single dangerous moment I do not act [in war], then I am doing nothing other than surrendering my neighbors." DBWE 10:371.

3: The Discovery of a Black Jesus

1 For a good summary of this formative period in Bonhoeffer's life and work, see the introduction to DBWE 10, pp. 1–50. See also the insightful narratives in Marsh, *Strange Glory*, 88–135; and Bethge, *Dietrich Bonhoeffer: A Biography*, 125–72.

2 DBWE 10:178–79.

3 DBWE 10:189–90.

4 DBWE 2. For a good summary, see the introduction by Wayne Whitson Floyd Jr. to DBWE 2, pp. 1–24: "*Act and Being* evidences Bonhoeffer's emerging practical concern to find for theology a methodology adequate and proper to its unique subject matter—and to the challenging terrain of its cultural and historical location. Despite its seemingly abstract philosophical cast, this work begs to be interpreted within the concrete, historical context of the cultural crisis in Germany between the world wars, which eventuated in the National Socialist rise to power in 1933" (p. 7).

5   See the narrative in Eberhard Busch, *Karl Barth: His Life from Letters and Autobiographical Texts*, trans. John Bowden (Philadelphia: Fortress, 1976), 60–125; Gary Dorrien, *Theology without Weapons: The Barthian Revolt in Modern Theology* (Louisville, Ky.: Westminster John Knox, 2000), 36–80; William H. Willimon, *Conversations with Barth on Preaching* (Nashville: Abingdon, 2006), 1–22.

6   Cited in Andreas Pangritz, *Karl Barth in the Theology of Dietrich Bonhoeffer*, trans. Barbara Rumscheidt and Martin Rumscheidt (Grand Rapids: Eerdmans, 2000), 36.

7   Barth, *Epistle to the Romans*.

8   Barth, *Epistle to the Romans*, 28.

9   Barth, *Epistle to the Romans*, 36. Willimon writes, "His theological insights demanded new ways of talking. Barth now worked in a style that many have regarded as 'expressionistic,' a style of theological writing with similarities to some of the expressionist novelists of the era who sought to break open the surface of language to reveal the real world underneath or beyond our normal modes of discourse. . . . Even now, a preacher who reads the second edition of *Romans* will find, in Barth's strident cadences, the invigorating work of a fellow preacher who has been gripped by the gospel and thereby freed from the artificial restraints of culturally subservient theologies of this and that. Here is theology meant to be preached." Willimon, *Conversations*, 16–17. See Willimon's summary of Barth's theological and corresponding homiletical transformation during the period after the war (9–22); see also Dorrien, *Theology without Weapons*, 43–71.

10 Barth, *Epistle to the Romans*, 366.

11 See the detailed examination of Barth's hermeneutical approach to Scripture and the response it evoked in Richard E. Burnett, *Karl Barth's Theological Exegesis: The Hermeneutical Principles of the Römerbrief Period* (Grand Rapids: Eerdmans, 2001), 3–11, 184–220.

12 Dorrien, *Theology without Weapons*, 66–73.

13 Karl Barth, *The Göttingen Dogmatics: Instruction in the Christian Religion*, ed. Hannelotte Reiffen, trans. Geoffrey W. Bromiley (Grand Rapids: Eerdmans, 1991).

14 Busch, *Karl Barth: His Life*, 154–60.

15 Barth, *Göttingen Dogmatics*, 14.

16 See Dorrien, *Theology without Weapons*, 71–80, 83. Daniel Migliore writes, "'God is God'—this is the theme of the Göttingen Dogmatics." Migliore, "Karl Barth's First Lectures in Dogmatics: Instruction in the Christian Religion," in Barth, *Göttingen Dogmatics*, xxvi. See also Migliore's introductory section on "Dogmatics in Service of Preaching" (xx–xxv).

17 Barth, *Göttingen Dogmatics*, 23.

18 Barth, *Göttingen Dogmatics*, 126–27.

19 Barth, *Göttingen Dogmatics*, 54.

20 DBWE 2:83–103. Here, I am indebted to the extended argument set forth in DeJonge, *Bonhoeffer's Theological Formation*, 57–58: "According to Bonhoeffer's first line of criticism, Barth's act-theology creates discontinuities at the level of the concept of God and, therefore, at the level of epistemology. The discontinuity at the level of the concept of God follows from Barth's act-concept of revelation and formal account of God's freedom. . . . Bonhoeffer takes Barth's various discontinuities as evidence of something amiss. Even if Barth successfully protects God's transcendence, he does not ground theoretically the continuous or historical aspects of the Christian life. Barth does not adequately reflect the faithful continuity of God's self-giving or the constancy of the life of faith that rests in it. Barth's act-theology, even if it solves the problem of transcendence, runs aground on the problem of historical existence." DeJonge shows that Bonhoeffer's critique of Barth reprises long-standing theological differences between the Lutheran and Reformed traditions around the doctrine of Christ and, thus, how revelation is construed and received (41–55). See the discussion of Barth's interpretation of the Lutheran/Reformed debate in Migliore, "Karl Barth's First Lectures," xxxiv–xlii. Migliore points out that Lutheran orthodoxy was Barth's preferred conversation partner in his early theological development.

21 DBWE 2:110–12. Clifford Green writes, "That the being of revelation is the being of Christ in the church-community as a community of persons expresses two points: its continuity of being as transcendent to the individual, and its contingent freedom which engages a person in existential encounter. Affirming the ontological thesis of being as prior to one's response to being, Bonhoeffer proposes the social category as a way to integrate dialectically the 'being' and 'act' dimensions of revelation in Christ." Green, *Bonhoeffer: A Theology*, 87, 67–104.

22 DBWE 2:30–31, 150–55.

23 DBWE 2:137.

24 *Luther's Works* 37:72. Cited in DBWE 2:82. DeJonge concludes that Bonhoeffer's interpretation entails an alternative to, rather than a misreading of, Barth's theology, standing with Barth in affirming God's transcendent revelation. He breaks from Barth, however, by articulating a Lutheran understanding of contingency through person-concepts of revelation and God rather than a Reformed understanding of contingency through an act-concept of revelation and subject-concept of God. See the thorough discussion in DeJonge, *Bonhoeffer's Theological Formation*, 101–28.

25 DBWE 2:111–12.

26 DBWE 2:115.

27 DBWE 2:120.

28 DBWE 2:130.

29 DBWE 2:129.

30 DBWE 2:130–31.

31 DBWE 2:133. The extensive secondary literature on Bonhoeffer's academic works has tended to focus on the theological and philosophical nature of the arguments set forth in *Act and Being*, particularly in relation to Barth's theology and the philosophy of Martin Heidegger. What I find interesting is how little attention is given to Bonhoeffer's finely articulated Lutheran theology of preaching as generated by God's self-giving in Christ present with and for the church as the community of faith across time.

32 DBWE 10:407.

33 DBWE 10:382.

34 DBWE 10:382–83.

35 DBWE 10:383.

36 DBWE 10:384–86.

37 DBWE 10:205.

38 DBWE 10:201.

39 DBWE 10:198–99.

40 DBWE 10:205.

41 See the excellent discussion of liberal Protestantism, its roots, and its developments in Garry Dorrien, *The Making of American Liberal Theology: Idealism, Realism, and Modernity, 1900–1950* (Louisville, Ky.: Westminster John Knox, 2003), 1–20, 356–521.

42 Reggie Williams notes that in 1930 there were more than 165,000 blacks living in Harlem, with conditions so tight that tenants were forced to sleep in shifts. Williams reports that the stock-market crash of 1929 put more than 300,000 African Americans out of work, while the number of unemployed blacks in Harlem quadrupled. Williams, *Bonhoeffer's Black Jesus*, 84, 95.

43 See the comments on the influence of German liberalism in early twentieth-century American theological education in Howard, *Protestant Theology*, 363–78.

44 DBWE 10:265–66.

45 DBWE 10:266.

46 DBWE 10:412.

47 DBWE 10:580–81.

48 DBWE 10:581.

49 DBWE 10:583–84.

50 See Eberhard Bethge, "Friends," in *I Knew Dietrich Bonhoeffer: Reminiscences by His Friends*, ed. Wolf-Dieter Zimmerman and Ronald Gregor Smith, trans. Kathe Gregor Smith (New York: Harper & Row, 1966), 46–52.

51 DBWE 10:261.

52 DBWE 10:260.

53 DBWE 10:585–88.

54 Marsh, *Strange Glory*, 114.

55 DBWE 10:281–83.

56 DBWE 10:283–84.

57   DBWE 10:284–85.

58   DBWE 10:285–86. There is no surviving record of a response from Bon-
     hoeffer to Rossler's letter.

59   DBWE 10:306.

60   DBWE 10:307–9. Reggie Williams comments on the differences and simi-
     larities between Germany and America in Bonhoeffer's disappointments:
     "In America, instead of German nationalism parading as Christian dis-
     cipleship, Bonhoeffer was grappling with modern theological liberalism
     in white American Christianity. Theological liberalism in America was
     optimistic about articulating a middle way between fundamentalism and
     atheism, re-conceptualizing what might be considered traditional, or even
     fundamentalist, Christianity in light of the influence of modernity within
     the broader white American society. . . . Liberal Christianity's civilizing
     scheme accommodated Christianity and American society, making little
     distinction between human achievement in modernity and industry and
     the civilizing virtues of Western Christian refinement. . . . The content in
     America was different and foreign, but the concept of Protestant culture
     was not." Williams, *Bonhoeffer's Black Jesus*, 18–19.

61   DBWE 10:310–11. See Dorrien's helpful discussion of the pragmatic tradi-
     tion in *Making of American Liberal Theology*, 172–246.

62   DBWE 10:312.

63   DBWE 10:312–14.

64   DBWE 10:313–14. See the discussion of the "great American tradition" in
     Hughes Oliphant Old, *The Reading and Preaching of the Christian Scriptures
     in the Worship of the Christian Church* (Grand Rapids: Eerdmans, 2007),
     6:440–558. Bonhoeffer was unaware the roots of such homiletical pragma-
     tism could be traced largely to the revivalism in America that arose follow-
     ing the Great Awakenings. Charles Finney had established himself as the
     outstanding figure of an informal school of preaching that characterized
     the American pulpit for a century and a half, cutting across theological and
     denominational lines. The optimism of the American frontier was the pre-
     vailing temper, disposition, and outlook. The place of Scripture in preach-
     ing was rather sparse, serving an instrumental purpose that contributed to
     the goals of revival and reform. The Bible could be approached either as a
     sourcebook of moral instruction and imperatives or as a simple plan of sal-
     vation. Evangelistic preaching was colored by a kind of romantic idealism
     that aimed to be inspiring—not necessarily the inspiration that is the work
     of the Spirit, but rather the inspiration of the preacher's personality and style.
     One's personal experience rather than formal theological and exegetical
     study was the best commentary on the Bible. Sermons thus leaned heavily on
     the use of illustrations gathered from the lives of preachers and listeners. Lib-
     eral theology and the liberal democratic way of life were inseparable within
     this homiletical strategy. See the excellent development of this topic in Ted

A. Smith, *The New Measures: A Theological History of Democratic Practice* (Cambridge: Cambridge University Press, 2007), 111–258.

65 See Dorrien's discussion of the social gospel and its influence in *Making of American Liberal Theology*, 73–93, 364–83.

66 See Marsh, *Strange Glory*, 122–26; see also the introduction to DBWE 10, pp. 32–35.

67 DBWE 10:281.

68 Williams, *Bonhoeffer's Black Jesus*, 24–25. See Garry Dorrien, *The New Abolition: W. E. B. Du Bois and the Black Social Gospel* (New Haven: Yale University Press, 2015), 294–95, 349–58, 483–85.

69 DBWE 10:314.

70 DBWE 10:258.

71 DBWE 10:268.

72 DBWE 10:293.

73 DBWE 10:314. See Williams' discussion of black lynchings in America, particularly the Scottsboro Case and Bonhoeffer's response. Williams, *Bonhoeffer's Black Jesus*, 20–21.

74 On Powell's preaching and leadership in response to the Great Depression, see the discussion in Williams, *Bonhoeffer's Black Jesus*, 79, 99–102; on the role of Scripture in the African American church, see Cain Hope Felder, "Race, Racism, and the Biblical Narratives," in *Stony the Road We Trod: African American Biblical Interpretation*, ed. Cain Hope Felder (Minneapolis: Fortress, 1991), 127–45; Vincent L. Wimbush, "The Bible and African Americans," in Felder, *Stony the Road*, 81–97. Richard Lischer writes, "The African-American tradition of interpretation, however, did not pass through the Enlightenment, never enjoyed the leisure of disinterested analysis, and therefore did not distance itself from the Bible or settle for moral applications. The cruelties of slavery made it imperative that African Americans not step *back* but step *into* the Book and its storied world of God's personal relations with those in trouble. Bereft of a remembered history of their own in a culture that valued historical consciousness, the enslaved Africans listened to the Bible and adopted a new history." Lischer, *The Preacher King: Martin Luther King Jr. and the Word That Moved America* (New York: Oxford University Press, 1995), 200 (emphasis in original).

75 DBWE 10:314–15. See the good summary of the importance of Powell's ministry and preaching in Dorrien, *New Abolition*, 3–15, 428–47.

76 DBWE 10:315. See the introduction to black preaching in Frank A. Thomas, *They Like to Never Quit Praisin' God: The Role of Celebration in Preaching*, rev. ed. (Cleveland: Pilgrim, 2013). On black preaching, the Bible, and "white" hermeneutics, see Cloephus J. LaRue, *I Believe I'll Testify: The Art of African American Preaching* (Louisville, Ky.: Westminster John Knox, 2011), 19–36, 57–70.

77 Letter to Martin Rumscheidt, December 17, 1986; cited in DBWE 10:31.

78 DBWE 10:269.

79 DBWE 10:315.

80 See the discussion in Marsh, *Strange Glory*, 112–21.

81 DBWE 10:282.

82 Williams, *Bonhoeffer's Black Jesus*, 20–21.

83 Williams, *Bonhoeffer's Black Jesus*, 21–25; Marsh, *Strange Glory*, 115–21.

84 Lischer describes King's prophetic calling as "a spokesman for the Lord whose ministry is not restricted to a single locale or to local issues. He travels with the freedom of the Spirit. . . . King overlaid his prophetic vision with imagery and verbal expressions suggestive of the Apostle Paul. . . . While Paul was in prison he wrote much of the canonical literature of the New Testament. When Martin Luther King Jr. was imprisoned in the Birmingham City Jail, he produced a canonical classic of prison literature." Lischer, *Preacher King*, 174, 184.

85 Martin Luther King Jr., "Letter from a Birmingham City Jail (1963)," in *A Testament of Hope: The Essential Writings and Speeches of Martin Luther King, Jr.*, ed. James Melvin Washington (New York: Harper One, 1986), 290.

86 King, "Letter from a Birmingham City Jail," 296–97. On King and the black social gospel, see Dorrien, *New Abolition*, 1–11, 25–26.

87 King, "Letter from a Birmingham City Jail," 298.

88 King, "Letter from a Birmingham City Jail," 299–300.

89 Williams writes, "Harlem Renaissance intellectuals shaped a literary movement that spoke about black culture, black political agency, and a black Jesus. Their descriptions of a black Jesus were disruptive to white supremacy and at times graphic, in their explicit rebukes of the oppressive and white Christ. Theology from the margins was, for its constituents, anti-venom to the toxic theological imagination of racist colonial Christianity. . . . The intellectual architects of blackness in Harlem portrayed Jesus in a way that decentered Europe and whiteness as the source of all saving knowledge." Williams, *Bonhoeffer's Black Jesus*, 54.

90 DBWE 10:318–19.

91 See the excellent survey of Harlem literature in Williams, *Bonhoeffer's Black Jesus*, 53–72: "In the death of Christ, God's power is revealed through Christ's empathetic identification with the outcast, exposing the white-centered, white supremacist as foes of God. Cullen's 'The Black Christ' is a unique analysis of the relationship between race and religion in the Harlem Renaissance. . . . These depictions [in black literature] are counternarratives to the pejorative descriptions of black humanity from the racializing worldview of white-supremacist Christianity. Like 'The Black Christ,' narratives of Jesus in the Harlem Renaissance demythologize the white-centered story of idealized white humanity by including black suffering within the narrative of Christ, child of God, cosufferer and redeemer" (72). See the discussion of Cullen's influence on Bonhoeffer in Josiah U. Young, "Theology and the Problem of Racism," in Jenkins and

McBride, *Bonhoeffer and King*, 75–76. Young writes, "Cullen helped Bonhoeffer to see that many young blacks thought their inherited Christianity blocked their self-esteem and their human rights. Bonhoeffer thought their militant rejection of their elders' strong eschatological faith was an 'ominous' consequence of the history of the Protestant church in the United States" (75).

92 As Reggie Williams describes it, "Theology at Abyssinian was developed within communal circumstances that provided Bonhoeffer with new sources to make sense of life. Some scholars describe a 'mental grid' as a complex process of filtering all of our learning through the experience of our social identity. Theologically the mental grid includes one's social environment in the process of determining individual or communal ways of knowing God. Bonhoeffer's experience of learning in Harlem was unique, as it required the modification of filters formed in Germany through which he was accustomed to seeing the world and understanding himself in it. For modification to happen, Bonhoeffer had to allow himself to be vulnerable to seeing himself and society from the perspective of others." Williams, *Bonhoeffer's Black Jesus*, 79.

93 See Barker, *Cross of Reality*, 195. Williams comments, "The gospel that he heard in Harlem caught his attention by its familiar theological claims of Christ-centeredness. But he found that to be Christ centered in Harlem required a different engagement with the world than that which he was familiar. The African-American Christian community at Abyssinian that Bonhoeffer encountered was indeed Christ centered, but Bonhoeffer needed to enter the context of their encounter with Christ to recognize and to reflect on the cultural implications of how this unique theological contribution described Christ-centeredness and what Christians in Harlem meant by this term." Williams, *Bonhoeffer's Black Jesus*, 40–41. A consequence is that Bonhoeffer's understanding of discipleship through his friendship with Laserre was shaped by his experience in Harlem. I am indebted to Williams for this insight (28–30).

94 DBWE 2:120. Michael Battle comments, "Dietrich Bonhoeffer's theology teaches that God is both being and action in the person of Jesus Christ. . . . *Act and Being* . . . demonstrates Bonhoeffer's attempt to battle his culture's modern European assumptions that one could never know God as an object beyond the human. Bonhoffer took a stand against the prevailing, transcendental category of 'object,' replacing in its stead the worshiping community of the church." The community that made this conviction concrete and visible for Bonhoeffer was Abyssinian Baptist Church. Battle shows that, for King, the Civil Rights Movement was essentially a worshiping community whose source was the preaching of the gospel. See Battle, "Reconciliation as Worshiping Community," in Jenkins and McBride, *Bonhoeffer and King*, 235, 237. See also Lischer, *Preacher King*, 10–12.

4: *Preaching as Theology*

1   See the following works: Bethge, *Dietrich Bonhoeffer: A Biography*, 173–
    256; Schlingensiepen, *Dietrich Bonhoeffer*, 76–113; Marsh, *Strange Glory*,
    136–56; introduction to DBWE 11, pp. 1–28. Bethge writes of this time:
    "Bonhoeffer's return to Germany represented a break in his development
    that was certainly sharper than the momentous and ecclesiastical upheaval
    that followed two years later. The second major phase of his career began
    now, not in 1933. The period of learning had come to an end. He now began
    to teach on a faculty whose theology he did not share, and to preach in a
    church whose self-confidence he regarded as unfounded. More aware than
    before, he now became part of a society that was moving toward political,
    social, and economic chaos." Bethge, *Dietrich Bonhoeffer: A Biography*, 173.

2   See the excellent discussion of Weimar Germany and preaching in Han-
    cock, *Karl Barth's Emergency Homiletic*, 62–91, 137–92.

3   See the helpful narratives in Victoria J. Barnett, *For the Soul of the People:
    Protestant Protest against Hitler* (Oxford: Oxford University Press, 1992),
    25–29; and idem, *Bystanders: Conscience and Complicity during the Holo-
    caust* (London: Praeger, 2000), 35–62; see the helpful editor's introduction
    by Dean G. Stroud, "Historical Context: Preaching in the Third Reich," in
    Preaching in Hitler's Shadow: Sermons of Resistance in the Third Reich, ed.
    Stroud (Grand Rapids: Eerdmans, 2013), 3–22. I have benefited from the
    discussion of recent scholarship from the perspective of historical theol-
    ogy in Paul R. Hinlicky, *Before Auschwitz: What Christian Theology Must
    Learn from the Rise of Nazism* (Eugene, Ore.: Cascade, 2013), 14–43. Hin-
    licky argues for the similarities between the Nazi Party and liberal Prot-
    estantism: "In large measure, liberal Protestantism was directed against
    the Lutheran defense of the confessional school and the 'Christian state'
    that defended it. Although liberal Protestants believed in the church as a
    community of believers with the state, they maintained it would ultimately
    be absorbed by the state. . . . Just as Judaism was fulfilled and replaced by
    Christianity, now Christianity receives fulfillment in National Socialism."
    Hinlicky, *Before Auschwitz*, 38–39, 43.

4   See the excellent discussion of leading figures and issues in Jack Forstman,
    *Christian Faith in Dark Times: Theological Conflicts in the Shadow of Hit-
    ler* (Louisville, Ky.: Westminster John Knox, 1992): "The Hitler enthusiasts
    believed their Führer ('leader') would bring an end to the political insta-
    bility of the Weimar Republic, reestablish freedom for the German people,
    rectify the unjust and oppressive terms of surrender in 1918, and make it
    possible once again to be proud to be German" (16–17). On preaching, see
    Hancock, *Karl Barth's Emergency Homiletic*, 152–56.

5   See the interpretation of this time period in Bonhoeffer's life in Bethge,
    Dietrich Bonhoeffer: A Biography, 192–205; see also the editor's introduction

and afterword in DBWE 11, pp. 20–29, 477–92; Marsh, *Strange Glory*, 149–51.

6   DBWE 11:37.

7   DBWE 11:38. See the excellent discussion of Bonhoeffer's relation to Barth during this time period in Andreas Pangritz, "Dietrich Bonhoeffer," 254–57. A good survey of Barth's early ethical work is provided in Nigel Biggar, "Barth's Trinitarian Ethic," in *The Cambridge Companion to Karl Barth*, ed. John Webster, Cambridge Companions to Religion (Cambridge: Cambridge University Press, 2000), 212–17.

8   DBWE 11:50.

9   DBWE 11:54–55. Stanley Hauerwas has argued that the heart of Bonhoeffer's work was an attempt to recover the visibility of the church in response to the modern project that had reduced Christianity to a set of beliefs that serve to make life "meaningful." See Hauerwas, *Performing the Faith*; and *State of the University*, 33–44. Hauerwas writes, "The Christian faith requires the shaping of a visible community constituted by material practices that give us ways to go on when we are not sure where we are." Hauerwas, *State of the University*, 40.

10   DBWE 11:62.

11   Gavin D'Costa has described this arrangement as the "Babylonian captivity of theology." See D'Costa, *Theology in the Public Square*, 1–37. For a summary of conditions in universities during this period, see Hancock, *Karl Barth's Emergency Homiletic*, 76–87. See also Robert Ericksen's work for a good summary of the "Dehn Affair" that demonstrates the growing threat to professors who did not support students' conservative, nationalistic desires. Ericksen, *Complicity in the Holocaust: Churches and Universities in Nazi Germany* (Cambridge: Cambridge University Press, 2012), 74–84. Bonhoeffer wrote in response to the case of Dehn (a professor of practical theology at Halle University), "Where such Protestant teaching . . . the church's proclamation of the judgment and mercy of God over all human action with an undermining liberalistic cultural criticism . . . is called into question, the church is attacked at its foundation" (DBWE 11:100).

12   DBWE 11:55. Hancock writes, "Professors who expressed openness to ideas like socialism, pacifism, or anything else deemed unGerman were subject to protests, jeering, demonstrations, slander, and threats from right-wing student organizations. Such events were already occurring well before the official Nazi student group became a significant presence at most universities. If nationalist students did not join the Nazi Party in the early 1930s, they were certainly well-disposed toward it, and the party made inroads with the professors as well." Hancock, *Karl Barth's Emergency Homiletic*, 80–81.

13   See "The History of Twentieth-Century Systematic Theology," in DBWE 11:177–244.

14   DBWE 11:228, 237.

15   DBWE 11:242–44. Wolf Krötke writes of Bonhoeffer's orientation to Luther during this time period: "Such an orientation became more urgent when the 'German Christians' began around 1933 to use Luther for their religious, anti-Semitic, and racist ideology in the name of God's revelation for the German people and ultimately for the destruction of the church in Germany. For Bonhoeffer, keeping and actualizing the foundations of the church was identical with articulating Luther's genuine understanding of the word of God in law and gospel, faith, the church and Christian action. He dedicated himself uncompromisingly. . . . Because Bonhoeffer was keen to reach his own conclusions on Luther's theology on the basis of Luther's writings, his path in the 1930s often collided . . . with what was called Lutheranism or Lutheran." Krötke, "Dietrich Bonhoeffer and Martin Luther," 54–55.

16   Barth, "The Strange New World within the Bible," in *Word of God*, 28–50.

17   DBWE 11:401–2.

18   DBWE 11:405–7.

19   DBWE 11:414–15.

20   See the summary of "positive Christianity" in Richard Steigmann-Gall, *The Holy Reich: Nazi Conceptions of Christianity, 1919–1945* (Cambridge: Cambridge University Press, 2003), 13–16.

21   DBWE 11:420–21. Barnett (in *For the Soul of the People*, 25–27) provides a good discussion of church/state matters in the months leading up to Hitler's appointment as chancellor in January 1933. See also Ericksen's description of postwar Weimar Germany and the memory of the war in *Complicity in the Holocaust*, 14–17. Doris L. Bergen writes, "Although twisted and offensive, German Christian teachings reflected a fairly stable set of beliefs built around a specific understanding of the church. The German Christians intended to build a church that would exclude all those deemed impure and embrace all 'true Germans' in a spiritual homeland for the Third Reich." Bergen, *The Twisted Cross: The German Christian Movement in the Third Reich* (Chapel Hill: University of North Carolina Press, 1996), 4. Such scholarship sheds light on the courage Bonhoeffer displayed in his preaching.

22   DBWE 11:425.

23   DBWE 11:422–27. See the important discussion of Bonhoeffer's theological development in relation to the ecumenical movement and the call to proclaiming the gospel of peace in Mark Thiessen Nation, Anthony G. Siegrist, and Daniel P. Umbel, *Bonhoeffer the Assassin? Challenging the Myth, Recovering His Call to Peacemaking* (Grand Rapids: Baker Academic, 2013), 17–49.

24   Reggie Williams sees a striking resemblance between Bonhoeffer's ministry with young people in the depressed part of Berlin and the work done by

Abyssinian Baptist Church in Harlem. Williams, *Bonhoeffer's Black Jesus*, 114–15.

25 DBWE 11:73. The most helpful interpretation for the significance of Bonhoeffer's work with youth during this period can be found in Root, *Bonhoeffer as Youth Worker*, 87–116.

26 DBWE 11:76.

27 DBWE 11:97.

28 DBWE 11:94.

29 DBWE 11:97–98.

30 DBWE 11:258–66.

31 Luther begins the section on the creed in *The Large Catechism* this way: "Thus far we have heard the first part of Christian Doctrine [Ten Commandments]. In it we have seen all that God wishes us to do or not to do. The Creed properly follows, setting forth all that we must expect and receive from God; in brief, it teaches us to know him perfectly." Luther, *Large Catechism*, 55.

32 DBWE 11:259.

33 DBWE 11:260, 262.

34 Richard Rother, a member of the confirmation class, writes, "On the same Sunday [of confirmation] the elections took place and everywhere in the north of Berlin political tensions ran high. But Pastor Bonhoeffer was beloved and respected by his congregation, and the confirmation ceremonies suffered no disturbances. Never before or after has Zion Church had such a strong congregation as when this gifted man was its pastor." Rother, "A Confirmation Class in Wedding," in Zimmerman and Smith, *I Knew Dietrich Bonhoeffer*, 57.

35 DBWE 11:428–30.

36 DBWE 11:431–33.

37 DBWE 11:416–17. The economic crisis in Germany during the early 1930s made a great demand on the church to demonstrate its continued social and moral usefulness. See Ericksen, *Complicity in the Holocaust*, 14–15.

38 DBWE 11:417.

39 DBWE 11:418–19.

40 DBWE 11:433–34.

41 DBWE 11:121–22.

42 DBWE 11:434–40.

43 Doris Bergen writes about this time in mid-1932 when politicians, pastors, and laypeople met in Berlin to plan how to capture the energies of Germany's Protestant churches for the National Socialist cause. The sources she cites show that Hitler suggested the name "German Christians." Bergen writes, "Members of the group then used their name to enforce the contention that they represented the only authentic fusion of German ethnicity and Christian faith." Bergen, *Twisted Cross*, 4–5.

44 DBWE 11:434–35.

45   DBWE 11:435. See Forstman's summary of the theological situation in Germany during the postwar period—that neither conservative nor liberal religion was satisfactory, kindling desires for a new cause for the sake of the German nation. Forstman, *Christian Faith in Dark Times*, 22–24.

46   DBWE 11:437.

47   DBWE 11:439–40.

48   DBWE 11:444–45.

49   DBWE 11:445–46. Bonhoeffer sets the proclamation of the gospel over against enthusiasm, experience, or perceived needs as the basis of the church's life—an external word that comes from beyond itself in Jesus Christ. See Hinlicky, *Before Auschwitz*, 180.

50   DBWE 11:450–65.

51   DBWE 11:459.

52   DBWE 11:239–332.

53   DBWE 11:328.

54   DBWE 11:329–32.

55   DBWE 11:333–41.

56   Here, Bonhoeffer follows the Christology of Luther, who interpreted Christ as both example and sacrament, or gift. See Hinlicky, *Luther and the Beloved Community*, 295–96, 355–56. See Christoph Schwobel, "The Creature of the Word: Recovering the Ecclesiology of the Reformers," in *On Being the Church: Essays on the Christian Community*, ed. Colin E. Gunton and Daniel W. Hardy (Edinburgh: T&T Clark, 1989), 116–37: "The Church as *creatura verbi divini* which is made possible by the Word of God and in which true faith is made possible is *one*" (127; emphasis in original). Here, Bonhoeffer arguably echoes Luther's understanding of faith and freedom. See Luther, "The Freedom of a Christian," in *Roots of Reform*, 467–538.

57   DBWE 11:339–40.

58   DBWE 11:132.

59   DBWE 11:356–57.

60   DBWE 11:359–60.

61   See Hinlicky's insightful discussion of recent scholarship on this matter in *Before Auschwitz*, 21–27. Forstman covers the leading historical voices in this argument. Forstman, *Christian Faith in Dark Times*, 51–72, 121–32.

62   DBWE 11:363–64.

63   DBWE 11:367.

64   DBWE 11:136–37.

65   DBWE 11:375.

66   DBWE 11:378.

67   DBWE 11:473.

68   DBWE 11:474–75.

69   Joseph Dunne writes, "Practical knowledge has been shown as a fruit which can grow only in the soil of a person's character and experience;

apart from the cultivation of this soil, there is no artifice for making it available in a way that would count. In exposing oneself to the kind of experience and acquiring the kind of character that will yield the requisite knowledge . . . one is at the same time a feeling, expressing, and acting person, and one's knowledge is inseparable from one as such." Dunne, *Back to the Rough Ground*, 358. The practical knowledge or judgment exercised by Bonhoeffer in preaching cannot be understood apart from his prior study and experience, that his preaching was informed by and also informed his life as a German citizen and his work in theology, pastoral ministry, and the ecumenical movement.

70 Hauerwas writes, "The pastoral task is prophetic, in so far as the means that are peculiar to the church's ministry help to remind the community of the story that makes the community prophetic. There can no more prophetic task than the preaching of the word and the serving of the Eucharist, for it is through them that the church is constituted as God's people in a world that does not know God." This is a good description of Bonhoeffer's "prophetic" ministry in Berlin during the chaos of late Weimar Germany. Hauerwas, *Christian Existence Today*, 161. See the good discussion of prophecy in the Reformation in David C. Steinmetz, *Taking the Long View: Christian Theology in Historical Perspective* (Oxford: Oxford University Press, 2011), 81–90. Steinmetz notes, "A prophet for them [the Reformers] was primarily a messenger from God, someone who like the ancient prophets of Israel carried an important and authoritative Word. In Luther's case, he was regarded as a prophet whose message had inaugurated a new evangelical age in the history of Christianity. . . . Luther was . . . understood as the recipient not of fresh revelations but of fresh insights into an ancient and settled revelation" (89–90).

71 DBWE 11:155.

5: *Preaching as Politics*

1 This chapter draws from *Dietrich Bonhoeffer Works; Berlin: 1932–1933*, ed. Larry L. Rassmussen, trans. Isabel Best and David Higgins, DBWE 12 (Minneapolis: Fortress, 2009); and DBWE 13. For helpful biographical information, see Bethge, *Dietrich Bonhoeffer: A Biography*, 257–418; Schlingensiepen, *Dietrich Bonhoeffer*, 114–76; Marsh, *Strange Glory*, 157–93.

2 For a good summary of the Pastor's Emergency League and Confessing Church, see Barnett, *For the Soul of the People*, 47–154.

3 Interpretations of the relation of National Socialism and Christianity are diverse and complex. I have benefited from the following: Steigmann-Gall, *Holy Reich*, 51–189; Bergen, *Twisted Cross*, 1–118; Ericksen, *Complicity in the Holocaust*, 24–93; Klaus Scholder, *The Churches and the Third Reich*, vol. 1, *1918–1934*, trans. J. Bowden (Minneapolis: Fortress, 1988); Michael Burleigh, *The Third Reich: A New History* (New York: Hill & Wang, 2000); Hinlicky, *Before Auschwitz*, 14–140.

4   On the struggle to define the gospel and preaching during this time, see
    Stroud's introduction to *Preaching in Hitler's Shadow*; Hancock, *Karl
    Barth's Emergency Homiletic.*

5   *Dietrich Bonhoeffer Works: Creation and Fall; A Theological Exposition of
    Genesis 1–3*, ed. John W. de Gruchy, trans. Douglas Stephen Bax, DBWE 3
    (Minneapolis: Fortress, 1997).

6   John W. de Gruchy, introduction to DBWE 3, pp. 2–5.

7   See the excellent discussion of the creation of the "academic Bible" in
    Legaspi, *Death of Scripture*, 3–52.

8   De Gruchy, introduction to DBWE 3, pp. 6–8.

9   DBWE 14:133–34.

10 DBWE 14:134.

11 De Gruchy writes, "Thus we see with these lectures a turning point in Bon-
    hoeffer's development from an abstruse academic theologian whose con-
    text was solely the university to a theologian for preachers." De Gruchy,
    introduction to DBWE 3, p. 8. See also the insightful discussion of Bon-
    hoeffer's reading of Scripture for the church in Brock, *Singing the Ethos of
    God*, 71–95; Webster, *Word and Church*, 87–112.

12 Commenting on Luther's exegesis of Genesis, Jaroslav Pelikan writes, "For
    Luther the Book of Genesis was a book for the church. . . . Genesis was a
    history of the people of God." Pelikan, *Luther the Expositor*, 91, 91–102. See
    also the excellent essay on Luther's theological reading of Scripture, partic-
    ularly Genesis, in Mickey L. Mattox, "Luther's Interpretation of Scripture:
    Biblical Understanding in Trinitarian Shape," in *The Substance of Faith:
    Luther's Doctrinal Theology for Today*, ed. Paul R. Hinlicky (Minneapolis:
    Fortress, 2008), 11–55. On the relation of Bonhoeffer, Luther, biblical inter-
    pretation, and Genesis, see Martin Kuske, *The Old Testament as the Book of
    Christ: An Appraisal of Bonhoeffer's Interpretation*, trans. S. T. Kimbrough
    Jr. (Philadelphia: Westminster, 1976), 18–40; see the excellent discussion of
    Luther's interpretation of Genesis in light of the new creation in Oswald
    Bayer, *Living by Faith: Justification and Sanctification*, trans. Geoffrey W.
    Bromiley (Grand Rapids: Eerdmans, 2003), 42–57.

13 Martin Ruter and Ilse Todt, afterword to DBWE 3:152.

14 DBWE 3:21.

15 DBWE 3:35.

16 DBWE 3:22–23.

17 Barker's *Cross of Reality* provides a good discussion of the increasingly
    ecclesial focus of Bonhoeffer's theological work during this time of transi-
    tion. Cf. 249–76. See Bethge's insightful narrative of this time in Bonhoef-
    fer's life and ministry. Bethge, *Dietrich Bonhoeffer: A Biography*, 221–55:
    "Preaching was the great event for him. His severe theologizing and critical
    love for his church were all for its sake, for preaching proclaimed the mes-
    sage of Christ, the bringer of peace. For Bonhoeffer nothing in his calling
    competed in importance with preaching" (234).

18 Steigmann-Gall, *Holy Reich*, 114–89; Barnett, *For the Soul of the People*, 30–44.

19 See the significant discussion of Hitler's theology in Hinlicky, *Before Auschwitz*, 90–140: "Hitler embraced the rationalist, watch-maker God typical of deistic (not 'theistic') thought whose stern and ruthless law he discovered anew in Darwinian natural selection. In this way, Hitler renounced the God identified by biblical narrative. This too is typically 'modern.' . . . I have come to see . . . that his [Hitler's] theology plays familiar chords within modernity and that it is not so strange at all" (140). See Marsh's comments: "The German Christian movement did not so much destroy as emerge from the ruins of the once grand Protestant liberal architectonic." Marsh, *Strange Glory*, 177.

20 Hinlicky, *Before Auschwitz*, 103–9.

21 Steigmann-Gall, *Holy Reich*, 13–50.

22 Cited in Steigmann-Gall, *Holy Reich*, 14.

23 The Augsburg Confession states, "Christ's kingdom is spiritual, that is, it is the heart's knowledge of God, fear of God, faith in God, and the beginning of eternal righteousness and eternal life. At the same time, it permits us to make outward use of legitimate political ordinances of whatever nation in which we live, just as it permits us to make use of medicine or architecture or food, drink, and air. Neither does the gospel introduce new laws for the civil realm. Instead, it commands us to obey the present laws, whether they have been formulated by pagans or by others, and urges us to practice love through this obedience." Robert Kolb and Timothy J. Wengert, eds., "Article XVI: Political Order," in *The Book of Concord: The Confession of the Evangelical Lutheran Church*, trans. Charles Arand et al. (Minneapolis: Fortress, 2000), 231; see the helpful essay on Luther's Two Kingdoms doctrine in David C. Steinmetz, *Luther in Context* (Bloomington: Indiana University Press, 1986), 112–26.

24 See the discussion in Barnett, *For the Soul of the People*, 128–54; Steigmann-Gall, *Holy Reich*, 29–41; Bergen, *Twisted Cross*, 21–43.

25 Burleigh, *Third Reich*, 256.

26 Ericksen, *Complicity in the Holocaust*, 24–37; Steigmann-Gall, *Holy Reich*, 51–85.

27 DBWE 12:101; see the insightful discussion in Hinlicky, *Before Auschwitz*, 141–54.

28 See Stroud's introduction to *Preaching in Hitler's Shadow*, 13–22; Hancock, *Karl Barth's Emergency Homiletic*, 154–80.

29 DBWE 12:443–44.

30 See Stroud's introduction to *Preaching in Hitler's Shadow*, 39–48. See also this essay on Bonhoeffer in light of the church/nation relation "after Christendom": Vigen Guroian, "Church and Nationhood: A Reflection on the 'National Church,'" in *Theology and the Practice of Responsibility: Essays*

on Dietrich Bonhoeffer, ed. Wayne Whitson Floyd Jr. and Charles Marsh (Valley Forge, Pa.: Trinity International, 1994), 171–96.

31 Steigmann-Gall, *Holy Reich*, 51–60, 84–85.

32 See Stroud's introduction to *Preaching in Hitler's Shadow*, 9–12.

33 Here, I am indebted to the excellent summary in Hancock, *Karl Barth's Emergency Homiletic*, 171–92; see also the insightful comments by Hinlicky on the struggle for the gospel in *Before Auschwitz*, 180–83.

34 Bonhoeffer's either-or approach toward proclaiming and hearing the gospel, the use of antitheses, has similarities to Luther's rhetoric of reform. See the excellent summary of Luther's use of language, in Peter Matheson, *The Rhetoric of the Reformation* (Edinburgh: T&T Clark, 1998), 111–38; see also the excellent study of Luther's use of biblical narratives for evangelizing, forming, and building up the church in Robert Kolb, *Luther and the Stories of God: Biblical Narratives as a Foundation for Christian Living* (Grand Rapids: Baker Academic, 2012).

35 DBWE 12:461.

36 DBWE 12:463–64.

37 DBWE 12:466.

38 DBWE 12:468.

39 DBWE 12:469–70.

40 DBWE 12:473.

41 DBWE 12:474.

42 DBWE 12:475.

43 DBWE 12:476.

44 DBWE 12:477.

45 DBWE 12:477.

46 DBWE 13:477.

47 DBWE 13:478–79.

48 See the detailed narrative in Bethge, *Dietrich Bonhoeffer: A Biography*, 300–323. Reggie Williams argues convincingly that Bonhoeffer's unique perspective among his peers on the Nazis' implementation of racism was due to the time spent in New York, particularly in Harlem. Williams, *Bonhoeffer's Black Jesus*, 120–32.

49 DBWE 13:24.

50 See the discussion of events in Steigmann-Gall, *Holy Reich*, 164–77.

51 DBWE 13:104.

52 See the narrative in Marsh, *Strange Glory*, 194–226.

53 DBWE 13:321.

54 DBWE 13:322.

55 DBWE 13:323.

56 DBWE 13:324–25.

57 DBWE 13:331.

58 DBWE 13:348–49.

59 DBWE 13:350–51.

60 DBWE 13:353–54.
61 DBWE 13:355.
62 DBWE 13:337.
63 DBWE 13:340–41.
64 DBWE 13:342–44.
65 DBWE 13:345.
66 DBWE 13:365–66.
67 DBWE 13:368–69.
68 DBWE 13:375–76.
69 DBWE 13:387.
70 DBWE 13:393.
71 DBWE 13:380.
72 DBWE 13:396.
73 DBWE 13:395–96.
74 Barker, *Cross of Reality*, 252–75.
75 Bonhoeffer's comment on the practice of racism in America, whites against blacks, reflects the fruit of his experience and reflection in New York. See Williams, *Bonhoeffer's Black Jesus*, 134–35.
76 Bonhoeffer is presumably responding to Nietzsche's criticisms of Christianity as a message to the weak and a religion of slaves. The sermon overturns Nietzsche and establishes Christ as the source of all values. See the discussion in Peter Frick, "Friedrich Nietzsche's Aphorisms and Dietrich Bonhoeffer's Theology," in *Bonhoeffer's Intellectual Formation*, 182–83.
77 DBWE 13:401–2.
78 DBWE 13:403.
79 DBWE 13:184, 189.

6: Preaching as Public Confession

1 On this period in Bonhoeffer's life, see Bethge, *Dietrich Bonhoeffer: A Biography*, 419–586; Schlingensiepen, *Dietrich Bonhoeffer*, 177–209; Marsh, *Strange Glory*, 227–62. Bethge's account is significant, since he was a member of the Finkenwalde community.
2 See Barnett, *For the Soul of the Nation*, 47–134: "At the end of the early period of the Third Reich, the Confessing Church was not a unified block of resistance to Nazism, but a scattering of individuals and parishes whose common creed was a Christianity undefiled by Nazism. How they practiced their Christianity was affected not just by the conflicts they had with the state but with each other. What continued to divide these Christians was an essential question of individual and institutional identity: To what, in their confession of faith, were they committing themselves and their church?" (71). This was the question continually raised by Bonhoeffer.
3 Here, I am indebted to Stanley Hauerwas, "No Enemy, No Christianity: Preaching between Worlds," in *Sanctify Them*, 191–200: "Indeed, the whole

point of Christianity is to produce the right kind of enemies. We have been beguiled by our established status to forget that to be a Christian is to be made part of an army against armies. . . . When Caesar becomes a member of the church the enemy becomes internalized. . . . [We] need to have a sense of where the battle is, what the stakes are, and what the long-term strategy may be. Yet this is exactly what most preaching does not do" (196).

4   DBWE 14:657. It is interesting that the writings Bonhoeffer produced from the Finkenwalde period are his most popular. *Discipleship*, *Life Together*, and *Prayerbook of the Bible* are typically read as devotional "classics" oriented to individual spirituality. Given the conditions in Germany, these books might be better read as works of resistance. When Bonhoeffer published these books in the years immediately following the shuttering of Finkenwalde, their intended audience was not only seminarians, pastors, and congregations of a Confessing Church fighting for its life; it also included the wider ecumenical church for which Bonhoeffer hoped Finkenwalde would serve as a model in a time for confessing. See the editor's introduction to *Dietrich Bonhoeffer Works: Life Together; Prayerbook of the Bible*, ed. Geffrey B. Kelly, trans. Daniel W. Bloesch and James H. Burtness, DBWE 5 (Minneapolis: Fortress, 1996), 3–24. The following chapter will discuss the writings produced from the Finkenwalde years.

5   DBWE 14:257.

6   DBWE 14:257.

7   DBWE 14:72–73.

8   See Barnett, *For the Soul of the People*, 51–71.

9   For a good discussion of Bonhoeffer, confessing the gospel, and the Confessing Church, see Robert W. Bertram, *A Time for Confessing*, ed. Michael Hoy (Grand Rapids: Eerdmans, 2008), 65–95. Bertram argues that Bonhoeffer saw the fundamental matter as evangelical freedom and not the exclusive confessional orthodoxy embraced by some members of the Confessing Church and Finkenwalde community: "The church, [Bonhoeffer] argued, was now having boundaries set *for* her, 'drawn against her from outside,' for instance, when seminarians were pressured by 'outsiders' to withdraw from the Finkenwalde community. Once that happened, must not these outsiders' self-imposed boundaries be recognized as the real boundaries they then become, for those outsiders? Then the self-imposed boundaries become barriers not to membership in some human organization, but to the body of Christ, barriers to Christ himself?" (79–80; emphasis in original).

10   DBWE 14:667.

11   DBWE 14:676.

12   See the insightful discussion by Dean G. Stroud in his introduction to *Preaching in Hitler's Shadow*, 3–50.

13   DBWE 13:135.

14   DBWE 13:152.

15 DBWE 13:191.

16 See the discussion in Marsh, *Strange Glory*, 220–26.

17 DBWE 13:217.

18 DBWE 12:284–85.

19 I am indebted to the excellent discussion of the Christology lectures in Andreas Pangritz, "Who Is Jesus Christ, for Us, Today?" in de Gruchy, *Cambridge Companion*, 134–53.

20 DBWE 12:300.

21 DBWE 12:301–2.

22 DBWE 12:317–18.

23 DBWE 12:366. See the discussion of Bonhoeffer's christological orientation to reality in Philip G. Ziegler, "God, Christ, and Church in the DDR—Wolf Krötke as an Interpreter of Bonhoeffer's Theology," in *Engaging Bonhoeffer: The Impact and Influence of Bonhoeffer's Life and Thought*, ed. Matthew D. Kirkpatrick (Minneapolis: Fortress, 2016), 201–20.

24 DBWE 14:84–85.

25 See the illuminating summary of Bonhoeffer's integrative way of teaching as practical theology in the editor's afterword to the German edition of DBWE 14, pp. 971–1015. Richard Lischer describes this way of forming preachers as a theologically grounded habitus, a quality of life uniting both theological understanding and spiritual wisdom. See Richard Lischer, *A Theology of Preaching: Dynamics of the Gospel*, rev. ed. (Eugene, Ore.: Wipf & Stock, 2001), ix–x.

26 Karl Barth, *Homiletics*, trans. Geoffrey W. Bromiley and Donald E. Daniels (Louisville, Ky.: Westminster John Knox, 1991). In this section I am indebted to the excellent study of Barth's homiletic in Hancock, *Karl Barth's Emergency Homiletic*.

27 Hancock, *Barth's Emergency Homiletic*, 171–73.

28 Hancock, *Barth's Emergency Homiletic*, 183.

29 Barth, *Homiletics*, 44.

30 Barth, *Homiletics*, 47–90.

31 Barth, *Homiletics*, 86–87.

32 Nicholas Lash writes, "Our ability to listen, and to speak, and hence our duty to do both things well, form part, we might say, of the 'shape,' the form or nature, that we have, as human beings, over time acquired. . . . To be human is to be able to speak. But to be able to speak is to be 'answerable,' 'responsible' to and for each other, and to the mystery of God." Lash, *Holiness, Speech and Silence: Reflections on the Question of God* (Aldershot: Ashgate, 2004), 57, 59.

33 Barth, *Homiletics*, 88. Hancock describes Barth's homiletic as practical theology: "The notes that were left behind do not reveal some kind of timeless universal homiletical blueprint we might label as 'Barthian' and then discard. Instead, they offer a glimpse at a self-consciously contextual, dialectical, theological, and temporary homiletic forged in the midst of

political and personal turmoil." Hancock, *Barth's Emergency Homiletic*, 327.

34   Barth, *Homiletics*, 89.

35   Barth, *Homiletics*, 89–90. Hancock concludes her study with the following comments: "Barth's practical advice to his students in the summer of 1933 undermined just about everything they had learned from Professor Pfennigsdorf about how to prepare a sermon—a minority report in relation to the homiletic theory and practice on display all around them. As such it was an emergency homiletic, a return to theological basics even with regard to practical questions, at a time when theological basics were in short supply." Hancock, *Karl Barth's Emergency Homiletic*, 322.

36   DBWE 14:341–43. See the discussion in chapter 3 on Bonhoeffer's critique of Barth's doctrine of revelation.

37   DBWE 14:509–14. One of the first studies of Bonhoeffer's homiletical work is still available in Fant, *Bonhoeffer*.

38   DBWE 14:510–11.

39   DBWE 14:512–13. See Bruce D. Marshall's excellent essay "The Church in the Gospel," *Pro Ecclesia* 1, no. 1 (1992): "The church is reformed in this view the same way the Protestant Reformers (among others) always said it is: by the gospel. The church's ongoing communal life is always subject to correction, at every point, by the gospel, but the church, precisely as the historically particular community on the way from Pentecost to the return of Christ, is itself part of the gospel in light of which its present speech and action are subject to reform. So the reform of the church's present belief and practice will very likely take a different concrete form than it would if the church did not belong to the gospel, if, in other words, the gospel could be spoken in abstraction from the church" (39–40).

40   DBWE 14:488. For an older but still helpful discussion of Luther on the Bible and the Word of God, see Pelikan, *Luther the Expositor*, 48–70.

41   On Luther as exegete and preacher, see David C. Steinmetz, "Luther and Formation in Faith," in *Educating People of Faith: Exploring the History of Jewish and Christian Communities*, ed. John Van Engen (Grand Rapids: Eerdmans, 2004), 252–62; Heiko A. Oberman, *Luther: Man between God and the Devil*, trans. Eileen Walliser-Schwarzbart (New York: Bantam Doubleday Dell, 1992); William H. Lazareth, *Christians in Society: Luther, the Bible, and Social Ethics* (Minneapolis: Fortress, 2001), 31–57; Oberman, "Preaching and the Word in the Reformation," *Theology Today* 18, no. 1 (1961): 16–29; John W. O'Malley, S.J., "Luther the Preacher," in *The Martin Luther Quincentennial*, ed. Gerhard Dünnhaupt (Detroit: Wayne State University Press, 1985), 3–16; Stephen H. Webb, *The Divine Voice: Christian Proclamation and the Theology of Sound* (Grand Rapids: Brazos, 2004), 141–46.

42   Martin Luther, *Sermons on the Gospel of John*, ed. Jaroslav Pelikan, vol. 22 of *Luther's Works* (St. Louis: Concordia, 1957), 66–67.

43 Johannes Schwanke, "Luther on Creation," in *Harvesting Martin Luther's Reflections on Theology, Ethics, and the Church*, ed. Timothy J. Wengert (Grand Rapids: Eerdmans, 2004), 78–98.

44 Martin Luther, "Preface to the New Testament," in *Martin Luther's Basic Theological Writings*, ed. Timothy F. Lull (Minneapolis: Fortress, 1989), 113. Oswald Bayer writes of Luther's practice of interpretation and preaching, "In this way, one is led deeply into the Bible—into the history between God and humanity witnessed by it and in turn formed by it. It is not only the history of Israel and the church, but—reflected in it, but reaching far beyond it—the whole history of nature and humanity: of the creation fallen, redeemed, and sighing for fulfillment." Bayer, "Luther as Interpreter of Holy Scripture," in McKim, *Cambridge Companion*, 79–80.

45 Ola Tjorhom, "The Church as the Place of Salvation: On the Interrelation between Justification and Ecclesiology," *Pro Ecclesia* 9, no. 3 (2000): 294–96.

46 In a discussion of Luther's influence on Bonhoeffer throughout his career, Wolf Krötke writes, "It would be impossible to understand how Bonhoeffer thought about God's word, Jesus Christ, and all other themes central to Protestant theology apart from Luther's insights, whether these played a direct or indirect role." Krötke, "Dietrich Bonhoeffer and Martin Luther," 79. Krötke also comments on the importance of Luther for Bonhoeffer during the time period that included Finkenwalde: "For Bonhoeffer, keeping and actualizing the foundations of the church was identical with articulating Luther's genuine understanding of the word of God in law and gospel, faith, the church and Christian action. . . . Because Bonhoeffer was keen to reach his own conclusions on Luther's theology on the basis of Luther's writings, his path in the 1930s often collided—both within and outside the Confessing Church—with what was called Lutheranism or Lutheran" (54–55). See also the good summary of Bonhoeffer's theology and work at Finkenwalde with reference to Luther in Barker, *Cross of Reality*, 277–302.

47 John Webster, *Holy Scripture: A Dogmatic Sketch* (Cambridge: Cambridge University Press, 2003), 78–85.

48 DBWE 14:95–96.

49 Jurgen Henkys summarizes Bonhoeffer's teaching in this manner: "For Bonhoeffer the range of theological disciplines develops within the overall framework of an integrative concept of theology. In the approach to theological work, the different theological disciplines are secondary rather than primary. The systematic theologian is thus able to bring his own specialization to bear in a more elementary theological fashion and engage in theology with his candidates in a way that makes the subject matter more urgent through its proximity. A decrease in the distance between human beings also involves a decrease in the distance between

the various disciplines." Henkys, editor's afterword to the German edition of DBWE 14, p. 982.

50   DBWE 14:111.

51   DBWE 14:171 (emphasis added).

52   DBWE 14:167 (emphasis in original).

53   DBWE 14:167. See the discussion of Bonhoeffer's seminar work on Luther's interpretation of Scripture in chapter 1. I have found the following discussions of Bonhoeffer's biblical interpretation helpful: Brock, *Singing the Ethos of God*, 71–97; Webster, *Holy Scripture*, 78–85. Both Brock and Webster point to Bonhoeffer's attempt to overcome modern academic divisions, reading the Bible as holy Scripture, which entails attentive listening to Christ present in the word. Faith, learning, and devotion are integrated within the life of the church.

54   DBWE 14:167–68. Lash writes, "The fundamental form of speech is prayer. . . . Contemplation is a deeper appropriation of the vulnerability of the self in the midst of the language and transactions of the world. The notion of 'vulnerability' neatly combines recognition of contingency, of the creature's absolute dependence on the mystery of God. . . (sentence trails off)." Lash, *Holiness, Speech and Silence*, 64–65. Stanley Hauerwas comments, "We are dying—and I mean quite literally dying—for examples of what reading Scripture theologically might look like. Scripture, vivified by the Holy Spirit, is the heart of the church. Without a heart we cannot live." Hauerwas, *Working with Words: On Learning to Speak Christian* (Eugene, Ore.: Wipf & Stock, 2001), 112.

55   DBWE 14:169.

56   Franz Posset, *The Real Luther: A Friar at Erfurt and Wittenberg* (St. Louis: Concordia, 2011), 64–69; Oberman, *Luther*, 169–74; Timothy J. Wengert, *Reading the Bible with Martin Luther* (Grand Rapids: Baker Academic, 2013), 8–24. See the insightful discussion of a liturgical hermeneutic/homiletic in F. Russell Mitman, *Worship in the Shape of Scripture* (Cleveland: Pilgrim, 2001), 23–29.

57   Oberman, *Martin Luther*, 169–71. See the discussion of Luther's attention to the "grammar" of Scripture as the language of the Spirit in Charles M. Wood, *An Invitation to Theological Study* (Valley Forge, Pa.: Trinity International, 1994), 103–7. Hauerwas notes, "Such a faith, that is, a faith in the resurrection of Jesus, also means that to speak Christian does not mean such speech cannot be understood by others who do not speak Christian. It does mean, however, that like us they will need to undergo training to hear what is being said and hopefully thereby become more eloquent and confident speakers." Hauerwas, *Working with Words*, 92.

58   Oswald Bayer, *Theology the Lutheran Way*, ed. and trans. Jeffrey G. Silcock and Mark C. Mattes (Grand Rapids: Eerdmans, 2007), 21–35, 67–85; Posset, *Real Luther*, 67–68. In the opening section of *Luther as Expositor*, Jaroslav Pelikan writes, "The history of theology is, of course, the most obvious

aspect of Christian history in which the interpretation of the Scriptures has figured very prominently—especially if the history of theology includes, as it should, the history of Christian preaching" (5).

59 See the discussion of integrity and constancy within one's agency as "intelligible action" in relation to the concrete narrative of Bonhoeffer's life in Hauerwas, *Work of Theology*, 77–89. Bonhoeffer's "experiment" with Finkenwalde was to provide a community where integrity and constancy could be cultivated in a manner appropriate to confessing Jesus Christ against the claims of Nazi Germany.

60 DBWE 14:95–96, 254. Stanley Hauerwas writes, "The distinction between theology and ethics certainly makes no sense to me if, as I have argued, most of theology is an exercise in practical reason. Perhaps even more problematic is the separation of 'pastoral' or 'practical' theology from theology proper. I am not denying that there may be some pragmatic reasons to distinguish between theology and practical theology, but if theology is in service to the church, if theology is one of the ways Christian holiness is made a reality, I do not think practical theology can be separated from theology." Hauerwas, *Work of Theology*, 109.

61 DBWE 14:413–33.

62 DBWE 14:414.

63 DBWE 14:417.

64 See the discussion in Stroud, *Preaching in Hitler's Shadow*, 39–50. For a theological assessment and critique of "relevance" in contemporary North American churches, see J. Todd Billings, *The Word of God for the People of God: An Entryway to the Theological Interpretation of Scripture* (Grand Rapids: Eerdmans, 2010), 31–148.

65 See the argument by Paul Hinlicky (in *Before Auschwitz*) that seeks to show the intellectual trajectory leading from liberal Protestant theology to the German Christians.

66 DBWE 14:413–14 (emphasis added).

67 DBWE 14:415.

68 DBWE 14:416 (emphasis added).

69 DBWE 14:417.

70 DBWE 14:417–18.

71 DBWE 14:417.

72 DBWE 14:417–18.

73 DBWE 14:419–20.

74 DBWE 14:420–21.

75 DBWE 14:421–22.

76 DBWE 14:423.

77 DBWE 14:424. Hauerwas writes, "To try to isolate the meaning of a word from its use is to assume that language is one thing and that what the language depicts is something quite other. As a result language and the world are understood to be externally related to one another in a manner that

language users are positioned as spectators rather than performers. The presumption that a dualism exists between language and the world hides from us that 'the world' is constituted by language and that there is no way to transcend language to speak about language." Hauerwas, *Working with Words*, 103. See the discussion in John W. Wright, *Telling God's Story: Narrative Preaching for Christian Formation* (Downers Grove, Ill.: InterVarsity, 2007), 15–76; chap. 1, "Homiletics as Biblical Hermeneutics," is particularly helpful.

78   DBWE 14:425–26.

79   DBWE 14:432–33. Wendell Berry writes of "standing by words" in the following manner: "My standpoint . . . is defined by the assumption that no statement is complete or comprehensible in itself, that in order for a statement to be complete and comprehensible three conditions are required: (1) It must designate the object precisely; (2) *Its speaker must stand by it: must believe it, be accountable for it, be willing to act on it*; (3) The relation of speaker, word, and object must be conventional; the community must know what it is." Berry, *Standing by Words*, 21 (emphasis added).

80   Bonhoeffer refused to reduce preaching to methodology, as the work of detached technicians whose aim is to make preaching "practical." As a practice of the whole church in service of the gospel, proclamation requires a particular kind of knowledge and character, a fitting kind of insightfulness and perception, judgment and discernment, imagination and affection. In preaching, the whole person is personally engaged with the church as a historical community with a particular calling and mission as given by God in Christ. See the excellent study on practical judgment in Dunne, *Back to the Rough Ground*, 275–366.

81   DBWE 14:490.

82   DBWE 14:492.

83   DBWE 14:493–95 (emphasis in original). See the excellent discussion of attending, assessing, and judging in Dunne, *Back to the Rough Ground*, 362–71. I have also benefited from Daniel J. Treier, *Virtue and the Voice of God: Towards a Theology of Wisdom* (Grand Rapids: Eerdmans, 2006), 183–206.

84   DBWE 14:504–6 (emphasis in original).

85   See the excellent discussion on the christological relation between sermon content and form in Richard Lischer, *The End of Words: The Language of Reconciliation in a Culture of Violence* (Grand Rapids: Eerdmans, 2005).

86   Bonhoeffer preferred the ancient homily form of the sermon that is scriptural, liturgical, and ecclesial in nature, a form of proclamation theology that follows the text verse by verse without imposing topical or thematic organization. See Walter J. Burghardt, S.J., "Homily," in *Concise Encyclopedia of Preaching*, ed. William H. Willimon and Richard Lischer (Louisville, Ky.: Westminster John Knox, 1995), 257–59.

87 DBWE 14:506–8. See the discussion on the use of words by ministers in Hauerwas, *Work of Theology*, 115: "To be in the ministry, to be a priest, to be a theologian is to be in the business of word care. . . . That we do not have control of the words we use I think is surely the case if you identify with that tradition of speech called Christianity. Theologians [or pastors] or priests or ministers do not get to choose what they are to think about. Better put, theologians do not get to choose the words they use. Because they do not get to choose the words they use they are forced to think hard about why the words they use are the ones that must be used. They must do the equally hard work of thinking about the order that the words they use must have if the words are to do the work they are meant to do."

88 See the summary of the Finkenwalde curriculum and its theological purpose of serving the gospel and church in the editor's introduction to DBWE 14, pp. 27–34.

89 DBWE 14:72–73.

7: A Forced Itinerary

1 Barnett, *For the Soul of the People*, 85–88.

2 For this chapter I have followed Bethge, *Dietrich Bonhoeffer: A Biography*, 587–680; Marsh, *Strange Glory*, 263–93; Schlingensiepen, *Dietrich Bonhoeffer*, 210–26. See also the introduction and afterword to *Dietrich Bonhoeffer Works: Theological Education Underground, 1937–1940*, ed. Victoria J. Barnett, trans. Victoria J. Barnett et al., DBWE 15 (Minneapolis: Fortress, 2012); *Dietrich Bonhoeffer Works: Discipleship*, ed. Geffrey B. Kelly and John D. Godsey, trans. Barbara Green and Reinhard Krauss, DBWE 4 (Minneapolis: Fortress, 2001); and DBWE 5.

3 See the narrative in Bethge, *Dietrich Bonhoeffer: A Biography*, 587–676.

4 Barnett, *For the Soul of the People*, 94–95: "Of the entire Protestant pastorate, 45 percent of the ordained ministers and 98 percent of vicars and candidates to the ministry had been mobilized by October 1944. The ranks of young Confessing Church Illegals were hardest hit. . . . Of the approximately 150 students who studied with Bonhoeffer, over 80 were killed in the war" (95).

5 Barnett, *For the Soul of the People*, 96–98.

6 Barnett, *For the Soul of the People*, 98–103: "The threat of Gestapo interrogation, of imprisonment in the dreaded Gestapo prisons or the camps, rumors about beatings and torture, and the concentration camps—all spread like a shadow over people's consciousness. Legalization and other concessions were, in a sense, the construction of political safeguards, attempts to create pockets of security for individuals and their families" (99).

7 DBWE 15:465–66.

8 DBWE 15:467.

9   The comments by Charles L. Campbell and Johan H. Cilliers on preaching as a "rhetoric of folly" helps toward understanding why Bonhoeffer, in
the context of Hitler's Germany, could find the command of the gospel to
love one's enemies as foolish: "The gospel is foolishness. Preaching is folly.
Paul's words have haunted us as we teach preaching in the midst of a world
shaped by almost overwhelming powers of domination and violence and
death. And the apostle's words have haunted us whenever we stand up to
preach with nothing but a word in the midst of a world shaped by armies
and weapons of mass destruction, by global technology and economy, by
principalities and powers that overwhelm both by their seductiveness and
their threat. Up against all that, preachers speak for a few minutes from the
pulpit. It seems like foolishness. In the face of those structures and institutions and systems and myths and ideologies that so often hold us captive
and prevent us from imagining alternatives to their deadly ways, preaching often seems like a weak and fruitless response." Campbell and Cilliers,
Preaching Fools: The Gospel as a Rhetoric of Folly (Waco, Tex.: Baylor University Press, 2012), 18.

10 DBWE 15:467, 470.

11 DBWE 15:471.

12 Nation, Siegrist, and Umbel, *Bonhoeffer the Assassin?*, 64–68. Bethge writes
of Bonhoeffer's struggles during this time: "Bonhoeffer was ashamed of the
Confessing Church, the way one feels shame for a scandal in one's own
family. This Confessing synod (1938) had approved the oath to the Führer
when it already knew of the impending order that non-Aryans must have
a larger 'J' stamped on their identity cards—an omen of worse things to
come, and the thing that finally moved his twin sister's family to flee. And
the threat of war against Czechoslovakia was growing. The possibility of a
gap between Bonhoeffer and the Confessing Church was becoming real."
Bethge, *Dietrich Bonhoeffer: A Biography*, 603. On the loyalty oath to Hitler, see Barnett, *For the Soul of the People*, 156–58.

13 DBWE 15:29. On the imprisonment of Confessing Church seminarians and
pastors, see Barnett, *For the Soul of the People*, 158–62.

14 DBWE 15:29.

15 "Preface to the Wittenberg Edition of Luther's German Writings (1539),"
in *Martin Luther's Basic Theological Writings*, 63–69; hereafter, "Luther's
Preface." Here, I am indebted to the discussion in Reinhard Hutter, *Suffering Divine Things: Theology as Church Practice* (Grand Rapids: Eerdmans, 2000), 72–75. Oswald Bayer writes, "In brief, we can sum up Luther's
remarks as follows: a theologian is a person who is interpreted by Holy
Scripture, who lets himself or herself be interpreted by it and who, having
been interpreted by it, interprets it for other troubled and afflicted people."
Bayer, *Theology the Lutheran Way*, 36, 33–68.

16 "Luther's Preface," 66.

17 "Luther's Preface," 66.

18   "Luther's Preface," 67–68.

19   DBWE 15:30.

20   DBWE 15:30, 31, 35.

21   For an extended example of such work, see William H. Willimon, *Pastor: The Theology and Practice of Ordained Ministry* (Nashville: Abingdon, 2002).

22   Geffrey B. Kelly and J. Burton Nelson write of Bonhoeffer's moral leadership with the churches in Germany, "The same churches that claim Bonhoeffer as one of their own because of his struggle against fascism might be disconcerted to see themselves bitterly denounced by him for their unwillingness to reform themselves in light of that tormented period in Christian history. Bonhoeffer's indictment of the churches for their failure either to prevent or bring to an end the repression of human rights and senseless, insane killings offers a lesson on how even well-intentioned churches can lose their vocation to be the prophetic Christ speaking peace against the demonic spirit of warlords. . . . Bonhoeffer demanded that the churches once again become, as they had always boasted they were, the presence and word of Christ for their people." Kelly and Nelson, *The Cost of Moral Leadership: The Spirituality of Dietrich Bonhoeffer* (Grand Rapids: Eerdmans, 2003), 125.

23   DBWE 15:39.

24   See the discussion in Robert J. Dean, *For the Life of the World: Jesus Christ and the Church in the Theologies of Dietrich Bonhoeffer and Stanley Hauerwas* (Eugene, Ore.: Pickwick, 2016), 93–95; Rowan Williams comments on Bonhoeffer's integrative understanding of piety, which unites prayer, language, and action: "Piety, in Bonhoeffer's eyes, is always something that tempts us to passivity unless it is anchored in a clear doctrine of the transforming word. Hence the spirituality, which he sought to inculcate at Finkenwalde, was inseparable from the call to resistance. To read the Bible together and to practice confession and meditation are necessary for human beings who are free to say no to the culture around them; they are ways of learning and absorbing the 'culture' of Christ's Body—not as a trivial alternative, an option alongside others, but as the resource out of which will come a humanity more fully equipped to be human alongside those whom the culture forgets or despises or terrorizes." Cited in Medi Ann Volpe and Jennifer Moberly, " 'Let Your Light So Shine': Rowan Williams and Dietrich Bonhoeffer," in *Engaging Bonhoeffer: The Impact and Influence of Bonhoeffer's Life and Thought*, ed. Matthew D. Kirkpatrick (Minneapolis: Fortress, 2016), 309–10.

25   DBWE 15:40.

26   DBWE 4.

27   Geffrey B. Kelly and John D. Godsey comment on Bonhoeffer's purpose in writing *Discipleship*: "He was determined to break the church out of its standard mode of compromise with, and accommodation to, political powers for the sake of its own survival as church. That self-serving,

ecclesiastical tactic—while eminently practical if the church's sole purpose was to be a sacramental system and an easygoing provider of grace—had convinced Bonhoeffer that the churches of Germany had, in effect, cheapened themselves." Editors' introduction to DBWE 4, p. 3.

28 Kelly and Godsey write in the editors' introduction to DBWE 4, p. 16: "The world of Bonhoeffer's original readers . . . was in open rebellion against the limits that constituted Christian values in a civil society. In *Discipleship*, Bonhoeffer attempts to confront the seductive lure held out to Germany's citizens, asking them to divorce themselves from what Nazi ideology portrayed as the less than fully Germanic world redeemed by Jesus Christ—a world portrayed as 'polluted' by subhumans like Jews and gypsies, in addition to those out of favor with the government through their dissenting ways. This to Bonhoeffer was a demonic attack on the real world, on real persons created in God's image, on the Christ."

29 DBWE 4:37.

30 DBWE 4:37–38. See the discussion of *Discipleship* in light of modern theology and ethics in Nation, Siegrist, and Umbel, *Bonhoeffer the Assassin?*, 128–36. See also the suggestive essay on Bonhoeffer's understanding of spirituality in light of *Discipleship* by Kelly and Nelson, *Cost of Moral Leadership*, 129–44: "Bonhoeffer understood the spiritual call to be part of this community as an invitation from Jesus Christ to become his communal form in every generation, suffering from the same rejection he experienced at the hands of a hostile world" (143).

31 DBWE 4:39–40.

32 DBWE 4:40.

33 DBWE 4:44–45.

34 DBWE 4:43.

35 DBWE 4:43.

36 The matter of "cheap grace" is not merely a doctrinal issue, as Robert J. Dean writes: "In the long run cheap grace had proven to be terribly costly to the church. Bonhoeffer attributes the hardening of individuals in disobedience and the collapse of organized churches to the peddling of cheap grace. The proliferation of cheap grace in Germany resulted in a comfortable, cultural Christianity. In surrendering the demands of discipleship in exchange for continuing influence and privilege in society, the church in Germany discovered that it lacked the resources to resist the false gods of Volk, Blut, and Boden." Dean, *For the Life of the World*, 77.

37 H. Gaylon Barker writes, "What Bonhoeffer saw was both the need for a new reformation as well as a new vision of the church and German life. Certainly the signs exhibited by the German Christians pointed out the real problem that had to be confronted, which was precisely what Bonhoeffer set out to do with *Discipleship*." Barker, *Cross of Reality*, 307.

38 DBWE 4:50. Nation, Siegrist, and Umbel (*Bonhoeffer the Assassin?*, 140) write, "It is important to note Bonhoeffer's distinction between true and

false models of Christological authority as well as the respective distinctions between true and false moral anthropologies, because these distinctions are what make it possible to bring together God's grace and human obedience to Christ's commandments while doing justice to both God's initiative and human response. The correct model of Christ's authority does justice to God as the divine subject, to Christ as God's freedom incarnate, and thus to God as the source of grace and empowerment. The model of Christ as moral teacher cannot do justice to the disciple's dependence upon God's gracious and active call in Jesus because it has employed an objectified and objectifying model of God and Christ. The model has reduced Christ to an object of reflection and his teachings to timeless moral values, principles, or absolutes. Thus this model, in not doing justice to Christ as the divine subject incarnate, reduces obedience to legalism and Christian freedom to self-grounded moral striving."

39   DBWE 4:53–55. Stanley Hauerwas writes, "Jesus issued this challenge not only through his teaching, but through his life. Indeed the very announcement of the reality of the kingdom, its presence here and now, is embodied in his life. In him we see that living a life of forgiveness and peace is not an impossible ideal but an opportunity now present. Thus Jesus' life is integral to the meaning, content, and possibility of the kingdom. For the announcement of the reality of this kingdom, of the possibility of living a life of forgiveness and peace with one's enemies, is based on our confidence that that kingdom has become a reality through the life and work of this man, Jesus of Nazareth. His life is the life of the end—this is the way the world is meant to be—and thus those who follow him become a people of the last times, the people of the new age." Hauerwas, *The Peaceable Kingdom: A Primer in Christian Ethics* (Notre Dame, Ind.: University of Notre Dame Press, 1983), 85.

40   See the magisterial narrative by Taylor in *A Secular Age.*

41   DBWE 4:50–51.

42   DBWE 4:51, 53.

43   DBWE 4:59. As Barker comments, "By linking justification and discipleship, Bonhoeffer provided the orientation that refuses to allow God to be separated from the world." Barker, *Cross of Reality*, 324.

44   Dean, *For the Life of the World*, 79.

45   DBWE 4:111–12.

46   DBWE 4:144–45.

47   DBWE 4:112–13.

48   DBWE 4:172.

49   DBWE 4:173. Campbell and Cilliers write of the experience of liminality, the state of uncertainty, and the quest for power to resolve and overcome uncertainty, "When power is abused to dominate or control—for instance, in the realm of politics—the result can be the total destruction or eradication of the object to which it is directed. When the object is human

beings (almost always the case) the outcome is truly evil: people are dominated and controlled, in fact *dehumanized*. Human dignity is sacrificed as justice, unity, and reconciliation are inverted through the operation of power. . . . The church, reckoning with the power of God, often tends to make itself (its structures, officials, theology [here I would add preaching]) as the final form of knowledge, if not God as such." Campbell and Cilliers, *Preaching Fools*, 64 (emphasis in original).

50 DBWE 4:173. Kelly and Nelson write, "The practical question thus became for Bonhoeffer how, in a non-triumphal Christianity, to prevent Christians and church communities from squandering their identity with Jesus Christ in the midst of their involvement with the secular. . . . A discipline of modesty in claims and humility in action was called for to help the church become liberated from itself and delivered from the stagnation of less than Christian forms of religious expression. The church had a mandate to preserve the mysteries of the Christian faith proclaimed by God's Word, not with a pathetic defensive frenzy, but with prayer, worship, and Christlike example." Kelly and Nelson, *Cost of Moral Leadership*, 43. Campbell and Cilliers offer a nuanced theological perspective on the "weakness" of the Word: "In God's compassion lies God's power—the foolish power of God's compassionate weakness. Such a theology of God's power in weakness, however, does not mean that those who believe in this God must forever be seeking vulnerability or suffering, or declare it to be an eternal state of affairs. . . . A theology of God's powerful weakness has nothing to do with masochism or a pathological compulsion to suffer. On the contrary, it is about the compassionate power of God continuously taking on new forms within reality. It is about the Spirit of Christ continuously busy with a deepened re-formation of form. The point of departure now is the broken-form of God in Christ; the aim is the re-formation of this form toward new expressions of the Spirit within reality. . . . The *church* is called to be just such a new pattern of pneumatic living." Campbell and Cilliers, *Preaching Fools*, 58 (emphasis in original).

51 DBWE 4:174. Campbell and Cilliers write, "Many God-images tend to smack of power and become reduced to human agendas. In fact, it is tempting to create a type of theology that promises control and power—a theology directly opposite to that of God's power in weakness. A God without controlling, dominating power is difficult to understand. . . . This lack of control is the true scandal. . . . It is therefore also for our own sake—our own salvation—that we need a God whose power comes through weakness, which suggests many surprising, and, for some, disturbing images and faces of God." Campbell and Cilliers, *Preaching Fools*, 56.

52 DBWE 4:184–85.

53 DBWE 4:186–87. Stanley Hauerwas writes, "Through Jesus' life and teachings we see how the church came to understand that God's kingship and power consists [*sic*] not in coercion but in God's willingness to forgive and

have mercy on us. God wills nothing less than that men and women should love their enemies and forgive one another; thus we will be perfect as God is perfect. Jesus challenged both the militaristic and ritualistic notions of what God's kingdom required—the former by denying the right of violence even if attacked, and the latter by his steadfast refusal to be separated from those 'outside.'" Hauerwas, *Peaceable Kingdom*, 85.

54 DBWE 4:188–89.

55 DBWE 4:189.

56 DBWE 4:189–91. Campbell and Cilliers write, "For the Word is vulnerable and fragile. Faithfully proclaimed, it does not control or coerce the outcome. It refuses to make others into objects or commodities. It refuses to take away human freedom. So it can be—has been—rejected and crucified. But this Word is vulnerable in another way as well. It relies on flawed human speech. Even the people of God have abused this Word. God's people have preached crusades and war. The church has used this Word in violent ways to abuse and manipulate and exclude. God's people themselves have often turned this Word into a kind of closed seriousness, which is in profound contradiction to the folly of the gospel." Campbell and Cilliers, *Preaching Fools*, 124.

57 DBWE 4:175–76. Stanley Hauerwas comments, "Jesus's instructions for the disciples' mission, however, remain true for any understanding of Christian evangelism. Too often concern for the status of the church tempts some to employ desperate measures to insure that the church will remain socially significant or at least have a majority of the population. But the church is not called to be significant or large. The church is called to be apostolic. Faithfulness, not numbers or status, should be the characteristic that shapes the witness of the church. Indeed it may well be the case in our time that God is unburdening the church so that we can again travel light." Hauerwas, *Matthew* (Grand Rapids: Brazos, 2006), 107.

58 DBWE 4:190–91.

59 DBWE 4:196–98.

60 DBWE 4:225–26.

61 DBWE 4:226–29.

62 DBWE 5. Dean writes, "The two works belong together, for not only do they emerge from the same period, but *Discipleship* and *Life Together* point to the same reality; for 'to be together as a group of people in that place [Finkenwalde] thus presupposed a willingness to stake one's life on faith in and obedience to the God revealed in Jesus Christ, to reject the Nazi gods of blood and soil, and to repudiate the Nazification of German Protestantism in the *Reichskirche*.'" Dean, *For the Life of the World*, 74. Dean is quoting Gary D. Badcock, *The House Where God Lives: Renewing the Doctrine of the Church for Today* (Grand Rapids: Eerdmans, 2009), 180–81.

63 DBWE 5:27.

64 DBWE 5:31–32.

65   Geoffrey Wainwright writes, "I see Christian worship, doctrine and life as conjoined in a common 'upwards' and 'forwards' direction towards God and the achievement of his purpose, which includes human salvation. They intend God's praise. His glory is that he is already present and within to enable our transformation into his likeness, which means participation in himself and his kingdom." Wainwright, *Doxology: The Praise of God in Worship, Doctrine, and Life* (New York: Oxford University Press, 1980), 10.

66   DBWE 5:28.

67   DBWE 5:45–46.

68   DBWE 5:45–46. See the discussion of Nazi practices of euthanasia to "purify" the German population and its challenge to the churches in Barnett, *For the Soul of the People*, 104–21.

69   DBWE 5:60–61. Barker writes, "Central to this approach to Scripture is the emphasis that is placed on God's work, God's story into which we are drawn, thereby making Christ's crucifixion our crucifixion. This fits with and reflects Bonhoeffer's basic orientation articulated in his earlier writings, where he made the distinction between Christianity and religion. Whereas religion leads from humanity to God, Christianity leads from God to the world. When expressed as the *theologia crucis*, this distinction reaffirms the posture that acknowledges that the initiative belongs to God and that God is committed to this world." Barker, *Cross of Reality*, 337. See also the insightful discussion of *lectio* in Eugene H. Peterson, *Eat This Book: A Conversation in the Art of Spiritual Reading* (Grand Rapids: Eerdmans, 2006), 23–118. For discussion of narrative reading and preaching that includes exegetical and homiletical examples, see Joel B. Green and Michael Pasquarello III, eds., *Narrative Reading, Narrative Preaching: Reuniting New Testament Interpretation and Proclamation* (Grand Rapids: Eerdmans, 2003).

70   DBWE 5:62. Peterson writes, "The story that is Scripture, broadly conceived, is the story of following Jesus. The Christian community has always read this story as not just one story among others but as the meta-narrative that embraces, or can embrace, all stories. If we fail to recognize the capaciousness of this form, we will almost certainly end up treating our biblical text anecdotally as 'inspiration' or argumentatively as polemic. . . . The Bible, the entire Bible, is 'relentlessly narratival.' And we cannot change or discard the form without changing and distorting the content. This biblical narrative gathers everything into it, providing a beginning and ending, plot and character development, conflict and resolution. For most of the Christian centuries, attentive readers of the Bible have understood that its many voices and points of view are all contained in the narrative form and are given coherence by it." Peterson, *Eat This Book*, 46–47. Stanley Hauerwas writes of the Christian narrative: "The alternative to explanation and understanding is descriptions made possible by truthful

stories. Descriptions, however, turn out to be extraordinary discoveries that demand constant reappropriation if we are not to be misled by our speech. For example, Christians are tempted to turn the description 'sin' into an explanation or understanding that makes sin but a manifestation of a 'deeper reality.' In like manner we often assume that fundamental moral descriptions, e.g., 'courage' or 'murder,' require a theory to sustain their meaning. But descriptions do not require a theory. Rather, we learn how they work and the kind of people we ought to be to sustain such descriptions by the practices and correlative narratives for a people to explain their way of life to themselves and others." Hauerwas, *Performing the Faith*, 145. *Discipleship* and *Life Together* do not attempt to explain or set forth a theory, but rather they offer extended narrative descriptions that require participation in particular practices to discern a correlative form of life that cannot be separated from the story of Scripture as read, preached, sung, prayed, and celebrated by the church.

71 Richard Lischer comments on preaching as articulating the "Grand Narrative" of the world. He notes how this has been perceived as functioning to dominate the narrative aspirations of other religions and worldviews, as a kind of "totalizing" discourse, from creation to consummation. Lischer points to three features of the Christian story that differentiate it from the Grand Narratives of modernity: (1) preaching tells the story in a perspectival manner; it is narrated by the fallible witness called "preacher," identifying itself as witness or confession, which testifies to its vulnerability; (2) the Christian narrative pivots on the crucifixion of Jesus; it speaks from and toward a theology of the cross; (3) the Christian narrative is eschatological and thus incomplete—a form of theology on the way that does not claim total knowledge. Lischer, *End of Words*, 101–2.

72 DBWE 5:62. Gerard Loughlin writes: "Christian truth has never been a matter of matching stories against reality. It has always been a matter of matching reality-stories against the truth: Jesus Christ. For the Christian Church it has always been a life-story that comes first, against which all other things are to be matched. This life-story is what 'truth' means in Christianity. Nor is this a matter of making up the truth, because it is the truth that makes up the story. The story is imagined for us before it is re-imagined by us: the story is *given* to us." Loughlin, *Telling God's Story: Bible, Church, and Narrative Theology* (Cambridge: Cambridge University Press, 1996), 32 (emphasis in original).

73 Peterson writes, "Liturgy preserves and presents the Holy Scriptures in the context of the worshipping and obeying community of Christians who are at the center of everything God has done, is doing, and will do. . . . It is useful to reflect that the word 'liturgy' did not originate in church or worship settings. In the Greek world it referred to public service. . . . As the church used the word in relation to worship, it kept this 'public service' quality—working for the community on behalf of or following

orders from God. As we worship God, revealed personally as Father, Son, and Holy Spirit in our Holy Scriptures, we are not doing something apart from or away from the non-Scripture-reading world; we do it *for* the world. . . . It is obedient, participatory listening to Holy Scripture in the company of the holy community through time." Peterson, *Eat This Book*, 74–75 (emphasis in original). See also the helpful discussion in Mitman, *Worship in the Shape of Scripture*: "What constitutes the community and community's conversation is the one Word, Jesus Christ, becoming enfleshed in the body of Christ through the conversation with the Scriptures that occurs in the worship event" (26).

74 DBWE 5:62–63.

75 See the essay on Bonhoeffer and the ministry of prophetic leadership in Kelly and Nelson, *Cost of Moral Leadership*, 51–82: "Bonhoeffer does not often use the word 'prophecy.' Nor does he speak directly at any length of the prophetic vocation of the Christian church community. Yet the Pauline pneumatological imagery that he used connects the Spirit's gift of freedom from law, sin, death, and secular idolatries with the prophetic vocation to speak with outrage against those secular powers that have oppressed those most vulnerable. Essentially, when Bonhoeffer urged his church to take a practical stand against Nazism he became indirectly an advocate of the radical prophetic vocation of the Christian church" (52). I would add that for Bonhoeffer the most essential aspect of prophetic ministry is a "standing by the Word" that is enabled by the Spirit. See also the excellent discussion of prophecy in Ellen F. Davis, *Biblical Prophecy: Perspectives for Christian Theology, Discipleship, and Ministry* (Louisville, Ky.: Westminster John Knox, 2013), 1–22.

76 DBWE 15:528.

77 DBWE 15:528–29.

78 DBWE 15:530.

79 DBWE 15:532–33.

80 Luther, *Word and Sacrament III*, vol. 37 of *Luther's Works* (St. Louis: Concordia, 1961), 72, cited in DBWE 15:532–33.

81 DBWE 15:533.

82 DBWE 15:275.

83 DBWE 15:276–77. Willimon writes, "Congregations need to believe that we preachers either do or do not believe our own witness and are attempting, as best we can, to embody that of which we speak. Who preaches seems to be very important for congregational receptivity to what is preached. Because of the nature of Scripture—words that demand performance and discipleship—congregations are right to want a preacher who not only talks to them, but also walks the faith with them." Willimon, *Pastor*, 158.

84 Hauerwas, *Performing the Faith*, 34.

8: *Preaching without Words*

1   Here I am following the narratives in Bethge, *Dietrich Bonhoeffer: A Biog-
    raphy*, 648–934; Marsh, *Strange Glory*, 294–384; Schlingensiepen, *Dietrich
    Bonhoeffer*, 227–378.
2   DBWE 15:217–45.
3   DBWE 15:217.
4   DBWE 15:219–21.
5   DBWE 15:225.
6   See the discussion in Williams, *Bonhoeffer's Black Jesus*.
7   DBWE 15:230–31.
8   DBWE 15:238.
9   DBWE 15:233.
10 DBWE 15:235–36.
11 DBWE 15:210, 215. See the account in Bethge, *Dietrich Bonhoeffer: A Biog-
    raphy*, 657–62.
12 DBWE 15:274.
13 Bonhoeffer wrote an essay after his return to Germany: "Essay about Prot-
    estantism in the United States of America." DBWE 15:438–64.
14 DBWE 15:275. For Bonhoeffer's continued following of Luther's "theology
    of the cross" during the war years, see Barker, *Cross of Reality*, 363–416.
15 Here I am following the editor's introduction to *Dietrich Bonhoeffer Works:
    Conspiracy and Imprisonment*, ed. Mark S. Brocker, trans. Lisa E. Dahill,
    DBWE 16 (Minneapolis: Fortress, 2006), 3–8.
16 Barnett, *For the Soul of the People*, 198–204.
17 Barnett, *For the Soul of the People*, 180–82, 198–200.
18 Barnett, *For the Soul of the People*, 95–97; Bethge, *Dietrich Bonhoeffer: A
    Biography*, 686–95.
19 Bonhoeffer's writings during this time include Bible studies, theological
    essays, reflections on the church's mission, sermon meditations, devo-
    tional pieces, ethical essays, and pastoral writings. The circular letters
    unite theological and practical concerns in ministering to pastors and con-
    gregations, who were profoundly affected by significant personal sacrifice
    and loss during the war. He also continued to engage in regular correspon-
    dence with individual pastors and seminarians, many of whom had been
    conscripted for military service. His correspondence also included fam-
    ilies and spouses of pastors and seminarians who had been killed in the
    war effort. See the editor's introduction to DBWE 16, pp. 4–5. A thread that
    runs through Bonhoeffer's writings during a time when he was in constant
    transition and eventually imprisoned is the faithfulness and goodness of
    God revealed in Jesus Christ.
20 Because of the scope of this book, Bonhoeffer as preacher and teacher
    of preachers, I have limited my remarks on his participation in the con-
    spiracy. See Sabine Dramm, *Dietrich Bonhoeffer and the Resistance*

(Minneapolis: Fortress, 2009). See also the editors' introductions to DBWE 8–15; Schlingensiepen, *Dietrich Bonhoeffer*, 234–378; Bethge, *Dietrich Bonhoeffer: A Biography*, 722, 934; Marsh, *Strange Glory*, 319–94. Bonhoeffer's participation in the resistance and conspiracy continues to be a controversial matter. See Nation, Siegrist, and Umbel, *Bonhoeffer the Assassin?*; and Dean, *For the Life of the World*, 241–51. Samuel Wells offers an insightful perspective on this matter: "Bonhoeffer's participation in the plot to kill Hitler was not a lonely hero's quest to save Germany even at the risk of his own soul; it was his much humbler participation in the communion of saints. It was not something Bonhoeffer did 'for'; it was something he did 'with.' In this lies its profound continuity with the previous threshold, the return to Germany a year earlier. The return to Germany was an incarnate expression of 'with': to have remained aloof and beyond Germany would still have permitted Bonhoeffer to work and be 'for' a new Germany. Yet it would not have permitted him truly to work and be 'with' Germany in its most benighted hour. Having committed himself to 'being with' Germany in 1939, it was not an incomprehensible step to begin to 'work with' those who sought to remove the single force that was propelling Germany deeper and deeper into the mire." Wells, "Bonhoeffer: Theologian, Activist, Educator," in *Interpreting Bonhoeffer: Historical Perspectives, Emerging Issues*, ed. Clifford J. Green and Guy C. Carter (Minneapolis: Fortress, 2013), 225. Bonhoeffer's commitment to "being with" was consistent with his theological understanding of preaching as serving the present Christ.

21 I am indebted to David Schnasa Jacobsen for this understanding of homiletical theology. See Jacobsen, *Homiletical Theology*, 3–55. See the collection of "German Christian" writings in *A Church Undone: Documents from the German Christian Faith Movement, 1932–1940*, ed. and trans. Mary M. Solberg (Minneapolis: Fortress, 2015). For example, National Bishop Ludwig Muller introduced a "German Christian" interpretation of the Sermon on the Mount as follows: he offers a version "for those who believe something isn't quite right about the Christian churches and Christianity itself, but who would like to make their own judgments about Christ and about what he wants. For you, my fellow Germans in the Third Reich, I have 'Germanized'—not 'translated'—the Sermon on the Mount" (386).

22 See Bonhoeffer's sermon meditation on Isaiah 9 for Christmas 1940. DBWE 16:611–16.

23 DBWE 5.

24 David F. Ford and Daniel W. Hardy write of the prophetic nature of the Psalms: "The prophets were the charismatic men and women who had the gifts of intimacy with Yahweh. Prophecy grew from within the liturgy, interpreting its message and relating it to the present situation. . . . The prophet is one who is typically so taken up into worship and the vision that is given by God to the people and for the people to God." Ford and Hardy, *Living in Praise: Worshipping and Knowing God* (Grand Rapids: Baker

Academic, 2005), 52–53. Bonhoeffer was arguably following the example of Luther, who saw the prophetic sense of the Psalms as testifying to the coming and works of Christ. See Oberman, *Luther*, 250–54. Oberman emphasizes Luther's reading of the Psalms as a "book of the church."

25 DBWE 5:155–56. See the excellent discussion of modes of prayer as ways of being formed before God in Don E. Saliers, *Worship & Theology: Foretaste of Glory Divine* (Nashville: Abingdon, 1994): "This reminds us of the central paradox of the Christian life itself. Christ, in and through the Spirit, prays for the world and for us in and through our prayers in his name. Hence, Christian liturgy both forms us in certain characteristic ways of being human, and brings these things to expression through the arts of worship" (28).

26 DBWE 5:156–57.

27 DBWE 5:157. Oswald Bayer provides a detailed discussion of Martin Luther's dependence upon prayer as both the means and the context for the study of theology. He notes that the monastic "love of learning and desire for God" are carried over into Luther's attempt to unite monastic and academic theology, liturgical spirituality and study, through daily use of the Psalms: "The study of theology as a way of prayer is neither contemplation nor action, but from first to last is all about waiting solely on God's work.... This perception in any case is no pure perception but is essentially sensory.... We perceive through sensory experience, which includes the outer senses, the emotions, the imagination, the memory, and the desires." Bayer, *Theology the Lutheran Way*, 10, 49. Elsewhere, Bayer writes, "Luther's use of the Psalter is the key in general to the understanding of his use of language, his linguistic power, as well as his experience of his world and life." Bayer, "Luther as Interpreter of Holy Scripture," 80.

28 DBWE 5:157. John Webster (*Word and Church*, 109) writes of Bonhoeffer's theological reading of Scripture: "First, hermeneutical and methodological questions are at best of secondary importance in the interpretation of Scripture. The real business is elsewhere, and it is spiritual, and therefore dogmatic. Correct interpretation cannot be detached from correct depiction of the situation in which we as readers go to Scripture and encounter God. The task of such a depiction is a dogmatic task, calling for the deployment of the concepts and language through which the church has sought to map out as best it can the astonishing reality of God's saving self-communication.... It is therefore true that a fittingly Christian hermeneutics 'requires the formation and transformation of the character appropriate to Christian disciples.'"

29 Rowan Williams comments on speaking with theological integrity: "Language about God is kept honest in the degree to which it turns on itself in the name of God, and so surrenders itself to God: it is in this way that it becomes possible to see how it is still *God* that is being spoken of, that which makes the human world a moral unity. Speaking of God is speaking

to God and opening our speech to God's; and it is speaking of those who have spoken to God and who have thus begun to form the human community, the unrestricted fellowship of holiness, that is the only kind of universal meaning possible without the tyranny of a 'total perspective.'" Williams, *On Christian Theology* (Oxford: Blackwell, 2000), 8 (emphasis in original).

30 See Paul L. Holmer, *The Grammar of Faith* (San Francisco: Harper & Row, 1978): "In so far as Christianity can be 'said' at all, theology and Scripture say it. But what is therein said, be it the words of eternal life, be it the creeds, or be it the words of Jesus Himself, we must note that like grammar and logic, their aim is not that we repeat the words. Theology must also be absorbed, and when it is, the hearer is supposed to become godly" (19).

31 DBWE 5:156–57. Stanley Hauerwas comments, "Prayer is the heart of Christian speech." He continues a discussion of learning to speak "Christian" or the language of faith: "Scripture, of course, is the source as well as the paradigm of Christian speech. What we say must be said faithful to the language of Scripture. That is a complex task because it is by no means clear how the many ways of expression in Scripture are to be said coherently. The investigation of that process is called theology." Hauerwas, *Working with Words*, 88, 92.

32 DBWE 5:162–77. See the discussion of Bonhoeffer's categorization of the Psalms in the editor's introduction to DBWE 5, pp. 144–53. Brock writes of Bonhoeffer's larger interpretive aim: "More constructively, Bonhoeffer has suggested that we must be prepared to understand Christian ethics as a structured facilitation of human cooperation with the divine sanctification of humanity. . . . Moral theology thus construed is not a program but a theologically attuned ear that directs the constant discovery of—and reorientation within—our place in creation. . . . Ethics thus serves human salvation as the processes of hearing, repentance, and sanctification." Brock, *Singing the Ethos of God*, 94.

33 DBWE 5:57–58. Kelly and Nelson write, "The practical dimension of the Psalms helps explain why Bonhoeffer cherished them as his principal form of prayer. Above all, the Psalms enabled him to cope with his own shifting moods amid all the vicissitudes of his ministry, including his imprisonment. The Psalms taught him that God was near in all the sorrows and joys, successes and disappointments that had marked his days." Kelly and Nelson, *Cost of Moral Leadership*, 232.

34 Editor's introduction to DBWE 5, pp. 146–49; Kelly and Nelson, *Cost of Moral Leadership*, 230–31; Bethge, *Dietrich Bonhoeffer: A Biography*, 641–43; Brock, *Singing the Ethos of God*, 198–99.

35 DBWE 15:496–526. Bethge considers the meditations on Psalm 119 as representing a new depth and clarity in Bonhoeffer's thought and language. Bethge, *Dietrich Bonhoeffer: A Biography*, 676.

36 DBWE 15:489.

37   DBWE 15:497–98.

38   DBWE 15:498–99. Brian Brock explains how Bonhoeffer interpreted the
      Psalms in a dynamic way: that the concept of instruction or command
      marks out a path and characterizes something continuous and ongo-
      ing. He contrasts this understanding with modern views of divine com-
      manding as occasional interventions: "Bonhoeffer stays quite close to
      the thought structure of the Psalms by interpreting commands within
      a dynamic view of human life and moral deliberation. Psalm 119 is rife
      with this imagery, as marked by the regular occurrence of terms such
      as 'walk,' 'way,' 'paths,' 'to restrain/turn back my feet,' 'let my steps be
      established by your word,' 'your word is a lamp to my feet,' 'to wander,'
      and 'to make haste, come quickly.' Bonhoeffer's aim is to discover how
      verbal meditation on Scripture facilitates the embodiment of faith."
      Brock, *Singing the Ethos of God*, 77.

39   Brock writes, "Christians must not give up the hope of God meeting
      them on the way, but must redouble their resistance to the temptation
      to discard some of the statutes by insisting on keeping all of God's com-
      mandments open and in play." Brock, *Singing the Ethos of God*, 82.

40   DBWE 15:504.

41   DBWE 15:505–7. Brock notes, "God's Word is thus not an ethical pro-
      gram but a heuristic, and a negative heuristic at that: it strips away our
      divergent self-referential hermeneutics to reveal our total dependence on
      God's presence, and so to direct us to his real (as opposed to imagined)
      presence." Brock, *Singing the Ethos of God*, 85.

42   Ford and Hardy write of praise and reading Scripture, "The fact of
      praise of God is a particularly good way of getting to the heart of the
      Bible because in praise there was the supreme attempt to acknowl-
      edge to God what was most fundamental for the community: God and
      God's activity. The explicit praise of the Bible concentrates in itself
      what was most distinctive and important for Israel and, with the addi-
      tion of the New Testament, for the Christian Church. Praise was the
      time of ultimate directness, of most active recognition of the presence
      and character of God." Ford and Hardy, *Living in Praise*, 31. Geof-
      frey Wainwright comments regarding the liturgical reading of Scrip-
      ture: "In and through the reading of the scriptures, the Church hears
      God's voice and message, and from its own side the Church speaks
      its response to God in prayer. . . . Liturgical use sets the proper atmo-
      sphere for the exegete and interpreter. The fundamental motivation of
      Christian exegesis and hermeneutics should be doxological." Wain-
      wright, *Doxology*, 150, 175, 176.

43   DBWE 15:508–9.

44   See the discussion of Bonhoeffer's understanding of the Holy Spirit and
      discipleship in Kelly and Nelson, *Cost of Moral Leadership*, 51–82.

45   DBWE 15:509–10.

46 DBWE 15:512–13. Williams comments, "Prayer . . . is precisely what resists the urge of religious language to claim a total perspective: by articulating its own incompleteness before God, it turns away from any claim to human completeness. By 'conversing' with God, it preserves conversation between human speakers." Williams, *On Christian Theology*, 13.

47 Walter Brueggemann writes, "In its liturgical life the church, led by the Spirit, engages in praise and obedience and so constitutes and is constituted as God's people. . . . What is under way is the formation of an alternative community. This work of the church is of course in response to the command of God and is indeed human work." Brueggemann, *Israel's Praise: Doxology against Idolatry and Ideology* (Philadelphia: Fortress, 1988), 28.

48 DBWE 15:513.

49 DBWE 15:515.

50 For an excellent discussion of faith, character, and constancy in pastoral ministry, see Willimon, *Pastor*, 299–336. Michael P. Knowles comments, "The preacher's silence is not occasioned by theological timidity, or by concern for preserving personal benefit or avoiding rejection, but by the recognition that even Jesus falls silent on the cross. Yet, because it is governed by the cross, that silence is neither final nor absolute: it is only temporary and provisional, ultimately reserved by its contingence upon the full dimensions of God's self-articulation in the person of Jesus, both crucified and risen. In very practical terms, preachers must therefore weigh their words carefully—not just for cadence and comprehensibility, but for the clarity of their testimony to an awkward, counterintuitive, glorious Christ." Knowles, *We Preach Not Ourselves: Paul on Proclamation* (Grand Rapids: Brazos, 2008), 261–62.

51 DBWE 15:515.

52 DBWE 15:515–16. David Ford and Daniel Hardy write about moralizing forms of Christianity that take the joy out of goodness: "This is perhaps the most devastating perversion of all. . . . Christianity of course has an ethic; but it is so all-involving and extraordinary that it can never be followed by setting it up as a duty to be carried out. The only way is to be filled with the Spirit, to be so taken up with the love of God that one can live with joyful discipline, extravagantly drawing on God's grace and risking the shame of constant failure and repentance." Ford and Hardy, *Living in Praise*, 180.

53 DBWE 15:517. See the excellent discussion of prayer, exegesis, and theological reflection in the life and work of the preacher in Thomas G. Long, *The Witness of Preaching*, 3rd ed. (Louisville, Ky.: Westminster John Knox, 2016), 58–112.

54 DBWE 15:521.

55 DBWE 15:526. Williams notes, "Religious practice is only preserved in any integrity by seriousness about prayer; and so, if theology is the untangling of the real grammar of religious practice, its subject matter is, humanly

and specifically, people who pray. If theology [which includes preaching] is itself a critical, even a suspicious discipline, it is for this reason. It seeks to make sense of the practice of dispossessed language 'before God.'" Williams, *On Christian Theology*, 13.

56 See the excellent discussion of "ethics as aesthetics" and the importance of perception in Brad J. Kallenberg, *Ethics as Grammar: Changing the Postmodern Subject* (Notre Dame, Ind.: University of Notre Dame Press, 2001), 49–82. For an Aristotelian perspective, see Dunne, *Back to the Rough Ground*, 298–308. I have also found the insightful essays by Pierre Hadot to be very helpful for understanding Bonhoeffer's unity of thinking, perceiving, discerning, acting, and speaking in a way of life conformed to Christ, who is known through the spiritual exercises of praying, reading, meditating upon, and obeying the Word. See Pierre Hadot, *Philosophy as a Way of Life: Spiritual Exercises from Socrates to Foucault*, ed. Arnold I. Davidson, trans. Michael Chase (London: Blackwell, 1995): "We must also associate our imagination and affectivity with the training of our thought. Here, we must bring into play all the psychagogic techniques and rhetorical methods of amplification. We must formulate the rule of life 'before our eyes,' . . . and see them in the light of this fundamental rule. This is known as the exercise of memorization . . . and meditation on the rule of life" (85).

57 Knowles summarizes this matter well: "The final test of faithful preaching, in other words, is the fact that preachers and hearers alike are changed by the saving action of God to which it testifies. They are conformed both individually and corporately to the pattern of Jesus' own death and vindication, and express in their lives together the contours of God's new creation and new humanity. Preaching is thus attended by 'glory'— by revelation of the character of God, and by the transformation that results from knowing and yielding to a characteristically gracious Savior." Knowles, *We Preach Not Ourselves*, 262. See also the excellent discussion of character, virtue, and wisdom in biblical interpretation in Treier, *Virtue and the Voice of God*.

58 DBWE 6. See the good discussion in Kaiser, *Becoming Simple and Wise*, 140–44.

59 DBWE 6:64.

60 See the excellent collection of essays in *Being Human, Becoming Human: Dietrich Bonhoeffer and Social Thought*, ed. Jens Zimmerman and Brian Gregor (Eugene, Ore.: Pickwick, 2010). John W. de Gruchy writes, "Bonhoeffer's humanism, so deeply rooted in Christ, then, is not an easy, superficial romanticism or philosophical idealism but an affirmation of life in its fullness amidst struggle and suffering. It is a Christian humanism fully cognizant of the depths to which humanity can plunge, the extent to which evil can run rampant. Fashioned through encountering evil, through struggle and suffering, it is a humanism of the cross." De Gruchy, "Dietrich

Bonhoeffer as Christian Humanist," in Zimmerman and Gregor, *Being Human, Becoming Human*, 17.

61 Jens Zimmerman argues that Bonhoeffer's teaching on biblical interpreta- tion and preaching are integral to his interpretation of ethics, which focuses on God's redemptive action in Christ to unite Christ and humanity: "The preacher, [Bonhoeffer] explains, has to show that the so called 'concrete situation' of any congregation is 'the general situation of every person before God, of every human being in his pride, his unbelief, his neglect of social responsibility, in his questioning.' . . . This discerning hermeneutic is complemented by Bonhoeffer's ecclesial, social view of the church as the new humanity. Being human is becoming human through participation in Jesus the Christ as his body the church. Bonhoeffer is concerned with 'how' this happens only insofar as he describes this participation as occurring in the sacraments of preaching, baptism, and the Eucharist." Zimmerman, "Being Human, Becoming Human," in Zimmerman and Gregor, *Being Human, Becoming Human*, 46.

62 DBWE 6:91.

63 DBWE 6:92–100; see Bonhoeffer's essay "What Does It Mean to Tell the Truth?" in DBWE 16:601–8. Kaiser concludes, "There is a reason Bonhoeffer spoke on many occasions of simplicity, simple faith, and simple obedience: these terms name something fundamental about the proper character and purpose of Christian life. In the same way, there is a reason he spoke of wis- dom and the human ability to reason and reflect on moral situations: such an emphasis recognizes the natural, penultimate context of discernment, without which the Christian life would be unintelligible. Moral discern- ment is not only a matter of faith, taking place within an ecclesial context; it is also a matter of human nature, implanted in the real and historical world." Kaiser, *Becoming Simple and Wise*, 119.

64 DBWE 6:81.

65 In my thinking about Bonhoeffer's "ethic of preaching," I have benefited from the excellent discussion in O'Donovan, *Self, World, and Time*: "With- out a key to the world's meanings we shall never be able to sift through the complex of information we receive about, and through, the world, and bring it to some kind of order. 'How shall a young man guard his way from corruption? By taking heed to it according to your word' (Ps 119:9). Practical reason looks for a word, a word that makes attention to the world intelligible, a word that will maintain the coherence and intelligence of the world as it finds its way through it, a word of God" (13).

66 See the helpful discussion in Jennifer Moberly, *The Virtue of Bonhoeffer's Ethics: A Study of Dietrich Bonhoeffer's Ethics in Relation to Virtue Ethics* (Eugene, Ore.: Pickwick, 2013), 157–62. Stanley Hauerwas writes, "For Bon- hoeffer, the source of the lie is always the penchant for abstraction. There- fore the true meaning of correspondence with reality is neither civility nor opposition to the factual, but rather the attempt to understand reality

without the real man—Jesus Christ. . . . The failure of the church to oppose Hitler was but the outcome of the failure of Christians to speak the truth to one another and the world." Hauerwas, *Performing the Faith*, 66–67.

67 DBWE 6:97.

68 See the discussion in Solberg, *A Church Undone*, 1–35. For an example of an ethic of preaching, see Charles L. Campbell, *The Word before the Powers: An Ethic of Preaching* (Louisville, Ky.: Westminster John Knox, 2002).

69 DBWE 6:92–93 (emphasis in original).

70 DBWE 6:356.

71 DBWE 6:352–54. See the excellent discussion in Lischer, *End of Words*.

72 DBWE 6:356–57. For a good example of the gospel as spoken and heard as "foolish," see Campbell and Cilliers, *Preaching Fools*.

73 DBWE 6:358–59. See the discussion on the need of the church for patience in Alan Keider, *The Patient Ferment of the Early Church: The Improbable Rise of Christianity in the Roman Empire* (Grand Rapids: Baker Academic, 2016), 1–132.

74 DBWE 6:396.

75 DBWE 6:397–99. Nicholas Lash comments, "Speech that has forgotten that the fundamental form of speech is conversation; forgotten that to be able to converse with others is to have been schooled in a culture of relationships; forgotten that all conversation and all culture are, ultimately, answerable not only to each other but to God—such speech would, in the long run, cease to be speech at all and, with this cessation, its utterers would be less than human." Lash, *Holiness, Speech and Silence*, 60.

76 DBWE 6:400–402.

77 DBWE 6:403–5. Here I have benefited from the discussion of Bonhoeffer's theological vision of preaching in Owens, *Shape of Participation*, 65–94. Brock helpfully defines Bonhoeffer's use of mandates as "a naming in faith of the main contours of God's saving work within a fallen world. . . . They function like 'focal images' in guiding analogical reasoning. . . . In themselves they are inconsequential. What matters is the 'obedience of faith rendered within them' [DBWE 6:389]. . . . Mandates are constantly revised descriptions of Scripture that help the faithful distinguish essential aspects of the many ways of humanity so that we can learn to discern between them." Brock, *Singing the Ethos of God*, 92–93. For an excellent critical interpretation of Bonhoeffer's use of mandates, see also Dean, *For the Life of the World*, 160–81: "Through his use of the term mandate, which refers not to any historic institution, but rather to the divine commission behind them, Bonhoeffer is able to avoid the pitfalls of orders language which often end up sanctioning the status quo" (166).

78 DBWE 8.

79 See the classic account in Bethge, *Dietrich Bonhoeffer: A Biography*, 799–934. See also the recent biography of Bonhoeffer by Marsh, *Strange Glory*, 319–94.

80 DBWE 8:362. Rowan Williams writes of how dogmatic language becomes
    empty and even destructive of faith when it is isolated from a lively and
    converting worship, a spirituality not afraid of silence and powerlessness:
    "The more God becomes functional to the legitimizing either of ecclesias-
    tical order or of private religiosities, the easier it is to talk of God; the easier
    it is to talk of God, the less such talk gives place to the freedom of God.
    And that suggests that there is an aspect of dogmatic utterance [including
    proclamation] that has to do with making it harder to talk about God."
    Williams turns to Bonhoeffer and notes, "Bonhoeffer's attack on the jargon
    of 'religion' is far from being a liberal reformist proposal that hard words
    be made easy or strange words familiar; he is concerned that the real moral
    and spiritual strangeness—and thus the judgment—of the gospel should
    again become audible." Williams points to words such as "incarnation"
    and "atonement" as examples of familiar words used by professional reli-
    gious talkers, words that "no longer bring the Church to judgment, and no
    longer do the job of dogma. They have simply become ideology." Williams,
    On Christian Theology, 84–85.

81 See the insightful essay by Barry A. Harvey, "A Post-Critical Approach to
    a 'Religionless Christianity,'" in Floyd and Marsh, *Theology and the Prac-
    tice of Responsibility*, 39–58: "Bonhoeffer's repudiation of religion as a for-
    mal strategy by means of which the post-modern world seeks to supervise
    the distinctively Christian practice of everyday life, opens the way for us
    to attend to the concrete ways we might refashion the body politic of the
    church. Bonhoeffer's deconstruction of religion as a viable theological cat-
    egory is also an invitation to, and an opportunity for, the church to reex-
    amine and reclaim its new religious (i.e., its political and social) existence
    and vocation as the body of Christ" (55).

82 DBWE 8:364–65. Bonhoeffer's prison writings have provoked a large body
    of scholarship by many interpreters from a variety of perspectives. See the
    editor's introduction and editor's afterword to DBWE 8. See also John W.
    de Gruchy's helpful essay "The Reception of Bonhoeffer's Theology," 93–
    112. See also the balanced essay by Peter Selby, "Christianity in a World
    Come of Age," in de Gruchy, *Cambridge Companion*, 226–45. A recent
    full-length study is Jeffrey C. Pugh's *Religionless Christianity: Dietrich
    Bonhoeffer in Troubled Times* (New York: T&T Clark, 2008); an older but
    still reliable guide is Ernst Feil, *The Theology of Dietrich Bonhoeffer*, trans.
    Martin Rumscheidt (Philadelphia: Fortress, 1985), 99–205. Kelly and Nel-
    son offer a good explanation of what Bonhoeffer attacked as "religion." On
    the one hand, religion believes in a "stop gap" god who helps Christians
    escape the world's trials, sufferings, and weakness. Yet this "god" did not
    command Christians to take responsibility or turn in repentance for their
    support of and complicity in the war effort, Nazi crimes, and concentration
    camps. This "god" may answer prayers for deliverance but did not summon
    Christian people into courageous acts of discipleship to stand with those

who suffered most. On the other hand, "religion" could also support belief in a "discarnate" god, one who remained removed from the world and was reduced to a "transcendent" symbol of authority, and who used fear, guilt, and shame to compel faith and obedience. A "discarnate" god produces abstract preaching, which Bonhoeffer vehemently opposed. Kelly and Nelson, *Cost of Moral Leadership*, 38–39.

83 DBWE 8:40.
84 DBWE 8:48–49.
85 DBWE 8:52.
86 DBWE 8:383–84.
87 DBWE 8:387.
88 DBWE 8:387.
89 DBWE 8:387–88.
90 DBWE 8:389.
91 DBWE 8:389.
92 Rowan Williams writes, "This will not be a conscious modernizing or secularizing of the terminology of dogma and liturgy; it is certainly not something that can be planned. It will be like Jesus' own language (and practice, we must assume) in that it effects the presence of God's peace with his creatures, and so, as Bonhoeffer says in a later letter (July 1944), it exposes the actual godlessness of the world. It is nonreligious in the sense that it is not primarily concerned with securing a space within the world for a particular specialist discourse. Whether or not it uses the word 'God,' it effects faith, conversion, hope. Bonhoeffer's paradigm . . . is the encounters in the gospels between Jesus and those he calls or heals; these are events in which people are concretely drawn into a share in the vulnerability of God, into a new kind of life and a new identity. They do not receive an additional item called faith; their ordinary experience is not reorganized, found wanting in specific respects and supplemented; it is transfigured as a whole." Williams, *On Christian Theology*, 40–41.
93 DBWE 8:390.

Conclusion

1 I am grateful to David Schnasa Jacobsen for the insightful term "theology on the way." See Jacobsen's introduction and "Homiletical Theology: Constructive Visions" in *Homiletical Theology*, 3–38.

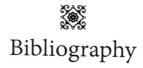

Bibliography

Augustine. *The Confessions.* Edited by John E. Rotelle, O.S.A. Translated by Edmund Hill, O.P. New York: New City Press, 1996.

————. *Teaching Christianity (De Doctrina Christiana).* Edited by John E. Rotelle, O.S.A. Translated by William P. Hill, O.P. New York: New City Press, 1996.

Badcock, Gary D. *The House Where God Lives: Renewing the Doctrine of the Church for Today.* Grand Rapids: Eerdmans, 2009.

Barker, H. Gaylon. *The Cross of Reality: Luther's Theologica Crucis and Bonhoeffer's Christology.* Minneapolis: Fortress, 2015.

Barker, H. Gaylon, and Mark S. Brocker, eds. *Dietrich Bonhoeffer Works: Theological Education at Finkenwalde, 1935–1937.* Translated by Douglas W. Stott. DBWE 14. Minneapolis: Fortress, 2013.

Barnett, Victoria J. *Bystanders: Conscience and Complicity during the Holocaust.* London: Praeger, 2000.

————, ed. *Dietrich Bonhoeffer Works: Theological Education Underground, 1937–1940.* Translated by Victoria J. Barnett, Claudia D. Bergmann, Peter Frick, and Scott A. Moore. DBWE 15. Minneapolis: Fortress, 2012.

————. *For the Soul of the People: Protestant Protest against Hitler.* Oxford: Oxford University Press, 1992.

Barnett, Victoria J., Mark S. Brocker, and Michael B. Lukens, eds. *Dietrich Bonhoeffer Works: Ecumenical, Academic, and Pastoral Work, 1931–1932.* Translated by Douglas W. Stott. DBWE 11. Minneapolis: Fortress, 2012.

Barth, Karl. *Church Dogmatics.* Edited by G. W. Bromiley and T. F. Torrance. Translated by G. T. Thompson. 14 vols. Edinburgh: T&T Clark, 1956–1977.

————. *The Epistle to the Romans.* Translated by Edwyn C. Hoskyns. 6th ed. Oxford: Oxford University Press, 1968.

————. *The Göttingen Dogmatics: Instruction in the Christian Religion.* Edited by Hannelotte Reiffen. Translated by Geoffrey W. Bromiley. Grand Rapids: Eerdmans, 1991.

————. *Homiletics.* Translated by Geoffrey W. Bromiley and Donald E. Daniels. Louisville, Ky.: Westminster John Knox, 1991.

————. *The Word of God and the Word of Man.* Translated by Douglas Horton. London: Hodder & Stoughton, 1928.

Battle, Michael. "Reconciliation as Worshiping Community." Pages 233–42 in *Bonhoeffer and King: Their Legacies and Import for Christian Social Thought.* Edited by Willis Jenkins and Jennifer M. McBride. Minneapolis: Fortress, 2010.

Bayer, Oswald. *Living by Faith: Justification and Sanctification.* Translated by Geoffrey W. Bromiley. Grand Rapids: Eerdmans, 2003.

————. "Luther as Interpreter of Holy Scripture." Pages 73–85 in *The Cambridge Companion to Martin Luther.* Edited by Donald K. McKim. Cambridge: Cambridge University Press, 2003.

————. *Theology the Lutheran Way.* Edited and translated by Jeffrey G. Silcock and Mark C. Mattes. Grand Rapids: Eerdmans, 2007.

Bergen, Doris L. *The Twisted Cross: The German Christian Movement in the Third Reich.* Chapel Hill: University of North Carolina Press, 1996.

Berry, Wendell. *Standing by Words: Essays by Wendell Berry.* Washington, D.C.: Shoemaker & Howard, 1983.

Bertram, Robert W. *A Time for Confessing.* Edited by Michael Hoy. Grand Rapids: Eerdmans, 2008.

Best, Isabel. Editor's introduction. Pages xiii–xxvi in *The Collected Sermons of Dietrich Bonhoeffer.* Edited by Isabel Best. Translated by Douglas W. Stott, Anne Schmidt-Lange, Isabel Best, Scott A. Moore, and Claudia D. Bergman. Minneapolis: Fortress, 2012.

Bethge, Eberhard. *Dietrich Bonhoeffer: A Biography.* Edited by Edwin Robertson and Victoria J. Barnett. Translated by Eric Mosbacher et al. Rev. ed. Minneapolis: Fortress, 2000.

————. *Dietrich Bonhoeffer: Theologian, Christian, Contemporary.* London: Collins, 1970.

————. "Friends." Pages 46–51 in *I Knew Dietrich Bonhoeffer: Reminiscences by His Friends.* Edited by Wolf-Dieter Zimmerman and Ronald Gregor Smith. Translated by Kathe Gregor Smith. New York: Harper & Row, 1966.

Biggar, Nigel. "Barth's Trinitarian Ethic." Pages 212–27 in *The Cambridge Companion to Karl Barth*. Edited by John Webster. Cambridge Companions to Religion. Cambridge: Cambridge University Press, 2000.

Billings, J. Todd. *The Word of God for the People of God: An Entryway to the Theological Interpretation of Scripture*. Grand Rapids: Eerdmans, 2010.

Bonhoeffer, Dietrich. *Dietrich Bonhoeffer Works*. English ed. 17 vols. Minneapolis: Fortress, 1996–2014. Volumes are cited in the notes and bibliography by editor and volume title.

Brian, Rustin E. *Covering Up Luther: How Barth's Christology Challenged the Deus Absconditus That Haunts Modernity*. Eugene, Ore.: Cascade, 2015.

Brock, Brian. *Singing the Ethos of God: On the Place of Christian Ethics in Scripture*. Grand Rapids: Eerdmans, 2007.

Brocker, Mark S. *Dietrich Bonhoeffer Works: Conspiracy and Imprisonment*. Translated by Lisa E. Dahill. DBWE 16. Minneapolis: Fortress, 2006.

Brueggemann, Walter. *Israel's Praise: Doxology against Idolatry and Ideology*. Philadelphia: Fortress, 1988.

Burghardt, Walter J., S.J. "Homily." Pages 257–59 in *Concise Encyclopedia of Preaching*. Edited by William H. Willimon and Richard Lischer. Louisville, Ky.: Westminster John Knox, 1995.

Burleigh, Michael. *The Third Reich: A New History*. New York: Hill & Wang, 2000.

Burnett, Richard E. *Karl Barth's Theological Exegesis: The Hermeneutical Principles of the Römerbrief Period*. Grand Rapids: Eerdmans, 2001.

Busch, Eberhard. *The Great Passion: An Introduction to Karl Barth's Theology*. Edited by Darrell L. Guder and Judith J. Guder. Translated by Geoffrey W. Bromiley. Grand Rapids: Eerdmans, 2004.

————. *Karl Barth & the Pietists: The Young Karl Barth's Critique of Pietism & Its Response*. Translated by Daniel W. Bloesch. Downers Grove, Ill.: InterVarsity, 2004.

————. *Karl Barth: His Life from Letters and Autobiographical Texts*. Translated by John Bowden. Philadelphia: Fortress, 1976.

Campbell, Charles L. *Preaching Jesus: The New Directions for Homiletics in Hans Frei's Postliberal Theology*. Grand Rapids: Eerdmans, 1997.

————. *The Word before the Powers: An Ethic of Preaching*. Louisville, Ky.: Westminster John Knox, 2002.

Campbell, Charles L., and Johan H. Cilliers. *Preaching Fools: The Gospel as a Rhetoric of Folly*. Waco, Tex.: Baylor University Press, 2012.

Charry, Helen. *By the Renewing of Your Minds: The Pastoral Function of Christian Doctrine*. New York: Oxford University Press, 1997.

Clements, Keith, ed. *Dietrich Bonhoeffer Works: London, 1933–1935*. Translated by Isabel Best. DBWE 13. Minneapolis: Fortress, 2007.

Davis, Ellen F. *Biblical Prophecy: Perspectives for Christian Theology, Disciple-ship, and Ministry*. Louisville, Ky.: Westminster John Knox, 2013.

D'Costa, Gavin. *Theology in the Public Square: Church, Academy, and Nation.* Oxford: Blackwell, 2005.

Dean, Robert J. *For the Life of the World: Jesus Christ and the Church in the Theologies of Dietrich Bonhoeffer and Stanley Hauerwas.* Eugene, Ore.: Pickwick, 2016.

de Gruchy, John W. "Dietrich Bonhoeffer as Christian Humanist." Pages 3–24 in *Being Human, Becoming Human: Dietrich Bonhoeffer and Social Thought.* Edited by Jens Zimmerman and Brian Gregor. Eugene, Ore.: Pickwick, 2010.

―――. *Dietrich Bonhoeffer Works: Creation and Fall; A Theological Exposi-tion of Genesis 1–3.* Edited by John W. de Gruchy. Translated by Douglas Stephen Bax. DBWE 3. Minneapolis: Fortress, 1997.

―――. *Dietrich Bonhoeffer Works: Letters and Papers from Prison.* Trans-lated by Reinhard Krauss, Nancy Lukens, Lisa E. Dahill, and Isabel Best. DBWE 8. Minneapolis: Fortress, 2010.

―――. "The Reception of Bonhoeffer's Theology." Pages 93–110 in *The Cam-bridge Companion to Dietrich Bonhoeffer.* Edited by John W. de Gruchy. Cambridge Companions to Religion. Cambridge: Cambridge University Press, 1999.

DeJonge, Michael P. "Bonhoeffer from the Perspective of Intellectual His-tory." Pages 197–204 in *Interpreting Bonhoeffer: Historical Perspectives, Emerging Issues.* Edited by Clifford J. Green and Guy C. Carter. Minne-apolis: Fortress, 2013.

―――. *Bonhoeffer's Theological Formation: Berlin, Barth, & Protestant The-ology.* Oxford: Oxford University Press, 2012.

de Lange, Frits. *Waiting for the Word: Dietrich Bonhoeffer on Speaking about God.* Translated by Martin N. Walton. Grand Rapids: Eerdmans, 1995.

Dorrien, Gary. *The Making of American Liberal Theology: Idealism, Realism, and Modernity; 1900–1950.* Louisville, Ky.: Westminster John Knox, 2003.

―――. *The New Abolition: W. E. B. Du Bois and the Black Social Gospel.* New Haven: Yale University Press, 2015.

―――. *Theology without Weapons: The Barthian Revolt in Modern Theol-ogy.* Louisville, Ky.: Westminster John Knox, 2000.

Dramm, Sabine. *Dietrich Bonhoeffer and the Resistance.* Minneapolis: For-tress, 2009.

Dunne, Joseph. *Back to the Rough Ground: Practical Judgment and the Lure of Technique.* Notre Dame, Ind.: University of Notre Dame Press, 1993.

Ericksen, Robert. *Complicity in the Holocaust: Churches and Universities in Nazi Germany.* Cambridge: Cambridge University Press, 2012.

Fant, Clyde E., ed. *Bonhoeffer: Worldly Preaching.* Nashville: Thomas Nelson, 1975.

Farley, Edward. "Can Preaching Be Taught?" *Theology Today* 62 (2005): 171–80.

————. *Practicing Gospel: Unconventional Thoughts on the Church's Ministry.* Louisville, Ky.: Westminster John Knox, 2003.

Feil, Ernst. *The Theology of Dietrich Bonhoeffer.* Translated by Martin Rumscheidt. Philadelphia: Fortress, 1985.

Felder, Cain Hope. "Race, Racism, and the Biblical Narratives." Pages 127–45 in *Stony the Road We Trod: African American Biblical Interpretation.* Edited by Cain Hope Felder. Minneapolis: Fortress, 1991.

Floyd, Wayne Whitson Jr. "Bonhoeffer's Literary Legacy." Pages 71–92 in *The Cambridge Companion to Dietrich Bonhoeffer.* Edited by John W. de Gruchy. Cambridge Companions to Religion. Cambridge: Cambridge University Press, 1999.

————, ed. *Dietrich Bonhoeffer Works: Act and Being; Transcendental Philosophy and Ontology in Systematic Theology.* DBWE 2. Translated by H. Martin Rumscheidt. Minneapolis: Fortress, 1996.

Ford, David F., and Daniel W. Hardy. *Living in Praise: Worshipping and Knowing God.* Grand Rapids: Baker Academic, 2005.

Forstman, Jack. *Christian Faith in Dark Times: Theological Conflicts in the Shadow of Hitler.* Louisville, Ky.: Westminster John Knox, 1992.

Frei, Hans W. *Types of Christian Theology.* Edited by George Hunsinger and William C. Placher. New Haven: Yale University Press, 1992.

Frick, Peter, ed. *Bonhoeffer's Intellectual Formation: Theology and Philosophy in His Thought.* Religion in Philosophy and Theology 29. Tübingen: Mohr Siebeck, 2008.

————. "Friedrich Nietzsche's Aphorisms and Dietrich Bonhoeffer's Theology." Pages 175–200 in Frick, *Bonhoeffer's Intellectual Formation.*

Green, Clifford J. *Bonhoeffer: A Theology of Sociality.* Rev. ed. Grand Rapids: Eerdmans, 1999.

————, ed. *Dietrich Bonhoeffer Works: Barcelona, Berlin, New York, 1928–1931.* Translated by Douglas W. Stott. DBWE 10. Minneapolis: Fortress, 2008.

————, ed. *Dietrich Bonhoeffer Works: Ethics.* Translated by Reinhard Krauss, Charles C. West, and Douglas W. Stott. DBWE 6. Minneapolis: Fortress, 2009.

————, ed. *Dietrich Bonhoeffer Works:* Sanctorum Communio; *A Theological Study of the Sociology of the Church.* Translated by Reinhard Krauss and Nancy Lukens. DBWE 1. Minneapolis: Fortress, 1998.

————. "Human Sociality and Christian Community." Pages 113–33 in *The Cambridge Companion to Bonhoeffer.* Edited by John W. de Gruchy.

Cambridge Companions to Religion. Cambridge: Cambridge University Press, 1999.

Green, Joel B., and Michael Pasquarello III, eds. *Narrative Reading, Narrative Preaching: Reuniting New Testament Interpretation and Proclamation.* Grand Rapids: Eerdmans, 2003.

Gregory, Brad S. *The Unintended Reformation: How a Religious Revolution Secularized Society.* Cambridge, Mass.: Belknap Press of Harvard University Press, 2012.

Guroian, Vigen. "Church and Nationhood: A Reflection on the 'National Church.'" Pages 171–96 in *Theology and the Practice of Responsibility: Essays on Dietrich Bonhoeffer.* Edited by Wayne Whitson Floyd Jr. and Charles Marsh. Valley Forge, Pa.: Trinity International, 1994.

Hadot, Pierre. *Philosophy as a Way of Life: Spiritual Exercises from Socrates to Foucault.* Edited by Arnold I. Davidson. Translated by Michael Chase. London: Blackwell, 1995.

Hancock, Angela Dienhart. *Karl Barth's Emergency Homiletic, 1932–1933: A Summons to Prophetic Witness at the Dawn of the Third Reich.* Grand Rapids: Eerdmans, 2013.

Harvey, Barry A. "A Post-Critical Approach to a 'Religionless Christianity.'" Pages 39–58 in *Theology and the Practice of Responsibility: Essays on Dietrich Bonhoeffer.* Edited by Wayne Whitson Floyd Jr. and Charles Marsh. Valley Forge, Pa.: Trinity International, 1994.

Hauerwas, Stanley. *Christian Existence Today: Essays on Church, World and Living In Between.* Durham, N.C.: Labyrinth Press, 1988.

———. *Matthew.* Grand Rapids: Brazos, 2006.

———. *The Peaceable Kingdom: A Primer in Christian Ethics.* Notre Dame, Ind.: University of Notre Dame Press, 1983.

———. *Performing the Faith: Bonhoeffer and the Practice of Nonviolence.* Grand Rapids: Brazos, 2004.

———. *Sanctify Them in the Truth: Holiness Exemplified.* Nashville: Abingdon, 1998.

———. *The State of the University: Academic Knowledges and the Knowledge of God.* London: Blackwell, 2007.

———. *The Work of Theology.* Grand Rapids: Eerdmans, 2015.

———. *Working with Words: On Learning to Speak Christian.* Eugene, Ore.: Wipf & Stock, 2001.

Haynes, Stephen R. *The Bonhoeffer Phenomenon: Portraits of a Protestant Saint.* Minneapolis: Fortress, 2004.

Hinlicky, Paul R. *Before Auschwitz: What Christian Theology Must Learn from the Rise of Nazism.* Eugene, Ore.: Cascade, 2013.

————. *Luther and the Beloved Community: A Path for Christian Theology after Christendom*. Grand Rapids: Eerdmans, 2010.

Holmer, Paul L. *The Grammar of Faith*. San Francisco: Harper & Row, 1978.

Holmes, Stephen R. *Listening to the Past: The Pace of Tradition in Theology*. Grand Rapids: Baker Academic, 2002.

Howard, Thomas Albert. *Protestant Theology and the Making of the Modern German University*. Oxford: Oxford University Press, 2006.

Hunsinger, George. *Disruptive Grace: Studies in the Theology of Karl Barth*. Grand Rapids: Eerdmans, 2000.

Hutter, Reinhard. *Suffering Divine Things: Theology as Church Practice*. Grand Rapids: Eerdmans, 2000.

Jacobsen, David Schnasa, ed. *Homiletical Theology: Preaching as Doing Theology*. The Promise of Homiletical Theology 1. Eugene, Ore.: Cascade, 2015.

————. Introduction. Pages 3–22 in Jacobsen, *Homiletical Theology*

Jenson, Robert W. *Systematic Theology*. Vol. 1, *The Triune God*. Oxford: Oxford University Press, 1997.

Johnson, Keith L. "Bonhoeffer and the End of the Christian Academy." Pages 153–73 in *Bonhoeffer, Christ, and Culture*. Edited by Keith L. Johnson and Timothy Larsen. Downers Grove, Ill.: IVP Academic, 2013.

Kaiser, Joshua. *Becoming Simple and Wise: Moral Discernment in Dietrich Bonhoeffer's Vision of Christian Ethics*. Eugene, Ore.: Pickwick, 2015.

Kallenberg, Brad J. *Ethics as Grammar: Changing the Postmodern Subject*. Notre Dame, Ind.: University of Notre Dame Press, 2001.

Keider, Alan. *The Patient Ferment of the Early Church: The Improbable Rise of Christianity in the Roman Empire*. Grand Rapids: Baker Academic, 2016.

Kelly, Geffrey B., ed. *Dietrich Bonhoeffer Works: Life Together; Prayerbook of the Bible*. Translated by Daniel W. Bloesch and James H. Burtness. DBWE 5. Minneapolis: Fortress, 1996.

Kelly, Geffrey B., and John D. Godsey, eds. *Dietrich Bonhoeffer Works: Discipleship*. Translated by Barbara Green and Reinhard Krauss. DBWE 4. Minneapolis: Fortress, 2001.

Kelly, Geffrey B., and F. Burton Nelson. *The Cost of Moral Leadership: The Spirituality of Dietrich Bonhoeffer*. Grand Rapids: Eerdmans, 2003.

King, Martin Luther, Jr. "Letter from Birmingham Jail (1963)." Pages 289–302 in *A Testament of Hope: The Essential Writings and Speeches of Martin Luther King, Jr.* Edited by James Melvin Washington. New York: Harper One, 1986.

Knowles, Michael P. *We Preach Not Ourselves: Paul on Proclamation*. Grand Rapids: Brazos, 2008.

Kolb, Robert. *Luther and the Stories of God: Biblical Narratives as a Foundation for Christian Living.* Grand Rapids: Baker Academic, 2012.

Kolb, Robert, and Timothy J. Wengert, eds. *The Book of Concord: The Confession of the Evangelical Lutheran Church.* Translated by Charles Arand, Eric Gritsch, Robert Kolb, William Russell, James Schaaf, Jane Strohl, and Timothy J. Wengert. Minneapolis: Fortress, 2000.

Krauss, Reinhard. "Discovering Bonhoeffer in Translation: New Insights from the Bonhoeffer Works, English Edition." Pages 71–78 in *Interpreting Bonhoeffer: Historical Perspectives, Emerging Issues.* Edited by Clifford J. Green and Guy C. Carter. Minneapolis: Fortress, 2013.

Krötke, Wolf. "Dietrich Bonhoeffer and Martin Luther." Pages 53–82 in *Bonhoeffer's Intellectual Formation.* Edited by Peter Frick. Religion in Philosophy and Theology 29. Tübingen: Mohr Siebeck, 2008.

Kuske, Martin. *The Old Testament as the Book of Christ: An Appraisal of Bonhoeffer's Interpretation.* Translated by S. T. Kimbrough Jr. Philadelphia: Westminster, 1976.

Larsen, Timothy. "The Evangelical Reception of Dietrich Bonhoeffer." Pages 39–57 in *Bonhoeffer, Christ and Culture.* Edited by Keith L. Johnson and Timothy Larsen. Downers Grove, Ill.: IVP Academic, 2013.

LaRue, Cloephus J. *I Believe I'll Testify: The Art of African American Preaching.* Louisville, Ky.: Westminster John Knox, 2011.

Lash, Nicholas. *Holiness, Speech and Silence: Reflections on the Question of God.* Aldershot: Ashgate, 2004.

Lazareth, William H. *Christians in Society: Luther, the Bible, and Social Ethics.* Minneapolis: Fortress, 2001.

Legaspi, Michael C. *The Death of Scripture and the Rise of Biblical Studies.* Oxford: Oxford University Press, 2010.

Lischer, Richard. *The End of Words: The Language of Reconciliation in a Culture of Violence.* Grand Rapids: Eerdmans, 2005.

———. *The Preacher King: Martin Luther King Jr. and the Word That Moved America.* New York: Oxford University Press, 1995.

———. *A Theology of Preaching: Dynamics of the Gospel.* Rev. ed. Eugene, Ore.: Wipf & Stock, 2001.

Long, Thomas G. "A New Focus for Teaching Preaching." Pages 3–17 in *Teaching Preaching as a Christian Practice.* Edited by Thomas G. Long and Leonora Tubbs Tisdale. Louisville, Ky.: Westminster John Knox, 2008.

———. *The Witness of Preaching.* 3rd ed. Louisville, Ky.: Westminster John Knox, 2016.

Loughlin, Gerard. *Telling God's Story: Bible, Church, and Narrative Theology.* Cambridge: Cambridge University Press, 1996.

Lull, Timothy F. "Preface to the Wittenberg Edition of Luther's German Writings (1539)." Pages 63–69 in *Martin Luther's Basic Theological Writings.* Edited by Timothy F. Lull. Minneapolis: Fortress, 1989.

Luther, Martin. "The Freedom of a Christian." Pages 467–538 in *The Roots of Reform.* Edited by Timothy J. Wengert. Vol. 1 of *The Annotated Luther.* Minneapolis: Fortress, 2015.

———. *The Large Catechism of Martin Luther.* Translated by Robert H. Fischer. Philadelphia: Fortress, 1959.

———. *Luther's Works.* Edited by Jaroslav J. Pelikan and Helmut T. Lehmann. 55 vols. St. Louis: Concordia, 1955–1986.

———. *Martin Luther's Basic Theological Writings.* Edited by Timothy F. Lull. Minneapolis: Fortress, 1989. See esp. "Preface to the Wittenberg Edition of Luther's German Writings (1539)."

MacIntyre, Alasdair. *Three Rival Versions of Moral Enquiry: Encyclopedia, Genealogy, and Tradition.* Notre Dame, Ind.: University of Notre Dame Press, 1990.

Mallard, William. *Language and Love: Introducing Augustine's Religious Thought through the Confessions Story.* University Park: Penn State University Press, 1994.

Marsh, Charles. "Bonhoeffer on the Road to King: 'Turning from the Phraseological to the Real.'" Pages 123–38 in *Bonhoeffer and King: Their Legacies and Import for Christian Social Thought.* Edited by Willis Jenkins and Jennifer M. McBride. Minneapolis: Fortress, 2010.

———. *Strange Glory: A Life of Dietrich Bonhoeffer.* New York: Alfred A. Knopf, 2014.

Marshall, Bruce D. "The Church in the Gospel." *Pro Ecclesia* 1, no. 1 (1992): 27–41.

Matheny, Paul Duane, Clifford J. Green, and Marshall D. Johnson, eds. *Dietrich Bonhoeffer Works: The Young Bonhoeffer, 1918–1927.* Translated by Mary C. Nebelsick. DBWE 9. Minneapolis: Fortress, 2003.

Matheson, Peter. *The Rhetoric of the Reformation.* Edinburgh: T&T Clark, 1998.

Mattox, Mickey L. "Luther's Interpretation of Scripture: Biblical Understanding in Trinitarian Shape." Pages 11–58 in *The Substance of Faith: Luther's Doctrinal Theology for Today.* Edited by Paul R. Hinlicky. Minneapolis: Fortress, 2008.

Metaxas, Eric. *Bonhoeffer: Pastor, Martyr, Prophet, Spy.* Nashville: Thomas Nelson, 2010.

Meuser, Fred W. "Luther as Preacher of the Word of God." Pages 136–48 in *The Cambridge Companion to Martin Luther.* Edited by Donald K.

McKim. Cambridge Companions to Religion. Cambridge: Cambridge University Press, 2003.

Migliore, Daniel L. "Karl Barth's First Lectures in Dogmatics: Instruction in the Christian Religion." Pages xv–lxii in *The Göttingen Dogmatics: Instruction in the Christian Religion.* Edited by Hannelotte Reiffen. Translated by Geoffrey W. Bromiley. Grand Rapids: Eerdmans, 1991.

Mitman, F. Russell. *Worship in the Shape of Scripture.* Cleveland: Pilgrim, 2001.

Moberly, Jennifer. *The Virtue of Bonhoeffer's Ethics: A Study of Dietrich Bonhoeffer's Ethics in Relation to Virtue Ethics.* Eugene, Ore.: Pickwick, 2013.

Moses, John A. "Bonhoeffer's Germany: Theadvet Political Context." Pages 3–21 in *The Cambridge Companion to Dietrich Bonhoeffer.* Edited by John W. de Gruchy. Cambridge Companions to Religion. Cambridge: Cambridge University Press, 1999.

Nation, Mark Thiessen, Anthony G. Siegrist, and Daniel P. Umbel. *Bonhoeffer the Assassin? Challenging the Myth, Recovering His Call to Peacemaking.* Grand Rapids: Baker Academic, 2013.

Oberman, Heiko A. *Luther: Man between God and the Devil.* Translated by Eileen Walliser-Schwarzbart. New York: Doubleday, 1992.

———. "Preaching and the Word in the Reformation." *Theology Today* 18, no. 1 (1961): 16–29.

O'Donovan, Oliver. *Finding and Seeking.* Vol. 2 of *Ethics as Theology.* Grand Rapids: Eerdmans, 2014.

———. *Self, World, and Time.* Vol. 1 of *Ethics as Theology.* Grand Rapids: Eerdmans, 2013.

Old, Hughes Oliphant. *The Reading and Preaching of the Christian Scriptures in the Worship of the Christian Church.* 7 vols. Grand Rapids: Eerdmans, 1998–2010.

O'Malley, John W., S.J. "Luther the Preacher." Pages 3–16 in *The Martin Luther Quincentennial.* Edited by Gerhard Dünnhaupt. Detroit: Wayne State University Press, 1985.

Owens, L. Roger. *The Shape of Participation: A Theology of Church Practices.* Eugene, Ore.: Cascade, 2010.

Pangritz, Andreas. "Dietrich Bonhoeffer: 'Within, Not outside the Barthian Movement.'" Pages 245–82 in *Bonhoeffer's Intellectual Formation.* Edited by Peter Frick. Religion in Philosophy and Theology 29. Tübingen: Mohr Siebeck, 2008.

———. *Karl Barth in the Theology of Dietrich Bonhoeffer.* Translated by Barbara Rumscheidt and Martin Rumscheidt. Grand Rapids: Eerdmans, 2000.

————. "Who Is Jesus Christ, for Us, Today?" Pages 134–53 in *The Cambridge Companion to Dietrich Bonhoeffer*. Edited by John W. de Gruchy. Cambridge Companions to Religion. Cambridge: Cambridge University Press, 1999.

Pasquarello, Michael, III. *Christian Preaching: A Trinitarian Theology of Proclamation*. 2006. Reprint, Eugene, Ore.: Wipf & Stock, 2011.

————. *Sacred Rhetoric: Preaching as a Theological and Pastoral Practice of the Church*. 2005. Reprint, Eugene, Ore.: Wipf & Stock, 2012.

————. *We Speak Because We Have First Been Spoken: A "Grammar" of the Preaching Life*. Grand Rapids: Eerdmans, 2009.

Pelikan, Jaroslav. *Luther the Expositor: Introduction to the Reformer's Exegetical Writings*. Companion Volume in Luther's Works. St. Louis: Concordia, 1959.

Peterson, Eugene H. *Eat This Book: A Conversation in the Art of Spiritual Reading*. Grand Rapids: Eerdmans, 2009.

Posset, Franz. *The Real Luther: A Friar at Erfurt and Wittenberg*. St. Louis: Concordia, 2011.

Pugh, Jeffrey C. *Religionless Christianity: Dietrich Bonhoeffer in Troubled Times*. New York: T&T Clark, 2008.

Rashkover, Randi. "The Future of the Word and the Liturgical Turn." Pages 1–25 in *Liturgy, Time, and the Politics of Redemption*. Edited by Randi Rashkover and C. C. Pecknold. Grand Rapids: Eerdmans, 2006.

Rassmussen, Larry L., ed. *Dietrich BonhoefferWorks: Berlin, 1932–1933*. Translated by Isabel Best and David Higgins. DBWE 12. Minneapolis: Fortress, 2009.

Robertson, Edwin. *The Shame and the Sacrifice: The Life and Martyrdom of Dietrich Bonhoeffer*. New York: Scribner, 1988.

Root, Andrew. *Bonhoeffer as Youth Worker: A Theological Vision for Discipleship and Life Together*. Grand Rapids: Baker Academic, 2014.

Rother, Richard. "A Confirmation Class in Wedding." Pages 57–58 in *I Knew Dietrich Bonhoeffer: Reminiscences by His Friends*. Edited by Wolf-Dieter Zimmerman and Ronald Gregor Smith. Translated by Kathe Gregor Smith. New York: Harper & Row, 1966.

Rumscheidt, Martin. "The Formation of Bonhoeffer's Theology." Pages 50–70 in *The Cambridge Companion to Dietrich Bonhoeffer*. Edited by John W. de Gruchy. Cambridge Companions to Religion. Cambridge: Cambridge University Press, 1999.

————. "The Significance of Adolf von Harnack and Reinhold Seeberg for Dietrich Bonhoeffer." Pages 201–24 in *Bonhoeffer's Intellectual*

Formation. Edited by Peter Frick. Religion in Philosophy and Theology 29. Tübingen: Mohr Siebeck, 2008.

Saliers, Don E. *Worship as Theology: Foretaste of Glory Divine*. Nashville: Abingdon, 1994.

Schlingensiepen, Ferdinand. *Dietrich Bonhoeffer 1906–1945: Martyr, Thinker, Man of Resistance*. Translated by Isabel Best. New York: T&T Clark, 2010.

Scholder, Klaus. *The Churches and the Third Reich*. Vol. 1, *1918–1934*. Translated by J. Bowden. Minneapolis: Fortress, 1988.

Schwanke, Johannes. "Luther on Creation." Pages 78–98 in *Harvesting Martin Luther's Reflections on Theology, Ethics, and the Church*. Edited by Timothy J. Wengert. Grand Rapids: Eerdmans, 2004.

Schwöbel, Christoph. "The Creature of the Word: Recovering the Ecclesiology of the Reformers." Pages 110–55 in *On Being the Church: Essays on the Christian Community*. Edited by Colin E. Gunton and Daniel W. Hardy. Edinburgh: T&T Clark, 1989.

Selby, Peter. "Christianity in a World Come of Age." Pages 226–45 in *The Cambridge Companion to Dietrich Bonhoeffer*. Edited by John W. de Gruchy. Cambridge Companions to Religion. Cambridge: Cambridge University Press, 1999.

Smith, Ted A. *The New Measures: A Theological History of Democratic Practice*. Cambridge: Cambridge University Press, 2007.

Solberg, Mary M., ed. *A Church Undone: Documents from the German Christian Faith Movement, 1932–1940*. Translated by Mary M. Solberg. Minneapolis: Fortress, 2015.

Steigmann-Gall, Richard. *The Holy Reich: Nazi Conceptions of Christianity, 1919–1945*. Cambridge: Cambridge University Press, 2003.

Steinmetz, David C. "Luther and Formation in Faith." Pages 253–69 in *Educating People of Faith: Exploring the History of Jewish and Christian Communities*. Edited by John Van Engen. Grand Rapids: Eerdmans, 2004.

———. *Luther in Context*. Bloomington: Indiana University Press, 1986.

———. *Taking the Long View: Christian Theology in Historical Perspective*. Oxford: Oxford University Press, 2011.

Stroud, Dean G. "Historical Context: Preaching in the Third Reich." Pages 3–50 in *Preaching in Hitler's Shadow: Sermons of Resistance in the Third Reich*. Edited by Dean G. Stroud. Grand Rapids: Eerdmans, 2013.

Taylor, Charles. *A Secular Age*. Cambridge, Mass.: Harvard University Press, 2007.

Thomas, Frank A. *They Like to Never Quit Praisin' God: The Role of Celebration in Preaching*. Rev. ed. Cleveland: Pilgrim, 2013.

Thompson, Christopher J. *Christian Doctrine, Christian Identity: Augustine and the Narratives of Character.* New York: University Press of America, 1999.

Tjorhom, Ola. "The Church as the Place of Salvation: On the Interrelation between Justification and Ecclesiology." *Pro Ecclesia* 9, no. 3 (2000): 285–96.

Treier, Daniel J. *Virtue and the Voice of God: Towards a Theology of Wisdom.* Grand Rapids: Eerdmans, 2006.

Volpe, Medi Ann, and Jennifer Moberly. "'Let Your Light So Shine': Rowan Williams and Dietrich Bonhoeffer." Pages 303–24 in *Engaging Bonhoeffer: The Impact and Influence of Bonhoeffer's Life and Thought.* Edited by Matthew D. Kirkpatrick. Minneapolis: Fortress, 2016.

Wainwright, Geoffrey. *Doxology: The Praise of God in Worship, Doctrine, and Life.* New York: Oxford University Press, 1980.

Wannenwetsch, Bernd. *Political Worship: Ethics for Christian Citizens.* Translated by Margaret Kohl. Oxford: Oxford University Press, 2004.

Webb, Stephen H. *The Divine Voice: Christian Proclamation and the Theology of Sound.* Grand Rapids: Brazos, 2004.

Webster, John. *Holy Scripture: A Dogmatic Sketch.* Cambridge: Cambridge University Press, 2003.

———. *Word and Church: Essays in Christian Dogmatics.* New York: T&T Clark, 2001.

Wells, Samuel. "Bonhoeffer: Theologian, Activist, Educator." Pages 221–36 in *Interpreting Bonhoeffer: Historical Perspectives, Emerging Issues.* Edited by Clifford J. Green and Guy C. Carter. Minneapolis: Fortress, 2013.

Wengert, Timothy J. *Reading the Bible with Martin Luther.* Grand Rapids: Baker Academic, 2013.

Williams, Reggie L. *Bonhoeffer's Black Jesus: Harlem Renaissance Theology and an Ethic of Resistance.* Waco, Tex.: Baylor University Press, 2014.

Williams, Rowan. *On Christian Theology.* Oxford: Blackwell, 2000.

———. *Why Study the Past? The Quest for the Historical Church.* Grand Rapids: Eerdmans, 2005.

Willimon, William H. *Conversations with Barth on Preaching.* Nashville: Abingdon, 2006.

———. *Pastor: The Theology and Practice of Ordained Ministry.* Nashville: Abingdon, 2002.

Wimbush, Vincent L. "The Bible and African Americans." Pages 81–97 in *Stony the Road We Trod: African American Biblical Interpretation.* Edited by Cain Hope Felder. Minneapolis: Fortress, 1991.

Wood, Charles M. *An Invitation to Theological Study.* Valley Forge, Pa.: Trinity International, 1994.

————. *Vision and Discernment: An Orientation in Theological Study.* Atlanta: Scholars Press, 1985.

Wright, John W. *Telling God's Story: Narrative Preaching for Christian Formation.* Downers Grove, Ill.: InterVarsity, 2007.

Young, Josiah U. "Theology and the Problem of Racism." Pages 69–77 in *Bonhoeffer and King: Their Legacies and Import for Christian Social Thought.* Edited by Willis Jenkins and Jennifer M. McBride. Minneapolis: Fortress, 2010.

Ziegler, Philip G. "God, Christ, and Church in the DDR—Wolf Krötke as an Interpreter of Bonhoeffer's Theology." Pages 201–20 in *Engaging Bonhoeffer: The Impact and Influence of Bonhoeffer's Life and Thought.* Edited by Matthew D. Kirkpatrick. Minneapolis: Fortress, 2016.

Zimmerman, Jens. *Incarnational Humanism: A Philosophy of Culture for the Church in the World.* Downers Grove, Ill.: IVP Academic, 2012.

————. *Recovering Theological Hermeneutics: An Incarnational-Trinitarian Theory of Interpretation.* Grand Rapids: Baker Academic, 2004.

Zimmerman, Jens, and Brian Gregor, eds. *Being Human, Becoming Human: Dietrich Bonhoeffer and Social Thought.* Eugene, Ore.: Pickwick, 2010.

Index

Aaron, 115–16
Adam, 60–61, 74, 103, 151
Advent, 50, 51, 68, 69, 88, 99, 114, 115, 123
African American Christian community, 227n93; *see also* black community
America, 65–66, 68, 71–73, 75–77, 79, 169–72, 224n60, 224n64, 225n73, 237n75; *see also* United States
anti-Semitism, 109, 170, 177
Aristotle, 213, 215
Aryan, 70, 83, 105, 109–10, 132, 141, 165, 246n12; Jesus, 83; leader; Paragraph, 110, 117; Reich Church, 115
Augustine, 8, 41, 45, 55–56; *Confessions*, 41, 45, 55

Babylon, 117
baptism, 55, 91, 102–3, 133, 134, 165, 178, 190–91, 262n61
Barcelona, 4, 35–39, 46, 52, 54–57, 68, 78, 213n8, 214n18, 214n19, 218n68, 220n77

Barth, Karl, 8, 13–15, 17, 19–20, 22, 27, 32, 35, 40, 42, 53–54, 58–60, 84–87, 94, 106, 107, 118, 132–34, 141, 205n6, 205n7, 205n8, 207n25, 208n27, 213n13, 214n22, 215n27, 215n28, 216n34, 219n71, 221n9, 221n11, 222n20, 222n24, 223n31, 229n7, 239n33, 240n35, 240n36; Göttingen lectures on Christian dogmatics, 59; on preaching, 15, 132–34; *Romans*, 58, 106–7
Bartimaeus, 182
Beatitudes, 47, 159
Berlin, 13–15, 17, 20, 22, 26, 32, 35–36, 38–39, 42, 55–58, 64, 85–88, 90, 93–95, 102, 104, 106, 111–13, 116, 118, 130, 132, 204n1, 204n3, 211n2, 212n4, 215n27, 218n65, 230n24, 231n34, 231n43, 233n70; University, 13, 35, 42, 85, 106, 204n3, 212n4
Bethel Confession, 118
Bethge, Dietrich Wilhelm Rudiger, 190
Bethge, Eberhard, 188, 190, 211n2, 215n34, 216n39, 220n77, 228n1, 234n17, 237n1, 246n12, 258n35

Bible, 6, 16, 18, 22, 24, 31, 38, 62–63,
68, 75, 84, 87–88, 90, 91, 96, 102,
104, 106–8, 111, 120–22, 125, 130,
138–40, 142, 145, 146, 171, 175–77,
182, 202n27, 207n21, 209n38, 212n5,
219n70, 224n64, 225n74, 225n76,
234n7, 240n40, 241n44, 242n53,
247n24, 252n70, 255n19, 259n42;
biblical interpretation, 25, 108, 138,
141, 207n21, 234n12, 242n53, 261n57,
262n61
Birmingham, 76–77, 226n84
black community, 76; *see also* African
American Christian community
Bonhoeffer, Dietrich: *Act and Being*,
3, 6, 7, 58–63, 79, 220n4, 223n31,
227n94; *The Cost of Discipleship*, 6,
154–57, 163, 166, 182, 238n4, 247n27,
248n28, 248n30, 248n37, 251n62,
253n70; *Ethics*, 6, 175, 182–84, 187,
189; exchange student in America,
65–79; first lecture course, 87;
homiletical theologian, 3, 13, 15,
33, 52, 56, 79, 104, 106, 107, 123, 150,
173, 195, 196, 212n4; imprisonment
and execution, 174; *Letters and
Papers from Prison*, 6, 175, 188; *Life
Together*, 6, 163–66, 238n4, 251n62,
253n70; pastoral assistant in Barcelona, 35; *Prayerbook of the Bible*,
175–76, 238n4; preacher and professor in Finkenwalde, 127; *Sanctorum
Communio* (dissertation), 6, 20, 26,
29, 35, 36, 48, 75, 79, 217n44, 217n49
Bonhoeffer, Karl Friedrich, 74
Bonn, 14, 84, 85, 132; University, 132
Bronish, Gotthelf, 32

catechesis, 65, 72, 193
Civil Rights Movement, 76, 227n94

Christ: black, 75, 78; body of, 47–48,
55, 135, 145, 162–63, 195, 216n44,
217n49, 238n9, 254n73, 263n81;
Christus praesens, 99, 100; incarnate Word, 157, 176; Lord, 3, 5, 20,
27, 31–32, 51–53, 78, 97–99, 113–14,
116, 120, 128, 135–36, 144, 154, 160,
165, 174, 176, 186–87, 296; love of, 27,
32, 159; lowliness of, 124, 175; mystery of, 131, 166–67; resurrection
of, 9, 48, 53, 60, 61, 93, 96, 102, 108,
131, 144, 164, 165, 196, 242n57; risen
Lord, 3, 5, 27, 113, 136, 176, 187, 196;
Son of God, 60, 110, 135, 163, 166,
167, 175, 176; Wisdom of God, 55,
56, 103; word of, 15, 25, 32, 99, 137,
142–44, 146, 149, 157, 187, 247n22;
see also Jesus
Christianity, 7, 15, 17–19, 41, 50, 52–55,
66, 70–72, 77, 78, 83, 85, 89, 98, 103,
109–10, 112, 123, 127, 129, 132, 142,
158, 162, 168, 169, 172, 183–85, 188,
195, 204n2, 218n68, 224n60, 226n89,
226n91, 228n3, 229n9, 230n20,
233n70, 233n3, 237n76, 237n2,
238n3, 245n87, 248n36, 250n50,
252n69, 253n72, 256n21, 258n30,
260n52; Christian community,
62, 163, 227n93, 252n70; Christian
doctrine, 18, 72, 130; Christian
humanism, 183, 261n60; dogmatic,
7, 184, 185; positive, 89, 110, 132,
230n20; practical, 7, 184, 185; "religionless" Christian, 188; "without
Christ," 195
Christmas, 64, 68, 90, 166–67, 177,
256n22
Christology, 26–27, 32, 98, 130–32,
134, 167, 232n56, 239n19
church: Abyssinian Baptist, 74, 75, 78,
90, 227n94, 231n24; black, 73–79;
Confessing, 105, 119, 126–27, 129,